The Law Enforcement Process

Man routinely judges the actions of others and expects to have his actions judged by other men.

Magnum Photos

The Law Enforcement Process

By Alan J. Butler
Pace University/Westchester

ALFRED PUBLISHING CO., INC.

Printed and bound in the United States of America

Library of Congress Cataloging in Publication Data

Butler, Alan J. 1912-
The law enforcement process.

Bibliography: p.
Includes index.
1. Law enforcement. 2. Criminal justice, Administration of. I. Title.
HV7921.B8 364 74-6878
ISBN 0-88284-015-0

DEDICATION

To my beloved wife, Dr. Grace K. Pratt-Butler — if it were not for her inspiration and encouragement, this would never have been written — and with all my love.

ACKNOWLEDGMENTS

The people listed below have all been influential in the development of my career as a police officer and teacher; and I am grateful for having known them and learned from them.

Dr. James Banks, Cuyahoga Community College
Dr. Algernon D. Black, Leader Emeritus, New York Society for Ethical Culture
Assistant Chief Inspector Charles F. Calby (ret.), New York City Transit Police Department
Dr. Anthone Colovas, Cuyahoga Community College
Chief Louis Cottell, Chief of Detectives, New York City Police Department
Dr. Donald L. Dahlstrom, University of Maine
Professor Joseph Dorinson, Long Island University
Chris Economachus, Professional Photographer
Dr. Felix M. Fabian, University of Nebraska
Dr. George T. Felkenes, University of Alabama
Dr. George Fuller, Kent State University
Chief Sanford Garelick, Chief of Department, New York City Transit Police Department
Eugene Hauman, New York City Transit Authority, Legal Division
Dr. Joseph Jablonski, Sinclair Community College
Dr. William J. Mathias, Georgia State University
Dr. Bernard J. Markowitz, Central Islip State Hospital
Deputy Chief Bernard J. Morris (Ret.), New York City Transit Police Department
Professor George Rosbrook, Lorraine Community College
Dr. Eugene Schwartz, Director of Criminal Justice, University of St. Louis
Professor Arthur Taliaferro, Cuyahoga Community College
Dr. Solomon Tanzer, Assistant Attorney-in-Charge, New York City Transit Authority, Legal Division
Professor James Todd, Lakeland Community College
Sergeant Henry Ulrich, New York City Police Department
Dean Richard H. Ward, John Jay College of Criminal Justice

SPECIAL ACKNOWLEDGMENTS

Dr. Louise Antz, Professor Emeritus, New York University

Dr. Grace K. Pratt-Butler, Professor of Education, Long Island University

Dr. John Corfias, President, Dyke College

Dr. Joseph J. Gross, Director of Criminal Justice, Pace University/Westchester

Dr. Paul Hahn, Director of Administration of Justice, Xavier University

Dr. Alfred M. Livingston, Vice-Chancellor, Cuyahoga Community College

Dr. Arthur Niederhoffer, John Jay College of Criminal Justice

Dr. Ivan Polk, Director of Criminology, Southern State Oregon College

Dr. Samuel Sherrid, Director of Criminal Justice, New York Institute of Technology

Dr. Thomas Stirton, Long Island University

Inspector Sidney Tatz (ret.), New York City Transit Police Department

Dr. Rene A. Wormser, (author, "The Story of the Law")

Dr. Earle Roberts, Director of Criminal Justice, Kent State University

CONTENTS

PART II: OPERATIONS

Introduction

Throughout man's recorded history he has lived under an elaborate system of controls imposed upon him by society. These controls serve to maintain the orderly functioning of society and peaceful relations between the citizen and the state and between one citizen and another.

Society's controls have been set forth in two ways. First, by a system of public and personal morality and ethics that attempts to convince each citizen of the rightness of certain kinds of behavior and the wrongness of other kinds. This first system is usually linked to and supported by an elaborate set of religious teachings, principles, and rituals. It has, in addition, enlisted the support of the health professions, which instill the conviction that it is healthier, both physically and mentally, to abide by the rules. If this first system, with its vast and awe-inspiring authority, does not exact the proper behavior of the society's citizenry, a second system is brought into play. This second system, which often proclaims the first as its basis and rationale, is the law enforcement process. In this second system, the concepts of right versus wrong, decent versus sinful, healthy versus sick, and normal versus deviant are replaced by the concept of legal versus illegal. If conscience, fear of punishment in an afterworld by an unseen and often unperceived God, and desire to avoid physical or mental debilitation are not sufficient to insure acceptable behavior, the second system, with its array of dissuasions and punishments, is counted on for some assurance of proper conduct.

Though there has been constant change and modification in the law, and though the law as it is written and interpreted has differed considerably from age to age and differs considerably from nation to nation, it is obvious that no society could exist or function successfully without it. It is just as obvious that no system of law could exist or function without the complex apparatus that gives life to the law and makes it an active instrument for assuring certain approved behaviors and eradicating other, disapproved, behavior.

This apparatus comprises:

a) the police, who serve as a symbolic and actual force for respect for and compliance with the law;

b) the courts, which were established as ideal and impartial adjudicators of alleged noncompliance with the law; and

c) a penal or correctional system, whose function is to provide retribution to and rehabilitation of those who have been found to have violated the law.

In the next several chapters we will examine the components of this apparatus and learn of their historical development, the concepts by which they now operate, and their organizations and functions. We will determine, after this examination, how American society serves itself and its citizens through the operation of its multifaceted law enforcement and criminal justice process.

The book is divided into two main parts. Part I, Foundations, presents the history and evolution of law and law enforcement agencies; and relates them to our present-day police, judicial and corrections system. Part II, Operations, uses the background information from Part I to examine crime, and the methods police use to respond to it. The chapter on police and society deals with the question of police relations with society in general. And the chapter on police administration treats the internal problems of police function and response. The book ends with a discussion of various law enforcement agencies and their related roles in serving to control crime and to help the general public.

I would like to thank several people for helping me write this book. My wife Grace spent hours reading and re-reading the manuscript. Her comments were invaluable. John Stout, social sciences editor at Alfred, stood by and assisted at each stage of the project's development. I would also like to thank Commissioner Louis J. Frank and Public Relations Officer Lt. Robert Yaccarino for their assistance and permission to use certain photographs from the Nassau County Police Department files. And finally, a special thank you is for Les Kaplan, writer and editor, whose assistance was absolutely essential to the completion of the book.

The Law Enforcement Process

Part I
FOUNDATIONS

1. *The Origin and Development of the Law*

2. *The Growth of Organized Law Enforcement*

3. *The Judicial System: Judges, Courts, and Trials*

4. *Corrections: Treating the Convicted Offender*

1

The Origin and Development of the Law

While every modern society is based upon a system of written laws, many of these written laws originated thousands of years ago in the unwritten customs, mores and folkways of peoples in diverse ancient lands. To a considerable extent, much of our everyday conduct is guided by these unwritten laws, and it is perhaps not an exaggeration to declare that our everyday conduct is influenced more by these unwritten laws that manifest themselves in conscience than by our conscious knowledge of written law. Study of anthropology, sociology and psychology will provide fascinating information and insight into these phenomena. We are concerned here, however, with the development of the written law and how it has affected the law as it is currently applied and enforced in the United States.

ORIGINS OF THE LAW

Middle Eastern and Mediterranean Beginnings

As in so many other areas, a search for origins takes us to the lands that gave birth to the three principal religions of Western culture.

The earliest record we have of a codified system of law and of the rules for their enforcement are the Codes of Hammurabi, dating from about 1955–1913 B.C. During these decades, Hammurabi, king of Babylon, caused these codes to be inscribed on a

The earliest record we have of a codified system of law and of the rules for their enforcement are the Codes of Hammaurabi. Here the god Shamash gives the laws to Hammaurabi.
The Granger Collection, New York

pillar of black diorite which was unearthed at Susa by archeologists during the winter of 1901–1902. As originally inscribed the Codes comprised some 4,000 lines divided into 282 clauses. They dealt with criminal, commercial and land law, and set forth elaborate rules for marriage, domestic relations and divorce. The Codes were characterized by three essential features:

a. jus talionis, a concept that has had a greater and more long-lasting grip on the popular imagination than almost any other (". . . if a freeman destroys the eye of another, his eye shall be destroyed. If anyone breaks a freeman's bone, his bone shall be broken . . .");

b. the sanctity of an oath before God; and

c. the necessity of providing written evidence in all legal matters.

The Codes of Hammurabi preceded by about six hundred years that other monumental source of law in our Judaeo-Christian civilization, the Mosaic laws. There are many similarities between the two, the essential difference being that the Codes never rose to the heights of moral passion that the laws of Moses did.

The Bible: Almost more than any other source, the Bible

serves a central function in our legal system, because we preserve in our society so much of the moral and religious underpinnings in secular law that we first learned from the Bible. The Bible does, however, present us with some difficulties, because it is necessary to differentiate between those laws that are fundamentally religious or ritualistic in nature and those ethical teachings that have been transferred to civil law and form its unchallenged core. Certain ritual laws such as, for example, those governing the rules of Kashruth are maintained primarily by Orthodox Jews; other ritual laws, such as the keeping of the Sabbath as a holy day, are observed as a religious obligation by observant Jews, but have also been transformed into various Sunday blue laws as a civic obligation. And, of course, a host of religious injunctions can be violated without committing offense against civil law. The most far-reaching Biblical injunctions, however, which are not unique to the Bible, are so basic to the operation of any civilized society that they have been adopted into the civil law with little hint of disputation. These are embodied largely in the Ten Commandments and give us an insight into one of the major distinctions in law of the nature of crime. Some crimes are considered *mala in se,* evils prohibited by their very foulness (murder, rape, arson, aggravated assault), while others are considered *mala prohibita,* conduct society has chosen to forbid as a violation of law because it goes against an accepted moral code (abortion, homosexuality, pornography, prostitution).

Another differentiation that gives us an insight into society and its attitude toward crime is the notion of Natural Law versus Human Law. Natural Law presupposes that by his very nature man follows certain laws that reflect God's eternal law. Natural Law forbids all vices and sins. Human Iaw, while it often reflects Natural Law, is instituted by man, but it is neither eternal nor unchangeable. Theoretically, the combination of Natural Law and Human Law will direct man's reason to act for the common good.[1]

The Sixth Commandment proclaims, "Thou shalt not kill." Murder is the supreme crime, condemned and punished in every society. Through the centuries there has been a gradually greater differentiation of the nature of the killing of one person by another, based largely on the circumstances of the act and the state of mind and motivation of the perpetrator of the act. Several degrees of homicide and manslaughter have been delineated and the thrust of this differentiation has been to limit as much as possible the number of persons doomed to execution for their crime. Through these same centuries sensitive critics have asked whether this commandment also enjoins the legal killing by the state of any of its citizens who has killed another of its citizens. The trend has moved away from capital punishment. Many nations have forbidden it as an unconscionable act. In the United States, the death penalty has been rarely invoked since 1957 and has not been invoked at all since 1967. The Supreme Court has edged ever closer to an unqualified elimination of the death penalty. In 1972, in *Furman v. Georgia* (408 U.S. 238), it declared capital punishment unconstitutional because of the capricious and arbitrary manner with which it had been imposed. It is currently slated to decide on the question of banning it completely on the ground that it constitutes "cruel and unusual punishment," which is expressly forbidden by the Constitution.

The Seventh Commandment says: "Thou shalt not commit adultery." All societies have postulated sexual union during marriage as the ideal and only permissible relationship. Laws forbidding every other kind of sexual relations have proliferated, but have been only fitfully observed and enforced. Contemporary attitudes are in a state of considerable flux. Many would contend that most of the sexual unions forbidden by law are consensual, that they can be forbidden but not prevented, and should, therefore, be the subject not of criminal sanction but of personal morality and conscience. Despite changing attitudes, the legal sanctions remain on the statute books and will likely continue to remain there.

The Eighth Commandment declares: "Thou shalt not steal." Unlike the strictures of the Seventh Commandment, there is no broad-based adherence to the proposition that anyone has the right to steal from another. This early and fundamental recognition of the right of private property is the basis for the greatest proportion of cases tried in our legal system.

The Ninth Commandment warns: "Thou shalt not bear false witness." This is most elemental in our legal code, where it is enshrined in the sanctions against perjury, libel, and slander, and in our accepted standard of social conduct.

The Tenth Commandment proclaims: "Thou shalt not covet." In one variation what a man shall not covet is his neighbor's wife, in another it is his neighbor's ox. It reinforces the injunctions of both the Seventh and Eighth commandments.

Greece: The beginnings of Greek law, like that of many other ancient peoples, can be traced to sacred customs revealed to man by the gods. Homer's epics, the *Iliad* and the *Odyssey,* the oldest Greek literature that we know, contain no word for "law," but often refer to conduct that is proper because it is ordained by "usage," "divine decree" and "rules of right." In time, these sacred customs were succeeded by collections of laws presented to the people by such lawgivers as Minos in Crete and Lycurgus in Sparta. The oldest of the Greek written codes to have survived is the Code of Gortyna, dating from about 450 B.C. It deals with such matters as family, slavery, property, gifts, mortgages and court procedures.

In the pre-Hellenic era, Greece consisted of separate city-states, each with its own constitution and set of laws. Because Greeks traveled freely from one city-state to another and the multiplicity of laws proved burdensome, some leaders advocated a unification of the separate sets of laws. About 620 B.C. Draco was appointed *thesmothete* (lawgiver extraordinary), with the task of codifying the laws of Greece and having them written down. To this day Draco is known for the severity of the punishments he prescribed, which included death for all crimes, including theft. Draco was once asked why he imposed the death sentence for such minor offenses as stealing a cabbage. He replied, "Small ones deserve that, and I have no greater penalty for the greater crime."[2] Although the penalties were severe, Draco's codification was considered a notable achievement because it regularized the laws and made them known to all, thus easing the oppression of the people by their rulers, who formerly had changed the law at whim to suit their needs.

Draco was succeeded by Solon (638–559 B.C.), whose reforms have had a lasting influence. Solon became archon (ruler) of Athens about 594 B.C. on a program of reform. He cancelled debts and mortgages, abolished serfdom and regulated weights and measures. He devised a system in which a general assembly of freemen passed the laws of Athens and instituted a court system in which juries were chosen from among these freemen. He lessened the harshness of the penalties prescribed by Draco, rescinding the death penalty for all crimes but murder. He imposed fines for rape and seduction, but legalized prostitution. Solon was ranked among the Seven Sages of ancient Greece and his name has come down to us as a synonym for wise rule, just as *draconian* has come down as a synonym for harshness.

As the period of the lawgivers came to an end, several trends could be discerned:

1. Laws began to be enacted by assemblies of legislators rather than by individuals
2. Some formerly sacred customs became adapted into law
3. The concept of precedent began to be established
4. The concept of equity was developed
5. There was a growing awareness of the need for prescribed public service by citizens
6. The ideal formed that one purpose the law should serve is the security and welfare of every citizen for the good of the state.

Some of these concepts took their most notable form in the writings of Plato (429–347 B.C.) and Aristotle (384–322 B.C.). Plato's writings introduced the concept of "public" as opposed to "private" and declared that the highest ideal was public service. One of his most famous books, *The Republic*, was written largely to explore the answers to two questions of overriding concern during his time: "What is the nature of virtue?" and "In what does man's happiness consist?" Plato developed the idea that justice was the central force of morality which impels man to do right.

In the *Laws,* he presented an amalgamation of the laws to Crete, Sparta and Athens that would lead to the best state possible in contemporary Greece. He categorized crimes according to the time during which they were committed (crimes committed at night were more serious than crimes committed during the day and the penalties for them were more severe). He discussed the degrees of homicide and differentiated between voluntary, involuntary and premeditated murder; in like fashion he suggested varying degrees of penalty.

Aristotle, Plato's most famous pupil, had several important influences on the law, not the least of which is his authorship of the constitution of Athens about 329 B.C. In his *Politics* there are several relevant themes. He opposed selfish class rule that was unresponsive to the needs of the people. He declared that the stability of the state depended on a fair economic and social order and declared that "poverty is the parent of revolution and crime." Perhaps most important of all, he noted the distinction between the rule of law and the rule of men, and recommended that where there was a choice the rule of law was always to be preferred. His definition of the law was: "The law is an agreement . . . between the citizens of their intending to do justice to each other, though not sufficient to make all the citizens just and good."[3]

Rome: The Roman contribution to the development of Western law, while not as lofty and philosophical as that of Greece, may have been more significant in its practical everyday applicability. Their most significant early contribution was the Twelve Tables, set down about 450 B.C. by a group of ten men called *decemvirs.* These Twelve Tables set forth the legal order, rules and institutions, and national law of the Romans. They dealt with such matters as ownership, inheritance, torts and judicial process. They remain the fundamental basis for much of our civil law and for the use of courts and judges to adjudicate disputes.

Approximately two centuries later, further codification of Roman law by Porcius Laeca added the rights of *habeas corpus* and of appeal. However, because these were turbulent times, both of these rights could be and often were suspended by a proclamation of martial law.

Rome's greatest contribution to the formation of much of European, English and American law came through the work of the Emperor Justinian (483–565 A.D.), who summarized many centuries of legal developments in what we know as the *corpus juris civilis,* or body of civil law, the most influential book of laws ever set down. Among the major concepts embodied in Roman law which have formed fundamental themes of our American legal system are the right of an accused to meet his accuser, the right to be considered innocent until proved guilty and the right to a fair trial. The Roman conception of law enacted in Justinian's compendiums reflect the statement of the function of law in society expressed three centuries earlier by the Roman jurist Celsus: "Law is the art of finding the good and the equitable."

European and English Developments

After the fall of the Roman Empire in 476 A.D., several centuries passed before meaningful additions to the development of law took shape. The first notable additions were the various *capitularies,* bodies of law promulgated by the Carolingian and Merovingian kings, chiefly by Charlemagne, in the interest of establishing uniform laws throughout the Holy Roman Empire. The capitularies of Charlemagne, set down in 785 A.D., enacted a complex body of laws dealing with crime, weights and measures, tolls, commerce, burial of the dead and emergency measures for dealing with pestilence and famine.

One of the more celebrated laws of the Holy Roman Empire was the *Constitutio Criminalis Carolina,* enacted in 1532 A.D., during the reign of Charles V. It contained 219 articles and regulated the standing and oath of judges, the character of witnesses, the penalties for different crimes and the circumstances under which torture was permissible.

Among the ancient Irish, before their conversion to Christianity, the tribes were ruled by *brehons,* who played the dual roles of judge and priest. The laws of the *brehons* resembled the legal codes of many other peoples of the time. They were formed into a formal code called the *Senchus Mor* about 440 A.D., which remained in force in Ireland until 1170 A.D. For many centuries the English tried to eradicate the *Senchus Mor,* but it was not until 1605 that it was abolished by James I.

The *Laws of Bretts and Scots* was a code of law in use among the Celtic tribes in Scotland. They are principally concerned with controlling crimes of violence. In 1305 Edward I issued an edict abolishing the Laws of Bretts and Scots.

The most direct and significant development of laws as it has affected the American system, however, can be traced to England, where the development of law began with the conquest of England, first by the Romans and subsequently by the Angles, Saxons, Jutes and Danes. A significant portion of this early law dealt with the ownership and inheritance of land.

In Anglo-Saxon times there were a number of different words used to denote what we conceive of as "law": *aew, riht, lagu,* and it is the last of these that has become "law." Common law definitions of crime were uncomplicated and most laws were designed to keep public order. During the ninth century, King Alfred, to insure stricter observance of the rules of society, drew up one of the memorable early codes of English law. He established a hierarchy of enforcement. The basic unit was the *tithing*, a group of ten families under the direction of a chief tithingman. Ten tithings were grouped together to form a *hundred*. Several hundreds comprised a *shire*. Alfred appointed as the chief law enforcement officer and magistrate the *shire-reeve*, an officer who has been transformed into our sheriff. Observance and enforcement of the law was incumbent upon every citizen. Every able-bodied man in the shire was armed, and when a crime was supposed to have been committed, the shire-reeve or one of his chief tithingmen would raise a *hue and cry*. Each citizen of the shire would then join in the *posse comitatus* (power of the county) in pursuit of the suspected violator of the law.

After the Battle of Hastings in 1066 A.D. had sealed the Norman Conquest, William, Duke of Normandy, divided England into 55 military districts. Among many innovations, William established the concept of *curfew*, a term derived from the French for "cover the fires." The shire-reeve was put in charge of each district and was given a military rank to go along with his civil rank. To aid the shire-reeve in carrying out his duties, the Normans introduced the role of *comes stabuli*, a position that has come down to us as constable.

Exactly one century after the Norman Conquest the *Leges Henrici*, issued by Henry I (1100–1135), offered two notable additions to the concepts of law. Among other things this document declared: "There will be certain offenses against the King's peace, arson, robbery, false coinage, and crimes of violence. These we deem to be felonious."[4] Not only did this indicate the first separation of crimes into the current categories of felonies and misdemeanors, it was also the first recognition of the fact that various crimes against the citizens of a state were also crimes against the state. Violation of the "King's peace" was punishable by *outlawry*. An *outlaw* was considered an enemy of the people and any citizen was justified in slaying him.

The most important early English document, and the one that most significantly spans the centuries and cultures between England and America, was the *Magna Carta*. The nobles of England, chafing under the despotic rule of King John, forced him to sign this memorable agreement on the fields of Runnymede in 1215. Magna Carta extended to the people freedom from arbitrary and despotic authority, protected them from unnecessary infringement of rights and liberties, and guaranteed them "due process of law." It restored local control of government, assured trial by jury, and assured every citizen that he would not "be taken or imprisoned or disposed or outlawed or banished or in any way destroyed . . . except by the legal judgment of his peers or by the law of the land."

In 1275 Edward I (1239–1307) issued the Statute of Winchester, which, besides formalizing earlier law enforcement practices, set forth the familiar stipulation that ignorance of the law was no defense against an allegation of having violated the law.

Edward III (1312–1377) promulgated the Statutes of Treason, defining as treason those acts which gave aid and comfort to the enemy. Counterfeiting was considered treason.

For several centuries after it was signed, the guarantees granted under Magna Carta were gradually eroded by the constant pressure of the English crown to reestablish its primacy. In 1487 Henry VII (1457–1509) established the Court of Star Chamber as a judicial instrument under which alleged offenders were charged, tried and sentenced without any right to present a defense. The Court of Star Chamber fell into disuse during the long reign of Elizabeth I, in which time England was united by the force of her personality and the pressures of foreign rivalries, but it was revived as an instrument of repression under Charles I (1600–1649). In 1628, Parliament, in a Petition of Right that revealed how seriously Magna Carta had been eclipsed, asked that no man be compelled to make loans to the king unwillingly or be imprisoned without observance of the laws and due process. The will of the people, declared the Petition of Right, was superior to the will of the king. Charles continued to use the Court of Star Chamber in defiance of the Petition and did not abolish it until 1648. By this time it was too late to avoid the civil war in which his armies were defeated and he was captured, tried, convicted and beheaded in 1649.

Charles was succeeded as ruler of England by Oliver Cromwell, who ruled as Lord Protector from 1653 to 1658. Cromwell divided England into 12 districts, each ruled by a provost marshal. There was total political suppression under martial law throughout this period. Cromwell died in 1658 and was succeeded by his son, Richard, who proved to be incompetent. Parliament therefore requested Charles II, son of the beheaded Charles I, to take the throne, but with restricted powers. He swore his adherence to Magna Carta, the Petition of Right and other statutes guaranteeing civil liberties.

In 1679 Parliament enacted the Habeas Corpus Act, which remains one of the cornerstones of English and American law, but the right of *habeas corpus* antedated Magna Carta, having been recognized in early Roman times. Until the reign of Henry VII *habeas corpus* had been used primarily in private disputes. Parliament's act required law enforcement officials to bring a prisoner before a magistrate to explain why he was being held. Upon the presentation of the evidence, the magistrate determined whether there was sufficient cause for the prisoner to be held or that he should be released. William Blackstone, whose *Commentaries on the Laws of England* exerted enormous influence on jurisprudence in the United States and is the chief source of our knowledge of English law, characterized *habeas corpus* as "the most celebrated writ in the English law."

In 1689, after James II fled England for Scotland, the English Bill of Rights was formalized when the crown was offered to William of Orange upon the condition that he accept it as the law of the land.

Even the most cursory review of the development of English law and law enforcement indicates why, when the Founding Fathers set about establishing a legal basis for American government, their first attempt resulted in the Articles of Confederation, with its weak and ineffectual central authority, and their second in our present Constitution, with its strong central authority whose prerogatives are hedged about by a system of checks and balances and our own Bill of Rights, which are concerned primarily with the protection of citizens from the encroachments of government.

United States

The Constitution of the United States is the oldest written constitution in the world and has formed the model for the constitutions of many nations that have come into being since it was promulgated. It was not, however, the first legal basis for the operation of government in the United States, having been preceded by the Articles of Confederation. The Articles, adopted in

The U.S. Constitution forms the legal basis for the operation of government in the United States. Here Washington presides at the Constitutional Convention, 1787.
The Granger Collection, New York

1781 upon the conclusion of the Revolutionary War, proved a weak instrument for effective government, as it reserved too many rights to the states and preserved too few for the central power. It was replaced by our current constitution in 1787, upon ratification by the thirteen original colonies. As originally framed the Constitution comprised seven articles and ten amendments, the latter commonly known as the Bill of Rights. For any study of the law enforcement process these ten amendments, which restrict the powers of the central authority from interfering with the lives of its citizens, are of transcendent importance. These ten articles are practical echoes of the affirmation in the Declaration of Independence that natural sovereignty rests with the people and the sovereignty of the state has been transferred to it by its citizens so that the state can serve them. Any understanding of Supreme Court decisions in the past several decades can be gained only by reviewing the contents of the Bill of Rights.

> *Article I:* Congress shall make no law respecting an establishment of religion, or prohibiting the free exercise thereof; or abridging the freedom of speech, or of the press; or the right of the people peaceably to assemble, and to petition the Government for a redress of grievance.

The courts have for generations passed judgments reversing

attempts to break down the walls separating church and state in the form of attempts to aid nonpublic education, or to introduce prayer, even in its most nondenominational form, into public schools. The freedoms of speech and press, while considered as absolutes by some, are hemmed in by legislative restrictions against obscenity and pornography, and a definitive Supreme Court opinion on the issue is still forthcoming. The right of peaceful assembly is commonly restricted by civil legislation or police regulation concerning the need for permits to hold rallies, marches and demonstrations, but the policeman, in his everyday activity, must be concerned with allowing these activities within the scope of an overriding need for public safety.

> *Article II:* A well-regulated Militia, being necessary to the security of a free State, the right of the people to keep and bear Arms, shall not be infringed.

Despite this clear-cut declaration, many states and the federal government have legislated against the right of private citizens to own and carry weapons except under license by state or local authorities. An increasing traffic in arms and the incidence of assassinations and gun-related deaths is currently giving momentum to a drive for national gun controls. Proponents of the right to bear arms, citing Article II as an absolute constitutional privilege, overlook the qualifying reference to a "well-regulated Militia," and ignore the lack of any motive for civil defense in the private purchase of small arms.

> *Article III:* No soldier shall, in time of peace be quartered in any house, without the consent of the Owner, nor in time of war, but in a manner prescribed by law.

A puzzling article, perhaps, because none of us has probably ever known of any attempt to quarter soldiers in private homes. The chief value of the article lies in its pointing the way for all the subsequent articles which gird the citizen with a protective barrier against the encroachments of governmental authority.

> *Article IV:* The right of the people to be secure in their persons, houses, papers, and effects, against unreasonable searches and seizures, shall not be violated, and no Warrants shall issue, but upon probable cause, supported by Oath or affirmation, and particularly describing the place to be searched, and the persons or things to be seized.

With the current concern over the continuing rise in crime, and the constant fear that this rise cannot be abated or reduced except by infringement of this basic article, the courts have continually had before them litigation centered on complaints that an accused or convicted person's rights have been violated in this regard. The courts have generally decided in favor of the citizen who claimed that he, his property, or his effects were subjected to "unreasonable searches and seizures."

> *Article V:* No persons shall be held to answer for a capital, or otherwise infamous crime, unless on presentiment or indictment of a Grand Jury, except in cases arising in the land or naval forces, or in the militia, when in actual service in time of war or public danger; nor shall any person be subject for the same offense to be twice put in jeopardy of life or limb; nor shall be compelled in any criminal case to be a witness against himself, nor deprived of life, liberty, or property, without due process of law; nor shall private property be taken for public use, without just compensation.

One of the most meaningful of the amendments, it has been often disputed, especially in regard to its safeguards against self-incrimination, as a refuge behind which criminals and traitors hide. Yet it is a bulwark against the unjust coercion of police and the force of governmental pressures.

> *Article VI:* In all criminal prosecutions, the accused shall enjoy the right to a speedy and public trial, by an impartial jury of the State and district wherein the crime shall have been committed, which district shall have been previously ascertained by law, and to be informed of the nature and cause of the accusation; to be confronted with the witnesses against him; to have compulsory process for obtaining witness in his favor, and to have the assistance of Counsel for his defense.

This article, which bears so critically on the manner in which justice is to be administered to a person accused of violating the law, has been the subject of some of the most far-reaching court decisions in recent years. Most of these have dealt with the right of the accused to counsel at every stage of his dealings with the criminal justice system. Given the current crowded conditions of our court calendars, which have kept many accused in prison for extended periods (if they could not raise bail), we can expect significant court rulings on this commonly practiced but not deliberate denial of the right to a "speedy" trial. Recognition of the problem led recently to the enactment in New York State of rules that will require all accused persons to be brought to trial within one year of arraignment.

> *Article VIII:* Excessive bail shall not be required, nor excessive fines imposed, nor cruel and unusual punishments inflicted.

The first clause, as indicated above in the comment on the denial to many of the right to a "speedy" trial, will be the subject of forthcoming court judgments, since many who languish in prison before going to trial are poor people who cannot raise bail. The last clause, forbidding "cruel and unusual punishments," animates the ongoing debate over capital punishment.

> *Article IX:* The enumeration in the Constitution, of certain rights, shall not be construed to deny or disparage others retained by the people.

One of the least celebrated but probably most momentous articles for its recognition of "natural" rights of the people. Where questions arise pitting the rights of the people against the rights of the state in new issues, the thrust of the Constitution is to judge in favor of the people.

> *Article X:* The powers not delegated to the United States by the Constitution, nor prohibited by it to the States, are reserved to the States respectively, or to the people.

This article has been predominantly a matter of major political concern for more than a century, serving as the basis of the lengthy, continuing and sometimes bitter debate over states' rights. Little noted is the last phrase, "or to the people," echoing so closely the concern of Article IX and the overwhelming interest of the framers of the Constitution that as many rights as possible shall be retained by the people. Because the Constitution does not in any of its clauses provide for the establishment of a police system, this article forms the basis for the right of each state to establish and operate a law-enforcement system.

One additional amendment, the Fourteenth, has had major influence on the criminal justice system. Adopted in 1866, in the wake of the Civil War, it contains several pertinent provisions:

1. Persons born or naturalized in the United States are citizens of the United States and of the states in which they are resident

2. No state shall deprive a person of life, liberty, or property without due process of law
3. Each person is entitled to protection under the law.

The Fourteenth Amendment returned to the federal government powers that the Supreme Court in the Dred Scott decision of 1852 had reserved to the states. The essence of this decision was that Negroes were not citizens and were not entitled to any of the privileges of citizenship.

For at least a century after the adoption of the Constitution, contemporary opinion, buttressed by considerable judicial opinion, asserted that the protection afforded by the Bill of Rights referred only to the relations between the citizen and the federal government, and that it could be limited in its equal application to all citizens. In his opinion rendered in the case of *Barron v. Baltimore* in 1833, Chief Justice John Marshall rejected the claim that the Fifth Amendment was applicable to state government and declared that it was applicable to the federal government only. The entire doctrine of "separate but equal" educational facilities in the South was predicated on just such an assumption, and the Supreme Court confirmed the validity of this doctrine in *Plessy v. Ferguson* in 1897. In the last twenty-five years, with the thrust of the civil rights movement reaching its crescendo, the courts and much current opinion have moved to the view that the Bill of Rights enjoined state governments as much as it did the federal government and that any failure by the state to afford each of its citizens equal justice under the law was unconstitutional. This Fourteenth Amendment is, therefore, important to the police officer in his understanding of and appreciation for major social and political transformations and his relation to these in the course of his everyday official duties.

CONTEMPORARY TRENDS

In the past several decades, and most especially during the term of Earl Warren as Chief Justice of the United States Supreme Court, numerous important decisions have focused on the rights of persons accused of having committed crimes. The thrust of most of these decisions has been to extend greater protection of the rights of the accused against the incursions of police power.

Among some segments of the police and the public these decisions have been characterized as handcuffing the forces of law and order and as contributing factors in the continuing rise in crime. They could more properly be considered guides to performing police duties more effectively and efficiently. The decisions place a great burden on the individual policeman and his department, but in complying with the requirements of these decisions, the police will find that those cases they bring to trial will be much more solid, with the likelihood of conviction more certain.

What are these decisions, and how do they affect the role of the police officer in his primary tasks of deterring crime or apprehending criminals who have committed crimes? Do they tilt in favor of the forces of crime against the forces of law and order? Do they shackle effective police enforcement of the law? A brief review will show that they concentrate upon guaranteeing to persons suspected of having committed crimes the protections enumerated in the Bill of Rights. The review will also show that these guarantees are entirely logical under a criminal justice system that is based upon the presumption of innocence. After all, if a person is innocent until proven guilty, it is entirely right and proper to ring him round with all the protection the Constitution confers upon him. A law enforcement system that cannot function except by the abridgement or abrogation of these protections needs to be improved to the point where it can.

Fourth Amendment Rights

Two major decisions are concerned with the legitimate use of evidence in a trial. Article IV of the Bill of Rights decrees that persons shall be secure against unreasonable search and seizure and that no search or seizure of persons, their homes, papers or effects shall be made except upon probable cause. In spite of these clearcut stipulations, law enforcement officers were not especially careful to avoid routine violations of them until the second decade of this century. Their searches and seizures might have been made illegally without warrants, but the evidence gathered in this manner was admissible in court. A drastic change in the definition of permissible evidence came in 1914 in the case of *Weeks v. United States* (232 U.S. 383). The plaintiff, Weeks, protested the use as evidence in his trial of letters and envelopes seized in his home without a warrant by a United States marshal. The Supreme Court, in a unanimous decision, held that evidence obtained by unreasonable search and seizure must be excluded from use in a trial in federal court.

For many years, little attention was given to this and subsequent rulings, since they applied only to the use of evidence in federal courts. It was not until 1961, in the landmark case of *Mapp v. Ohio* (367 U.S. 643), that the decision banning the use of evidence obtained illegally was extended to trials in state courts and made applicable to state, county, city, and town police officers. The story behind this momentous decision began on May 23, 1957, when three police officers attempted to enter the Cleveland, Ohio, home of Dolree Mapp. They had received information that a person connected with a bombing was hiding there. Miss Mapp refused to permit the police officers to enter without a warrant. The officers left and returned about three hours later, displaying a piece of paper purported to be a warrant. Miss Mapp took the paper and placed it in her bosom, but the police officers removed it by force and proceeded to a thorough search of the premises, which turned up a cache of pornographic materials. The person the officers had ostensibly come in search of earlier was not found. Miss Mapp was arrested and later convicted in an Ohio court on a charge of possessing pornographic materials. The case was appealed to the United States Supreme Court. The state of Ohio contended that though the search might have been illegal the evidence it uncovered was permissible in court. Ohio law specifically permitted the admission of such evidence in its own courts. The state's attorneys also pointed to a Supreme Court decision of 1949, *Wolf v. Colorado* (338 U.S. 25), which indicated that the decision in *Weeks v. United States* was applicable to federal and not to state courts. In spite of past decisions, the Supreme Court reversed itself and insisted unequivocally that the exclusionary rule (evidence obtained through an unreasonable search is inadmissible at trial) was applicable to state courts as well under the provisions of the Fourth Amendment as guaranteed by the Fourteenth Amendment.

Fifth Amendment Rights

Article V of the Bill of Rights guarantees among other things that no person "shall be compelled in any criminal case to be a witness against himself." This guarantee underlies the right of any person accused of a crime or taken into custody for that crime to remain silent. A major case that preceded both the Escobedo and Miranda decisions (which we shall discuss shortly) and went part way toward laying the framework for those momentous decisions was that of *Malloy v. Hogan* (378 U.S. 1). In this case, a petty gambler named Malloy, after having been arrested, having pleaded guilty to the charge of pool selling and having served 90 days of a one-year prison sentence was called more than one year later to testify at an inquiry into gambling and other illegal activities in Hartford County. When asked several questions about his arrest and conviction, Malloy refused to answer "on the grounds that it may tend to incriminate me." Malloy was adjudged in contempt of court and was remanded to prison until he indicated his willingness to answer the questions put to him. The superior court in which he was called to testify refused his petition for a writ of habeas corpus and Connecticut's Supreme Court of Errors affirmed this decision.

The United States Supreme Court, upon review of the case, declared in a 7–2 decision that the due process clause of the Fourteenth Amendment guaranteed Malloy the protection of the Fifth Amendment's privileges against self-incrimination.

Sixth Amendment Rights

Several other major decisions hinge upon the right of all persons accused of crimes to be represented by counsel and have had the effect of advancing the implementation of this right to the earliest moments when a citizen becomes enmeshed as a suspect in a potential criminal trial.

Article VI of the Bill of Rights declares that a person accused of a crime shall have the right "to have the assistance of Counsel for his defense." The landmark case in this connection is *Gideon v. Wainwright* (372 U.S. 335, 1963). The central figure was Clarence Earl Gideon, a seldom employed drifter who had been in and out of prison most of his life. In June, 1961, he was arrested for breaking and entering a pool hall in Panama City, Florida. Two months later, when Gideon's case came to trial, he said that he was not ready to stand trial because he did not have an attorney. He requested the court to appoint counsel for him, but the court refused, declaring that the statutes of Florida provided for the appointment of counsel in capital cases only. Gideon conducted his own defense, was found guilty at his trial and sentenced to serve five years in the state prison. The Florida Supreme Court refused his petition for dismissal of this conviction.

In a handwritten petition to the Supreme Court for habeas corpus, he declared, "I, Clarence Earl Gideon, claim that I was denied the rights of the 4th, 5th, and 14th amendments of the Bill of Rights." In granting Gideon's petition, the Supreme Court held that the Fourteenth Amendment's due process clause guarantees that the Sixth Amendment stipulations apply in state trials in both capital and noncapital cases.

The right of persons suspected of having committed a crime is not limited, however, to having counsel at their trials. A series of decisions set forth the doctrine that these persons have the right to counsel whenever their involvement with the police begins to focus upon determining their possible guilt in a case. One of the major decisions in this area is *Escobedo v. Illinois* (378 U.S. 478), issued in 1964. Danny Escobedo was arrested for the murder of his brother-in-law. He made no statement while in custody, but engaged an attorney, who filed for a writ of habeas corpus in state court and had his client released. The police arrested Escobedo again about ten days later. Escobedo made repeated requests to see his attorney. Though the attorney was present at police headquarters, he was refused permission to see his client. During this second detention Escobedo was subjected to persistent questioning. He was not advised of his right to remain silent, and finally he made some damaging statements, which were subsequently admitted as evidence in his trial. Escobedo was convicted of murder. He appealed to the Illinois Supreme Court, which affirmed his conviction. In a 5–4 decision, the United States Supreme Court held that

> where, as here, the investigation is no longer a general inquiry into an unsolved crime but has begun to focus on a particular suspect, the suspect has been taken into police custody, the police carry out a process of interrogations that lends itself to eliciting incriminating statements, the suspect has requested and been denied an opportunity to consult with his lawyer, and the police have not effectively warned him of his absolute constitutional right to re-

> main silent, the accused has been denied "the assistance of Counsel" in violation of the Sixth Amendment to the Constitution as "made obligatory upon the States by the Fourteenth Amendment," *Gideon v. Wainwright,* 372 U.S., at 342,

and that no statement elicited by the police during the interrogation may be used against him at a criminal trial.

The Supreme Court advanced the accused's right to counsel and to the protection of the safeguards of the Bill of Rights still further in the 1966 case of *Miranda v. Arizona* (384 U.S. 436). Ernesto Miranda was arrested at his home in Phoenix, Arizona, on a charge of kidnapping and rape. He was removed to a police station, identified by the complainant and then brought to an interrogation room in the detective bureau. He was not advised of his right to remain silent or to have an attorney present, but was subjected to two hours of intensive questioning, after which the detectives emerged with a signed confession. At his trial, this written confession was admitted into evidence over the objection of defense counsel. Miranda was found guilty of the charges against him. The United States Supreme Court, in another 5–4 decision, reversed the trial court's verdict on the grounds that Miranda's rights were violated during the time that he was held in pre-trial custody and that all evidence obtained during this time, including his signed confession, were not properly admissible. The court held that whenever a suspect is held in custody without the presence of legal counsel, that custody is in itself coercive, that the suspect has the right to remain silent at the moment of arrest and must be so advised, and that a voluntary and trustworthy confession must be elicited not only with a lack of coercion but with the full knowledge on the part of the accused of his Constitutional rights.

While holding that statements or confessions made by an accused in custody could be considered legally coercive, certain procedures, if followed, could assure that these statements of confessions could be made voluntary and trustworthy, and therefore admissible as evidence in court.

> Immediately, upon any detention which curtails freedom of movement and which involves police custody, the person must, in the absence of a clear, intelligent waiver of the constitutional rights involved, be warned prior to any questioning that he has a right to remain silent, that any statement he does make may be used

> as evidence against him, and that he has a right to the presence of an attorney, either retained or assigned. Further, the government must be prepared to prove that the individual understood the advice and by voluntary affirmative act knowingly and intelligently waived his rights. If the individual indicates "in any manner whatsoever" that he does not wish to talk, the interview must cease. Persuasion or trickery of any sort to induce a person to speak despite his reservations will invalidate any statement taken.

Another important case, *United States v. Wade* (388 U.S. 218), decreed in 1967 that a person taken into custody for a crime shall have the right to have counsel present when he is placed in a police line-up.

The case began with the arrest of Wade on charges of conspiring to rob a bank and for the robbery itself. The arrest was based essentially on an identification of Wade by two bank employees through mug-shot photographs. Fifteen days after his arrest, an FBI agent arranged to have the two bank employees observe Wade and half a dozen other prisoners in a police line-up, but failed to notify Wade's attorney of the line-up. Both employees identified Wade at the line-up as the bank robber, and later identified Wade in the courtroom as the robber and as the man they had picked out of the police line-up. Wade's attorney moved for a directed judgment of acquittal, or the striking out of the bank employees' courtroom identifications, on the ground that the conduct of the police line-up without notice to and in the absence of Wade's appointed counsel violated his Fifth Amendment privilege against self-incrimination and his Sixth Amendment right to the assistance of counsel. The motion was denied and Wade was convicted.

The Supreme Court, in its decision, rejected the argument that the line-up violated Wade's Fifth Amendment privilege, but affirmed the Sixth Amendment's guarantees of an accused's "right to counsel not only at his trial but at any critical confrontation by the prosecution at pretrial proceedings where the results might well determine his fate and where the absence of counsel might derogate from his right to a fair trial."

The 1965 case of *Pointer v. Texas* (380 U.S. 400) was a landmark Sixth Amendment case centering on the right of an accused to confront the witnesses against him. Pointer was arrested together with another man and taken before a state judge in Texas for a preliminary hearing on a charge of robbery by assault. At this hearing an assistant district attorney examined witnesses; neither of the defendants, both laymen, had the assistance of counsel. The victim of the robbery testified in detail and identified Pointer as the man who had robbed him. Pointer was indicted on the charge of robbery. Before the case came to trial, the victim moved to California. During the trial the state offered the victim's testimony at the preliminary hearing as evidence against Pointer, rather than his direct, in-person testimony. Pointer's attorney objected on the ground that this was a denial of Pointer's right to the "confrontment of the witnesses against the Defendant." In its review the United States Supreme Court declared

> The Sixth Amendment is part of what is called our Bill of Rights. In *Gideon v. Wainwright,* in which this Court held that the Sixth Amendment's right to the assistance of counsel is obligatory upon the States, we did so on the ground that a provision of the Bill of Rights which is fundamental and essential to a fair trial" is made obligatory upon the States by the Fourteenth Amendment.
>
> We hold today that the Sixth Amendment's right of an accused to confront the witnesses against him is likewise a fundamental right and is made obligatory on the States by the Fourteenth Amendment.

This decision, while couched in terms of the accused's right to confront the witnesses against him, is double-edged in its pointing to the fact that at the preliminary hearing Pointer was not represented by counsel, in violation of other Sixth Amendment guarantees of protection.

Although the Supreme Court during the tenure of Earl Warren as Chief Justice made historic decisions in many areas—notably in the area of education, with its banning of segregated education through *Brown v. Board of Education,* and in the area of voting rights, with its rule of "one man, one vote" in *Baker v. Carr*—it is in the area of the Court's decisions in cases resolving the conflicts between individual rights as guaranteed by the Bill of Rights and police responsibility to maintain law and order that the individual policeman needs to give his most careful attention. The law enforcement officer should study these decisions and evaluate them in terms of (*a*) his personal and professional involvement with them; (*b*) the relationship of departmental directives to the expanded concepts of these decisions; and (*c*) the various interrelationships among himself, his department, his community, and the state.

TYPES OF LAW

While this book, concerned as it is with the successful functioning of the criminal justice officer through an understanding of society and its citizens, focuses upon criminal law, it is essential to learn some of the length and breadth of the law.

In its broadest definition, as given by *Black's Law Dictionary,* law is "that which is laid down, ordained, or established," and "that which is obeyed and followed by all citizens, subject to sanctions or legal consequences."[5]

On the basis of the functions they serve, laws may be thought of in several ways: mandatory, prohibitive, or protective. Prohibitive law is characterized by language that decrees, essentially, "thou shalt not." Mandatory law says "thou shalt." Protective law is a combination of both, having both prohibitive and mandatory features; it centers especially around the relationship of government and citizen.

The following are some other categories of law:

Common Law. Law that is derived from or is based upon custom or usage rather than statutes enacted by legislatures. Common law is at the heart of the English legal system and exerts considerable influence on the American system. Common law grows by the constant arising and settling of litigation in the courts.

Statutory Law. The law that is written and passed by various legislatures in the form of laws, codes and ordinances. Statutory law is often written in response to situations in society that require standards of permissible and impermissible conduct.

Constitutional Law. The law found within State and Federal constitutions that creates and regulates governments. These laws are broadly prescriptive and deal in the broadest terms, although sometimes specifically, with the basic precepts of government. Constitutional law is fundamental and takes precedence over all other law.

Civil Law. The law that governs private relationships and describes the procedures for settling disputes between individuals. A violation of civil law is a tort.

Case Law. Law which is established as the result of cases tried and adjudicated in courts. It often involves the setting of precedents.

Criminal Law. Law that deals with crimes and defines actions that violate the public peace, safety, and welfare. Though the victim of any crime is a person or persons, the state tries the perpetrator of the crime on the supposition that a crime against any of its citizens is a crime against the state. Criminal law specifies punishments to be imposed upon violators of the law.

Administrative Law. Outlines the functions, duties and responsibilities of officers or units of government, and is applicable only to members of that unit.

SUMMARY

The law that America's citizens live by is complex. The United States Constitution is at the center and around this are the constitutions of the fifty states. These various constitutions lay the ground rules by which the governments operate and by which their various legislatures enact the statutes that govern almost every aspect of the citizen's life. In one way or another, each citizen must abide by the laws of the federal government, the state government, county, city and town governments, plus the rules and regulations of numerous agencies, bureaus and commissions.

This multiplicity of law has derived essentially from three sources. The first is the earliest formulation of rules of law in the ancient Middle East in the Codes of Hammurabi and the Mosaic laws of the Old Testament. The second is the theoretical and practical summations of the law found in the writings of the Greek philosophers and the statutes of lawgivers, and in the Twelve Tables of Rome's *decemvirs* and the *Code of Civil Law* compiled by the Emperor Justinian almost eight centuries later. The third is the development of the English common law dating from Anglo-Saxon times and taking shape in the continuing struggle among England's people, its nobility and its crown. The notable documents of this struggle are Magna Carta, the Petition of Right and the Bill of Rights.

America's Constitution was drawn up in an attempt to establish a government that would provide its citizens with the best features of these earlier influences and would protect them from the greatest dangers discerned in the past, particularly excessive government control over the life and freedom of its citizens. America's Bill of Rights is the primary bulwark against excessive governmental encroachment on the rights of its citizens. Throughout America's history the laws of all its governing units have been written in accordance with the strictures of the Constitution. But this Constitution has not been a stagnant document. It has from time to time been adjusted by the addition of Constitutional amendments. And it has continuously been analyzed, interpreted and transformed through judicial opinion to reflect the realities of life. At this very moment the Supreme Court has under consideration a host of cases in which it will decide what the Constitution means for the citizens of the United States on the eve of the nation's Bicentennial.

The law enforcement officer must be aware of the foundations of America's laws and must appreciate how the law functions to serve both the individual citizen and the needs of society in a world that is ever changing in its political, social, cultural, and economic forces.

NOTES

1. A. C. Germann, Frank D. Day, Robert R. J. Gallati, *Introduction to Law Enforcement and Criminal Justice*. Springfield, Ill.: Charles C. Thomas Publisher, 1973, p. 17.
2. Rene A. Wormser, *The Story of the Law*. New York: Simon and Schuster, 1962, p. 3.
3. Aristotle, *Politics*, Book 3.9, 1280b 10-12.
4. Germann, Day, and Gallati, *op. cit.*, p. 50.
5. Henry Campbell Black, *Black's Law Dictionary*. St. Paul, Minn.: West Publishing Co., 1951, p. 1028.

STUDY QUESTIONS

1. Of the three major ancient sources of American law — the Bible, Greek philosophy and Roman codifications — which has had the greatest influence?
2. Is the concept of *jus talionis* still applicable in contemporary law?
3. How valid are the moral sanctions of the Bible as elements of secular law? How are they changing or being modified?
4. Is capital punishment a useful instrument of the law?
5. Why is the right of habeas corpus so central to our concept of legitimacy?
6. Discuss the relationship between the development of the law and the development of the police power in England.

7. Compare America's Bill of Rights and England's Bill of Rights. What are the similarities and differences?
8. What would life in the United States be like if the Bill of Rights had not become part of the Constitution?
9. What role has the Fourteenth Amendment played in extending the guarantees of the Bill of Rights?
10. Discuss the effects of recent Supreme Court decisions on the criminal justice system's capacity to prevent or repress crime.

2

The Growth of Organized Law Enforcement

Although it is safe to assume that in every age there has had to be a body of men charged with the enforcement of the law, history gives little detail of early developments. In ancient, simpler times, enforcement of the laws, and they too were less numerous than the myriad we have now, was left to parents, family, and tribal leaders. The laws, and their enforcement, were concerned primarily with the protection of life, limb and property. As society grew more complicated and governmental structure more complex, laws proliferated and covered an ever greater scope of human endeavor. Law became concerned not only with the relationships between people but with the relationships between people and their government. Of course, it was government that dictated the proper relationship and saw to its enforcement.

THE BEGINNINGS OF LAW ENFORCEMENT

Early evidence of organized enforcement of the law is sometimes vague, and we can only surmise that those who perceived or received the law saw to it that the law was obeyed, by persuasion if possible, by force if necessary.

Early Development

We know from the Bible that the ancient Hebrew kingdoms were ruled by kings, priests, and judges. However, the first evidence in ancient times of what can be clearly recognized as a police agency is found in Egypt about 1400 B.C. There the pharaoh Amenhotep set up custom houses and a marine patrol to guard against smuggling. In the 6th century B.C., Cyrus established a system of roads and postal delivery in Persia; Darius divided the empire into provinces, each of them ruled by a *satrap* (a lesser prince), who was given the power to levy and collect taxes.

Law enforcement in ancient Greece was entrusted to a group of men called *ephors*. Five were elected each year in Sparta and were given almost unlimited power to regulate the conduct of their fellow citizens, supervise education, levy fines and other punishments, arrest and try transgressors. Because citizens had no recourse against the power of the ephors, who combined in their own persons the role of investigator, judge, jury and executioner, except to vote against them in a subsequent election, and because Sparta was an authoritarian state, the system led to the enrichment of greedy and corrupt enforcers beyond the reach of their fellow citizens.

Augustus, the first emperor of Rome, established the Praetorian Guard in 27 B.C. from members of his legions with the specific task of protecting the life and property of the Emperor. The *praefectus urbi* was given the authority to establish rules concerning public order, fire risks, religious observances, meetings, the activities of prostitutes, beggars and foreigners. The *praefectus* had at his disposal *curatores urbi,* magistrates responsible for sections of the city, and they in turn were aided by *stationarii* (the residents of a city block) and *vigiles* and *lictores* (who patrolled the streets and enforced the laws set down by the *praefectus urbi).*

The maintenance of security in medieval France was entrusted by the king to a group of marshals. In 875 A.D., they developed a body of armed men known as *maréchaussée*. During the reign of Francis I (1494–1547) a military force of mounted archers was formed to protect the highways, and out of this has developed France's modern *gendarmerie*.

England

The people of Anglo-Saxon England lived primarily in *tuns,* small communities that have given us the word *towns*. Toward the end of the ninth century, King Alfred established a system of policing that had a far-reaching effect. Tuns were grouped into *tithings,* tithings into *hundreds,* and hundreds into *shires,* the origins of present-day counties. Each shire was led by the *shire-reeve,* or sheriff, as chief law enforcement officer.

In one of his early embodiments during the reign of King Canute (1016–1035), the sheriff achieved his position by virtue of his strength, courage and accomplished use of weapons. The sheriff's duties were manifold and some of them remain the duties of law enforcement officers to this day: *1*) collecting taxes; *2*) presiding at local courts; *3*) maintaining prisons; *4*) apprehending criminals; *5*) serving writs and summonses; *6*) drafting jurymen. The sheriff earned his living by keeping a portion of the revenues he collected for the king as his own. Because of the broad powers vested in him, the position gradually became one much abused and the sheriff became a figure of oppression. The famous legends of Robin Hood indicate the oppressive nature of the office during the 13th and 14th centuries. Sheriffs were finally shorn of much of their power during the reign of the Tudors (1485–1603), and during this period many of the sheriff's primary duties were assumed by the justice of the peace.

Systematic law enforcement began in the 12th century with the issuance in 1181 of the Assize of Arms by Henry II (1133–1189). This first step in the establishment of a national guard was followed in 1275 by the issuance of the first Statute of Winchester by Edward I (1239–1307). However, it is the second Statute of Winchester, issued in 1285, that forms the basis of the criminal justice system as we know it today. This second statute imposed penalties on those "who protected or concealed criminals"; recognized the increase in "robberies, murders, and arsons"; reenacted the assize of arms and decreed that all citizens must participate in the *hue and cry;* and established a *watch and ward* system of protection. The watch and ward specified the number of men assigned to guarding the gates of the towns. The watch was a position akin to that of patrolman; the constable was a supervisor of the watch.

The watch and ward system remained in effect for several centuries and was augmented by three additional forms of police protection against crime. The merchant police were essentially a group of private watchmen whose main duties were to prevent the stealing of private property and to locate and recover private property that had been stolen. The parochial police were a group of guards hired by the parishioners of various churches to protect them against assault. The military police were a government-operated force led by the provost marshal. As in modern times, we can discern the nature of the problems requiring police intervention from the responses made to them.

In spite of continuing measures, crime in England increased, not because of an innate tendency toward criminality in people but because of a series of developments that led to the general debasement of life for many of England's citizens. In the 14th century the development of the weaving industries on the continent convinced the English lords that the land would be put to more profit if it were inhabited by sheep rather than by people. They established the enclosure system, fencing off huge tracts of

In 18th century London deteriorating slums became the breeding grounds for the foulest of crimes.
The Granger Collection, New York

land for the raising of sheep and forcing large numbers of farmers off the land and into the cities. There they lived in ever more crowded and dismal conditions, earning a fitful living from trade and handicraft. In the 18th century the Industrial Revolution replaced huge numbers of workers with machines. Those workers who were let go crowded in ever greater numbers into deteriorating slums, which became breeding grounds for the foulest of crimes. Those workers who were retained to operate the machines were exploited fearfully, working long hours under miserable conditions. By the middle of the 18th century, London and other large cities were generally unsafe. Violent crime abounded; highwaymen accosted travelers with impunity; juvenile crime was a phenomenon noted for the first time. The response was typical: citizens armed themselves and formed vigilante groups. The courts imposed long prison sentences, banished many to the colonies, and set severe physical punishments. By gradual escalation, the death penalty, which had previously been rarely imposed, came to be used to punish 160 different crimes. Still there was no abatement in the rise in crime.

This situation existed until the time of Sir Henry Fielding (1707–1754), a distinguished jurist of his day whom we know better as the author of *Tom Jones* and other notable novels. In 1748 Fielding was appointed magistrate for Middlesex and Westminster. While serving in this capacity, he conceived of the idea of preventing crime through the action of an organized police system. In 1751 he wrote *An Enquiry into the Cause of the Late Increase in Robberies*, in which he proposed the following: *1*) policing was a municipal function; *2*) men recruited for policing should be well paid; *3*) a mobile patrol was needed to police the highways; *4*) runners were needed to get to the scene of a crime quickly; *5*) a separate police court should be established. Together with his brother, John Fielding, he organized the Bow Street station, which functioned from 1754 to 1780 with three distinct units: foot patrol, horse patrol and the famous Bow Street Runners, who eventually became little more than bounty hunters, interested primarily in collecting rewards for their captives and confiscating their booty. Fielding's system remained in effect for almost half a century, but gradually proved inadequate to the needs of an increasingly complex society.

A modern police system, recognizable as the model for contem-

A modern police system recognizable as the model for contemporary police systems, came into being through the ingenuity and efforts of Sir Robert Peel (1788–1850).
The Granger Collection, New York

porary police systems, came into being through the ingenuity and efforts of Sir Robert Peel (1788–1850). As British Home Secretary during the Prime Ministry of the Duke of Wellington, Peel proposed to Parliament in 1829 "An act for Improving the Police In and Near the Metropolis." This Metropolitan Police Act, as it has come to be called, is generally credited with being the basis for all subsequent police organizations in England and the United States. Parliament accepted Peel's recommendations, and on September 29, 1829, Peel began the formal operation of his new organization with 1000 men divided into 17 districts, each with a population of 80,000 people. Each of these divisions was organized into eight patrol sections, and in each of these patrol sections there were eight beats.

In addition to organizing this prototypical police organization, Peel developed a set of principles by which they were to function which are worth examining even today, both for their contemporary relevance and also to note how far short of their achievement many departments still fall.

1. Police must be a stable organization set up along the lines of the military.

2. Police must be under governmental, not private, control.

3. Police effectiveness will be established by the absence of crime, not by success in apprehending criminals.

4. Crimes must be publicized.

5. Police assignments must be made according to time and location.

6. An effective policeman maintains control of his temper at all times.

7. The policeman must maintain a good appearance, which commands the respect of citizens.

8. Police efficiency is achieved by enrolling and training proper recruits.

9. Each policeman must be assigned an identification number.

10. Police headquarters should be centrally located and easily accessible.

11. Policemen should be hired on a probationary basis, and retained only upon the successful completion of training and commendable performance of duties.

12. Police should maintain complete and proper records.

Adherence to these principles by all police agencies today would do much to improve and perfect the police contribution to an efficient and worthwhile criminal justice system.

United States

Inevitably, the colonists brought to America the police methods they had learned in England, which were then tempered by the requirements of life in the various parts of the continent. The colonial South was characterized largely by flat land that was sparsely settled by English farmers. When the first counties were set up in Virginia in 1634, the office of sheriff was introduced to the United States. The colonial North had less farmland; it was colder and more barren. There were greater concentrations of native Indians to deal with. The English colonists here were more likely to have been townspeople, and so they established new towns on American soil, with the watch and ward system of law enforcement. The American West, which developed primarily in the post-Colonial era, shared characteristics of the North and the South. A vast, unsettled land, the West had large stretches given over to farming and ranching, with the police role largely in the hands of the county sheriff. To maintain, support and protect these far-flung lands, and to keep essential contact with the federal government, small towns dotted the landscape; here police protection was afforded by the town marshal.

In the cities, the first response to crime was the establishment in Boston of a night watch in 1636. A rattle watch, so called because the participants sounded rattles to announce their presence and to frighten off would-be criminals, was organized in New York in 1658. The selectmen of New Haven chose two constables for one-year terms in 1673. Philadelphia set up its night watch in 1700. In these cities, all males over the age of 16 were required to participate without pay.

Until the beginning of the 19th century, police activity was confined to these nighttime duties and there was no daytime policing. A Philadelphia ordinance of 1833 established the first daytime police activity. Organized daytime police roles were established in Boston in 1838, in Cincinnati in 1842, and in New York in 1844. Only New York's police department, however, was modern in the sense that it was organized along the lines of reform suggested by Sir Robert Peel. Other such modern departments followed New York's: Chicago in 1851, Cincinnati in 1852, Philadelphia in 1855, Baltimore in 1857, and Detroit in 1865. The detective unit as a separate entity in police departments is found first in Detroit in 1866, then in New York in 1882, and in Cincinnati in 1886.

Unfortunately, many early police departments were characterized by incompetence, inefficiency, and political corruption, which resulted eventually in the Civil Service Act of 1883.

The first state to organize its own law enforcement agency was Texas, which, in 1835, established the Texas Rangers. Their primary role was to enforce the laws and protect the state's borders. As originally constituted, the Texas Rangers comprised three companies of 56 men each under the command of three captains and a major. The Arizona Rangers were organized in 1901, the New Mexico Mounted Police in 1903, and the Pennsylvania State Constabulary in 1905.

Some attempts were made to establish private police forces. One notable example was the Coal and Iron Police of Pennsylvania, created by industrialists to prevent and forcibly break up

The Sandusky, Ohio police in 1909 are typical of many municipal police forces in America in the beginning of the 20th century.
The Granger Collection, New York

labor strikes. The Pennsylvania State Legislature abolished this force in 1935.

The United States constitution does not provide for the establishment of a federal law enforcement agency. Although it reserves to the federal government certain powers of enforcement over activities related to interstate commerce, coinage, weights and measures, and postal service, it does not specifically ordain that this enforcement role be played by a police agency. Accordingly, the involvement of the federal government in a variety of police activities and agencies has come largely in response to perceived needs for the prevention of certain activities and enforced compliance in other activities.

The Judiciary Act of September, 1789, established a system of federal courts, the office of Attorney General, and the position of federal marshal. Thirteen United States marshals were then appointed for four-year terms.

The Revenue Cutter Service was organized in 1789 to prevent smuggling. The Post Office inspection system was organized in 1829 to prevent mail fraud; a Division of Inspectors was established in 1878, and the post of chief inspector was created in 1886. The Secret Service took shape from 1842 to 1865 to fight counterfeiting. The Internal Revenue Service was not established until 1865. Besides its major responsibility in administering the collection and disbursement of federal income taxes, it controls the collection of taxes for alcohol, tobacco and firearms.

The accumulation of powers to a federal agency in response to growing needs can be seen vividly in the growth of the Secret Service. For approximately half a century after it was organized to fight counterfeiting its duties remained the same. In 1894, in response to threats on the life of President Grover Cleveland, the Secret Service was given a part-time role in protecting the life of the president. In 1901, upon the assassination of President William McKinley, this protective role became full-time. In 1913, the Secret Service was assigned to the protection not only of the president, but of the president-elect. In 1917, its role was extended still further to the protection of the president's family. After a generation of stability, the Secret Service role was extended once again in 1951 to include protection of the vice-president.

The growth of the role of the Attorney General is another instructive example. In 1861 he was given control over and responsibility for United States district attorneys and marshals. The Department of Justice, which is the federal agency now headed by the Attorney General, was not organized, however, until 1870. It did not have its own law enforcement agency until 1909, when Congress established a Bureau of Investigation. This agency proved rather ineffectual until it began to be headed in 1924 by J. Edgar Hoover; it was renamed the Federal Bureau of Investigation in 1935. The Department of Justice also administers the Immigration and Naturalization Service and the Bureau of Narcotics and Dangerous Drugs, among other agencies.

MODERN POLICE AND THE LAW

First Amendment guarantees of free speech and assembly are fundamental to our society and help to distinguish it from authoritarian and totalitarian regimes. While some police may look upon these rights as bothersome—the police officer may interpret freedom of speech to mean allowing the open advocacy of the overthrow of the government by violent means and freedom of assembly to mean the promotion of violent mass demonstrations—his official duty will require him to act in a manner that protects the freedoms of speech and assembly and to prevent any outbreak of violence. He has the primary obligation to protect speakers whose views may be offensive to him and to control the behavior of listeners and bystanders who may heckle or even try to silence the speaker, even though he may be in sympathy with their views and actions. From a host of Supreme Court decisions the policeman may conclude that an arrest is proper only under the following circumstances:

1. When the speaker incites his audience to commit a crime.
2. When the speaker uses obscene language.
3. When the speaker challenges one or more persons in his audience in terms that would provoke a fight.
4. When the speaker causes a crowd to gather that interferes with the primary function of that street for pedestrian or vehicular traffic.

While the policeman may arrest a speaker under the conditions described above, his superior officers are permitted to regulate the conduct of speakers to insure as much as possible that these conditions will not prevail. They do so under the general licensing or permit powers granted them on the basis of their need to assure the well-being of the community. Some of the tools available to the police administrator for enforcing his obligations to the community are:

1. The need to obtain a permit for any gathering.
2. The right to assign suitable or permissible areas.
3. The right to enforce ordinances against any "breach of the peace."

The police administrator's right to control public gatherings to ensure public safety must be exercised with restraint and decisions should be made as broadly and liberally as possible.

The other generally used control stems from the various laws defining "breach of the peace," "disorderly conduct," "harassment" and refusal to obey a police officer's legitimate requests. The police officer must be circumspect about invoking his powers and must be certain that the action he is taking comes in response to actual violations of law and not personal reactions to events with which he is not in sympathy. While he must be aware that arrests based upon occurrences arising out of a demonstration may be dismissed, he must not neglect his duty and fail to take action where it is called for.

Arrest and Detention

When one thinks of appropriate police action, he is most likely thinking of an arrest. Arrest has been defined in various ways by criminal codes, laws, and court decisions at both state and federal levels. In *Black's Law Dictionary,* arrest is defined as "taking, under real or assumed authority, custody of another for the purpose of holding or detaining him to answer a criminal charge or civil demand."[1] A simple guide for the police officer to remember is that when he detains a person and his actions indicate an intention to deprive that person of his liberty, he has made an arrest. No force or violence, or threat of it, is necessary; implicit in an arrest is the deprivation of liberty.

A large proportion of arrests are made by warrant, "a written order issued and signed by a magistrate, directed to a police officer or some other person specially named, and commanding him to arrest the body of a person named on it, who is accused of an offense."[2]

These are restrictions, with qualifications, governing both the officer and the private citizen in making an arrest or "taking into custody." Laws pertaining to police jurisdiction, its powers and limitations, are quite similar throughout the states. An arrest may be made by a peace officer without a warrant for a crime, felony or misdemeanor, committed in his presence. He can also make an arrest without a warrant in cases of felonies committed outside his presence if he has *reasonable* cause to believe that a felony has been committed and that the person whom he wishes to take into custody has committed that felony. Any citizen may arrest another citizen for a felony committed in his presence; unlike the policeman, however, he cannot make an arrest for a felony committed outside his presence.

With or without a warrant, arrest must be made only upon "probable cause"; arrest from mere suspicion is unconstitutional. Force as necessary to effect an arrest is valid, but excessive force is illegal. Resisting a lawful arrest or interfering with a lawful arrest is a criminal offense, yet any person is justified in resisting an illegal arrest and may legally resist it with whatever force is necessary. False arrest is a dangerous action for the police officer, who is liable for subsequent damages as a result of litigation.

A corollary to arrest is detention. Detention should not be confused with taking into custody, which is the essential element of arrest. It simply means that for just and probable cause a police officer may detain, question, and "frisk" a citizen without this action constituting deprivation of liberty, which is the definition of arrest. New York State enacted stop and frisk laws on July 1, 1964. "A police officer may in appropriate manner approach a person for purposes of investigation and possibly criminal behavior even though there is no probable cause to make an arrest."[3] The New York State Supreme Court not only concurred with this viewpoint, but extended it to include action in private living quarters. A qualifying factor that must be kept in mind by the police officer is the extent of discovery of anything illicit during a frisk. This was spelled out in a recent California State Supreme Court Decision:

> Accordingly we hold that an officer who exceeds a pat down without first discovering an object which feels reasonably like a knife, gun, or club must be able to point to specific and articulable facts which reasonably support a suspicion that the particular suspect is armed with an atypical weapon which would feel like the object felt during the pat down.[4]

In other words, it is safe to assume that any object found during a pat down must be considered a potential weapon in order to justify further action on the part of the officer. If an officer arrests a suspect in spite of an object not feeling like a weapon, it is considered a justifiable arrest. This interpretation of stop and frisk can be extended to the discovery of illicit or illegal possessions.

Law enforcement agencies must be alert to the dangers of exercising their powers of detention excessively. In their zeal to prevent crime, and sometimes under media and public pressure, they may adopt a policy, even if only temporarily, of preventive detention, holding for shorter or longer periods persons suspected of being about to or able to commit a crime. This is, on its face, a perversion of police powers. As James Ahern points out:

> Preventive detention is a violation of a defendant's Constitutional rights. As such it is likely to alienate him further and drive him more deeply into criminal behavior. In addition, preventive detention exposes a subject to the corroding influences of incarceration which, as it does nothing to rehabilitate him (and in principle should not, since he has not been convicted of a crime) is counterproductive.[5]

Another qualification, referring specifically to an in-custody arrest is that a "frisk, as in the case of the classic stop and frisk situation, can permissibly graduate into a full-blown search if the police have a reasonable belief that the person in custody is armed and that the officer is in danger."[6]

Many police departments maintain a file of "field interviews," which include questioning a suspicious person on the street or a stop and frisk. The police administrator should be aware of the latitude granted by the U.S. Supreme Court, so that there will be no abuse of the privilege and so that he will be made more fully aware of crime conditions, victims and participating victims, and the officer's own effectiveness. It is generally recommended that the police administrator insist on maintaining field interview files.

Warrants

We have been concerned thus far with arrest and detention, which involves the taking into custody for longer or shorter periods persons seen committing crimes or suspected of having committed crimes. This confrontation occurs rather infrequently in police work. A far greater proportion of police encounters with citizens come as a result of search or arrest mandated by the issuance of a warrant. A warrant is issued by a judge upon application by a police officer, subject to a number of requirements. All police officers should be acutely aware of these requirements, since any search or seizure effected without a warrant is subject to challenge and review in the courts, and any search or seizure that goes beyond the bounds indicated in the warrant may also be challenged. The requirements are:

1. The warrant must be issued by a qualified court officer.
2. It must specify the area, place, address or person to be searched.
3. It must specify the evidence being sought.
4. It may be issued only for probable cause.
5. The person seeking the warrant must attest to the likelihood of the evidence sought being found in the location that will be the subject of the search.

Seeking a warrant is often a time-consuming process, and some police officers and perhaps many among the public feel that the necessity of obtaining a warrant works against the interests of law enforcement by allowing known or suspected criminals to get rid of evidence before a properly warranted search can be carried out. There are circumstances, however, in which a house can be entered and searched without a warrant. These are:

1. A police officer is permitted to enter and search a house if he is in hot pursuit of a fleeing violator.
2. A police officer is permitted to enter and search a house if a felony is being committed at the very time he wishes to make entry.

The state of California, which has often been a pacesetter in the field of the administration of justice, has found an unusual way of speeding up the process of obtaining a warrant. The state legislature permits California police officers to affix the signature of a judge to a warrant after obtaining such authorization from him upon petition by telephone. Thus far, this procedure has worked well and the legislation has not been challenged.

Rights of the Arrested

Supreme Court decisions in the series of landmark judgments described in the previous chapter have had a significant effect upon the police officer's contact with citizens he arrests and takes into custody.

To avoid having any arrest declared in violation of a citizen's constitutional rights, police officers carry with them a series of written warnings which they will read to the person they arrest immediately upon taking that person into custody. They will inform him of the following:

1. "You have the right to remain silent."
2. "Any statement you make may be used against you in court."
3. "You are entitled to counsel."
4. "If you cannot afford to retain counsel, one will be furnished to you."
5. "You will be permitted to have counsel while in custody any time you are questioned."

Any person taken into custody may wish to speak to his arresting officers, or later to detectives who are investigating his case. It is recommended that should the person wish to speak, the police officers should follow up these warnings with questions such as these:

1. "Do you understand the meaning of the rights that have just been outlined to you?"
2. "If you understand these rights and their effect upon you in possible trial proceedings, do you still wish to talk to us?"

The New York City Police Department requires that officers carry such a card or note at all times. The officers are instructed to read the list of rights in a loud, clear voice. To make sure that the person understands them the officer is to wait for a reply or acknowledgment of each of the warnings. Although corroboration is not required, the officer should try to have a witness present. At any future trial this insert or card containing the list can be introduced as evidence that the warnings were indeed given.

An important point to remember is that the warnings made mandatory by the Miranda decision are not necessarily "applicable to misdemeanors involving only fines or small jail penalties."[7] To be safe however, even in such circumstances, if the officer thinks it important, he would be wise to read the necessary warnings.

All police officers should be aware of the consequences of failure to read the list. Any infringement of a citizen's right means that *no* evidence whatsoever can be presented in court. This is known in the legal profession as the *exclusionary rule*. It does not matter what the circumstances of the case are; if the court considers an officer's action contrary to the Bill of Rights' protective guarantees, all evidence obtained through such improper action, whether oral, material, or direct, must be excluded as evidence in a court trial.

Many arguments have been presented concerning the exclusionary rule. It has been asserted that it permits many guilty persons to go free to prey on society once again, that it hampers law enforcement officers in their efforts to protect citizens from criminals. There are convincing arguments for the rule, however. The right of privacy is basic to a free society; it is a constitutional guarantee which must be recognized and upheld. To permit violations of this privacy in order to obtain evidence is to ignore a fundamental right of a free people. Evidence obtained illegally is not excluded from a trial proceeding because it is untrustworthy, but because it was obtained through the misconduct of a law enforcement officer. In a system of laws, all actions by law enforcement officers must be made within the law, and no person should be sent to jail for a violation of the law through the actions of law enforcement officers which are themselves in violation of the law.

The law enforcement officer takes exception to the inference of misconduct on his part by the court. He feels that his efforts are often unappreciated and disparaged and that reversals of convictions reflect negatively on him. His disillusionment with the judicial system and the resulting cynicism are readily apparent. In spite of these feelings, he must—and usually does—continue to uphold his oath of office.

Another problem facing the officer is determining at what point he may interrogate a suspect, and under what circumstances. He must be keenly aware of his responsibilities stemming from the decisions in the Escobedo and Miranda cases, but not completely inhibited by them. Guideline notes in another federal court decision hold that generally, if the officer takes no overt action by actually placing someone under arrest, or letting that person know that he is in custody, then he may receive a voluntary statement or confession without having first informed that person of his rights. "Courts have regarded the intent or knowledge of the officer as irrelevant so long as it is *unvoiced*, i.e., not stated to the suspect. . . . The mere subjective assertion of a suspect that he considers himself under arrest is not enough."[8] Furthermore, when a suspect has actually been placed under arrest and informed of his rights, ". . . any reasonable verbal acknowledgment of understanding, or willingness to speak, is acceptable."[9]

The rules a police officer must follow today may, at times, seem frustrating. He may view these rules, and the judicial decisions on which they are based, with mistrust, and feel that they limit him in his attempt to enforce the law by making quick and effective arrests. He should keep in mind, however, that by following the rules in the event of an arrest, he will be building a stronger case for adjudication in the courts. Judicial decisions and the law enforcement officer's role are not in conflict; they function with the same goal in mind: to keep society safe from the depredations of criminals. There is growing evidence that in the near future cooperation and mutual understanding between the courts and the criminal justice officer will increase. Such a prediction is not unqualified, but it may be assumed that:

1. There will be greater leeway for warrant requests that require the use of wiretapping equipment.
2. There will be a more sympathetic approach by the courts toward warrant requests relative to search and seizure.
3. The admissibility of evidence secured under an acceptable warrant will be viewed more favorably.
4. Confessions, provided they fall within established guidelines, will not be construed as strictly as they have in the past.
5. The use of sophisticated technological and miniaturized instruments, insofar as eavesdropping and wiretapping are concerned, will be given more latitude. In Chapter 3 we will discuss the relationship between the law enforcement officer and the courts more fully.

SUMMARY

Law enforcement in the form of a separate specialized force whose members give exclusive attention to this mission is a fairly recent development, dating back little more than a century.

In ancient times obedience to the law was the concern of family leaders, tribal elders and the monarchy. In Greece a body of men called ephors combined the duties of investigator, judge, jury and executioner. In Rome the Emperor Augustus formed the praetorian guard to regulate the conduct of Rome's citizens and protect the life and property of the emperor.

Most of the developments leading to the formation of the law enforcement system we know can be traced to England, where in Anglo-Saxon times the people were divided into tithings, hundreds, and shires. The statutes of Winchester established the hue and cry as a citizen obligation and the watch and ward system as a means for maintaining public safety. Developments during the centuries, most notably the enclosure system and the Industrial Revolution, led to an ever increasing rise in crime. Though citizens armed themselves and formed vigilante groups, and though the penalties for violating the law became ever harsher, crime flourished. It became apparent in the 18th century that an attempt had to be made to organize a force that would give its attention to fighting crime. Sir Henry Fielding organized the Bow Street Runners, a force which soon degenerated into a group of bounty hunters. The most significant development was the Metropolitan Police Act formulated by Sir Robert Peel in 1829. This was the basis for the establishment of the London police. At the same time Robert Peel established a set of standards for the police which are still valid today.

United States law enforcement has its roots essentially in English history. The Constitution does not provide for the establishment of any police force, and most state and local police forces have been established under the "implied powers" clause of Article X of the Bill of Rights. The Federal government itself was not provided with a police force but was enjoined by the Constitution to provide for stable weights and measures, postage and currency. Most of the developments in the federal police role have come in response to needs perceived as American life has grown more complex.

In the states and the municipalities developments followed a recognizable pattern. In the South, settled by farmers, the sheriff was the chief law enforcement officer. In the North, settled by townspeople, the watch and ward system was employed. Until the 19th century this proved adequate, but in this century one city after another formed a regular police force, many patterned after the standards of the Peelian reform.

Although his duties are primarily grounded in Peelian standards and goals, the contemporary policeman must be sensitive to rights and responsibilities; he must know his prerogatives to arrest, detain, stop and frisk, or question a suspect. He must know the uses of the warrant and when he may engage in pursuit, search or arrest without a warrant.

Because of a series of Supreme Court decisions he must be sensitive to the rights of the accused and must inform the accused of his rights. Adherence to procedures will not only stem abuses but make for a more solid record in the event of a court trial.

Looking back through the growth of law enforcement organizations we can see that as society grew more complex, so did the duties of the law enforcement officer. Simultaneously, the growth of social consciousness and the value of human rights has made it necessary for today's law enforcement officer to be vigilant concerning court decisions and decrees which may affect his job as well as vigilant to preserve the peace.

NOTES

1. Henry Campbell Black, *Black's Law Dictionary*. St. Paul, Minn.: West Publishing Co., 1951, p. 140.
2. *Ibid.*, p. 141.
3. *Terry v. Ohio,* 392 U.S. 1, 44 Ohio op (2d) 353, 88 Sct 1868 (1969).
4. *People v. Collins*, 1 Cal. (3d) 658, 83 Cal. Rptr. 179, 463 (2d) 403 (1970).
5. James F. Ahern, *Police in Trouble*. New York: Hawthorn Books, 1971, p. 159.
6. International Association of Chiefs of Police, *Law Enforcement Legal Review*, No. 12, June 1973, p. 6.
7. National District Attorneys' Association Bulletin, *Confessions and Interrogations after Miranda, Chicago*, 1970, p. 6.
8. *Ibid.*, p. 7.
9. *Ibid.*, p. 52.

STUDY QUESTIONS

1. What are some contemporary forms of the English *hue and cry, watch and ward* and *posse comitatus?*
2. Discuss the relationship between social upheaval and the rise in crime. What is the proper police role in times of social unrest?
3. What is the significance of the Peelian reform?
4. How are the English antecedents of American law enforcement still reflected in various American regions?
5. What constitutes "probable cause"?
6. Why should persons arrested and accused of crimes have any rights?
7. What is the *exclusionary rule?* Should persons accused of crimes be protected by it?

8. What are the differences between a police arrest and a citizen's arrest?
9. When may a police officer forego reading an accused his rights?
10. Should a police officer accept a confession from a person he has arrested before reading him his rights?

3

The Judicial System: Judges, Courts, and Trials

A singular peculiarity has marked man from the very beginning. Alone among the creatures of this earth, as well as we can tell, he routinely judges the actions of others and expects to have his actions judged by others. From the earliest records and literature that have survived, including the Egyptian *Book of the Dead*, we learn that man has believed in a day of judgment, a time when all his actions on earth will be weighed in the balance and some affirmative or negative evaluation will be made. These early writings indicate that man expected this judgment to be made after his death, not during his lifetime. His good behavior and righteous conduct on earth were motivated by his desire for an affirmative evaluation of his life's record and a judgment that would grant him a pleasant and peaceful afterlife.

Apparently this proved inadequate to the task; man's conduct on earth needed to be judged on earth. His conduct during life was to be judged during his lifetime, and he would receive his rewards and his punishments during his lifetime. The transition was simple; instead of being judged in an afterlife by a god or gods, he was judged in this life by his king, the divinely ordained representative of the gods on earth, or by agents of the king.

In this chapter we will examine the development, organization and functioning of the United States judicial system. Once again the major early influence is the English system, traced from its rough beginnings in the shire courts through the development of circuit judges, justiciars and justices of the peace. Unlike the other systems discussed in the chapter America's judicial system is founded on the constitutionally based separation of federal and state courts. In the following pages we will examine the distinctions which are important to the law enforcement officer. Special emphasis is given to the case of *Marbury v. Madison*, in which for the first time the Supreme Court asserted the right of judicial review.

The final parts of Chapter 3 examine the trial process itself, identifying the nature and roles of the main participants and outlining the procedure of an actual court trial. Attention is also focused on the pleas the defendant may make and the nature and consequences of each plea.

EARLY DEVELOPMENTS

The earliest evidence that we have of courts are to be found in the ancient Middle East. In Egypt and Babylonia, the courts were semi-ecclesiastical institutions which used religious ritual as a basis for judgment. The ancient Hebrews were ruled by a triumvirate of kings, priests and judges, and, as we see in the Old Testament *Book of Judges*, at certain times the judges were the supreme rulers of their people, even controlling the appointment of kings. Both before and during the Christian era the supreme tribunal of the Jews was the Sanhedrin, consisting of approximately 70 members drawn from the priests, tribal elders and scribes.

In Greece, the judicial system centered on the jury, which was drawn by lot and usually comprised some 500 freeman. This jury acted as judge as well, and the trial they witnessed was not cast in the form of the adversary system we know today but was a series of addresses by accomplished orators.

The court system in Rome began as an offshoot of priestly convocations, but became a secular institution over the course of several centuries. The judge was called *magistratus* or *judex*, and served essentially as an arbiter or referee of disputes.

ENGLISH COURT HISTORY

The beginnings of a court system in England are once again

clouded in developments early in the Anglo-Saxon period. When a person was accused of a crime, his guilt or innocence was determined in one of several ways: trial by oath, trial by combat, or trial by ordeal. Under the system of trial by oath, the accused would come before the court and swear to his innocence. He would bring with him as many friends as he could who would likewise attest to his innocence. In this phenomenon, called *compurgation*, sufficient numbers of citizens attesting to the innocence of the accused resulted in his acquittal on the charges made against him. Compurgation remained an acceptable procedure in English courts until 1834. This may seem a rather naive method of determining the guilt or innocence of a person accused of a crime, but in a related form, the use of character witnesses, compurgation still echoes in our judicial system. Trial by combat, in which disputants would attempt to determine whose claim was right by armed personal combat, remained in force in England until 1819. Trial by ordeal involved the accused allowing himself to be tested by, for example, fire or water. He might allow his arm to be burned with a hot iron. One month later he would reappear for an examination of the arm. If it showed no sign of damage from the hot iron, he was proved innocent; if, however, the arm showed signs of a wound, infection, or scarring, he was proved guilty.

During this same period, a system of penalties for offenses began to be established, consisting of fines, rendition, servitude and restitution. Criminals were often stigmatized; that is, they were branded with some sign to indicate the offense they had committed. The scarlet letter that Hester Prynne was forced to attach to her clothing in Nathaniel Hawthorne's famous novel was an echo of stigmatizing brought to the New World by the Puritans.

Until the 11th century all law enforcement and adjudication remained in the hands of the sheriff. In 1072 the crown introduced *vicecomes* (circuit judges) who would travel about the country to try cases. In 1166 the jury system was introduced to England in the Assize of Clarendon. This early jury differed from ours in that it was essentially an investigative body. The justices ordered the jurors to investigate the case in dispute and return with a sworn verdict. During the reign of Edward I, the power of the court was taken over by the Lord Chancellor, who remains to this day the highest judicial officer of the British crown.

Various judicial officials, some of whom have come down to us in slightly altered form, date from this Anglo-Saxon period. The *justiciar* was closest to what we today call a judge. He was the head of the royal judicial system, chief administrative and legal assistant to the king, and his agent in all functions during the king's absence. Following the justiciar, we encounter an officer of the crown known as the *conservator of the peace*, whose functions consisted of receiving indictments, suppressing riots and disturbances, serving as trial judge, and punishing malefactors. Sir William Shareshull, who was Chief Justice of the King's Bench from 1350 to 1361, became active in the development of a new type of local court officer, who came to be known as a *justice of the peace*. This position is today more typical of the American system of jurisprudence than the English, and is the cause of some concern and debate because many such justices are not lawyers or even trained in the law.

The modern court evolved from rough beginnings in Anglo-Saxon and Norman times. The earliest court was the shire court, presided over by the earl or, in his absence, the sheriff. There were also courts in such smaller governmental units as villages, boroughs, and towns; even the hundreds sometimes had their own courts.

The king's court was known variously as *curia regis*—the chief court of the king—*cura regis* and as the *coram rege*. Assize courts were similar to circuit courts in the United States in that certain judges traveled from court to court to try cases. *Oyer and terminer* was originally a writ directing the assize judges to inquire into certain crimes. In some areas of the United States, the higher criminal courts are still called "courts of oyer and terminer."

AMERICAN COURT HISTORY

The basis for the judicial systems of the United States is the Constitution. Article III, Section 1, states: "The judicial power of the United States, shall be vested in one supreme court, and in such inferior courts as the Congress may from time to time ordain and establish." From this origin stems the federal judicial system. The Tenth Amendment, as previously cited, declares that "powers not delegated to the United States by the Constitution, nor prohibited to it by the States, are reserved to the States." From this origin, and from the various state constitutions, stem the various state judicial systems.

Article III indicates also the jurisdiction of the federal judiciary system:

1. Treaties with other nations and states.
2. Conflicts involving ambassadors, public ministers and consuls.
3. Maritime and admiralty cases.
4. Litigation to which the United States is party.
5. Disputes between the states.
6. Disputes between a state and the citizens of another state.
7. Litigation between citizens of different states.
8. Claims by citizens of one state against another state in which the claim involves state land.
9. Claims of a citizen of a state against the state.
10. Disputes between U.S. citizens and foreign nations or the citizens of foreign nations.

In view of the prominent political role that the Supreme Court has always played, especially in the controversial and far-reaching decisions in the past couple of decades, it is important to point out the origins of the Court's role in deciding what is the law of the land. The constitution did not give the Supreme Court the right of *judicial review*—the right to examine the law in the light of current litigation and determine its constitutional validity. The Court adopted this right in the famous case of *Marbury v. Madison* in 1803. Chief Justice John Marshall's opinion determined that Congress's legislative action was unconstitutional, and established that it was the Supreme Court that had the right to make this judgment.

ANATOMY OF THE AMERICAN COURT SYSTEM

The organization of the U.S. judicial system is fairly simple, consisting as it does of the Supreme Court, the Courts of Appeal, District Courts, and Special Courts.

The organization of the various state court systems is also fairly simple, consisting of a state supreme court, an appellate court, and a primary court, in which courses of judicial action are initiated. Some states, however, maintain two primary court systems, one civil and one criminal. Those states that separate civil and criminal actions usually refer to the criminal branch subdivisions as juvenile courts, traffic courts, magistrate courts, county courts, family courts, and so on. The most prevalent courts of limited criminal jurisdiction are those conducted by justices of the peace. These courts may be convened almost any place. They are not courts of record, however, and usually hold only preliminary hearings. A court of record is one in which a court stenographer is present and in which all testimony and evidence is recorded. If a person wishes to appeal a decision made in the court of a justice of the peace, he must take his case to a court of original jurisdiction and record.

The courts of the United States are divided into three levels of juridiction. *Courts of limited jurisdiction* are those whose legal jurisdiction covers only a particular class of cases or cases where the amount of controversy is below a prescribed sum or which is subject to specific exceptions. *Major trial courts* are those having unlimited general jurisdiction in civil and/or criminal cases. *Appellate courts* include those courts of last resort and intermediate appellate courts. These are courts having jurisdiction of appeal and review, with original jurisdiction conferred only in special cases.

Courts of limited jurisdiction are divided into three subcategories: juvenile, probate and other. Juvenile courts are those which deal primarily with delinquent and neglected children. In various places such courts are called Juvenile Courts, Family Courts, Juvenile and Domestic Relations Courts, Domestic Relations Courts and so forth. The jurisdiction of these courts can include crimes committed by persons under legal age, juvenile status offenses, offenses against children, probation of minor delinquents, adoption, custody, or disposition of minor and mentally incompetent children, child neglect or abandonment, child and wife support, and paternity.

Probate courts are also called Orphans Courts, Surrograte's Court, or Courts of Ordinary. The subject jurisdiction varies from place to place, but usually includes estate settlement, probate and contest of wills, adoption, commitment of the insane, administration of the affairs of orphans, mental defectives and incompetents, guardianship of minors, apprenticeship, receivership, change of name proceedings and the administration of trusts.

Other courts are various state and local courts with limited jurisdiction such as justices of the peace, district magistrates justice courts, county, municipal and city courts.

Major trial courts are given different names in different states and sometimes may be known by different names in different parts of the same state. Some of these names are: Circuit Courts, District Courts, Superior Courts, Chancery Courts, County Courts, Common Pleas Courts, Supreme Court (only in New York State) and Criminal Court (only in Indiana).

Appellate courts are divided among intermediate appellate courts and courts of last resort. Twenty-four states have intermediate appellate courts, and in fifteen of them the name used is Court of Appeals. Some other names for such courts are Appellate Court (Maryland), Court of Special Appeals (Massachusetts), Appeals Court (New Jersey). Courts of last resort are invariably called Supreme Court, except in New York, Kentucky, Maryland, and the District of Columbia (where it is the Court of Appeals), West Virginia (where it is the Supreme Court of Appeals), Maine and Massachusetts (where it is the Supreme Judicial Court). In Texas and Oklahoma there are separate courts of last resort for civil and criminal cases.

COURTS IN OPERATION

The court system begins to function long before either the plaintiff or the defendant steps foot into the courtroom. But all the actions taken prior to the opening of a trial in court have a significant bearing on the conduct of that trial and any judgments made on it during the appeals process.

The first step is arrest, the taking into custody by the police or by a fellow citizen of a person accused of having committed a crime. The arrest is followed by the booking. This is the recording in the law enforcement record-keeping system of the essential facts in the case: the date and time of the alleged crime, the name of the person arrested, the charge on which the person is held, and the name of the persons, police or private citizen, who made the arrest. Usually, a person is booked for a specific crime. There are times, however, when a person is held on an "open charge," or "for investigation," or on "suspicion of ...."

After a person is booked, he is arraigned. This means that he is brought before the court to be charged with the offense he is accused of having committed and is asked to plead to the charge made against him. The charge is made in the form of an *indictment, presentment, information,* or *formal complaint,* and the answer the accused makes to any one of these must be made in open court.

Pleas

There are several different pleas that the accused can enter during his arraignment.

Guilty. The accused may plead guilty to the offense charged. Under certain circumstances the court may disallow this plea and enter a not guilty plea instead. Often the guilty plea is made by arrangement among the court, the prosecution and the defense to a charge of a lesser offense than the one originally given. This plea, the result of what has come to be known as *plea bargaining,* is brought before the court to be charged with the offense he is is accepted usually as an expedient to save the time and money involved in a trial. However, if the guilty plea is made to the original charge, and the offense is serious, the court will accept it only after questioning the accused closely as to his understanding of the charge, the consequences of his plea, and the forthrightness and voluntariness of the plea.

Nolo contendere. This Latin phrase translates roughly into "I do not wish to contest (the charge)." The accused does not admit his guilt, but indicates that he is ready to accept the punishment meted out to persons found guilty of that offense. This readiness to accept conviction and sentencing is usually based on the desire to avoid trial, with its inevitable entry into the public record of all the facts of the case.

Nolle prosequi. This is a plea made not by the accused but by the plaintiff or the prosecutor, either of whom may decide not to proceed further in a trial or who determine that the charges cannot be proved. Often a *nol pros* is necessary if vital evidence is lost or destroyed or if a key witness is unavailable.

Stand mute. The accused may remain silent, refusing to make any answer to the charge. In such an event the court will enter a plea of not guilty.

Not guilty. The accused may enter a plea of not guilty, asserting his innocence of the charge made against him, or he may raise certain defenses: insanity, self-defense, statute of limitations, double jeopardy.

Plea Bargaining

Of the pleas that may be entered at the time of arraignment, the most significant and sought after is the guilty plea. A case which has been opened by an arrest can be closed expeditiously without the need for investing the time and expense of a jury trial. For this reason, the guilty plea is the subject of serious negotiation among all parties concerned. The plea is sought for another significant reason: the difficulty of obtaining conviction in jury trials for the charge leveled against the defendant. Of all the persons convicted of crime in the United States, fewer than 10% are convicted as a result of a jury's verdict; more than 90% are convicted by their own guilty pleas.

What is involved in the guilty plea? Essentially, the person against whom the charge is made makes an admission in open court of every element of the charge. Because of the consequences of the plea, it must be made intelligently, voluntarily and without coercion. The court will question the person who enters a guilty plea searchingly to determine: *a)* that he clearly understands the charge, *b*) that he is aware of the defenses he can make against the charge and the arguments in mitigation of his act that he may raise, and *c*) that he is entering the plea freely, without reservation and with complete understanding of the consequences. The court will also inform the accused that in entering a plea of guilty he is waiving several rights guaranteed to him in the Bill of Rights: *a*) the right against self-incrimination, *b*) the right to a trial by jury, and *c*) the right to be confronted by the witnesses against him. Only after the court is convinced that the guilty plea is made with a thorough understanding of all these factors will it accept the guilty plea.

Plea negotiation to extract a guilty plea from an accused is dangerous for all concerned and should be handled with great circumspection.

First, the pressures on an accused to plead guilty are severe, and an innocent person may enter this plea for fear of being found guilty after a trial and facing a more severe penalty for having gone to trial.

Second, the guilty plea may evoke a sentence from the judge that is unsuited to the nature of the crime committed or to the needs of the person accused of the crime.

Third, either the prosecution or the defense may be poorly served by the determination of the case, since one or the other is relinquishing a sworn commitment to see that justice is done.

If all the persons accused of crimes elected to go to trial, however, the courts would be loaded beyond their capacity to function. Therefore, prosecuting attorneys are under constant pressure to obtain guilty pleas, to lighten their workload and that of the courts. The negotiation they conduct is, however, hazardous. The prosecution cannot obtain a negotiated guilty plea without in some measure revealing the strength of its case. To convince the defendant and his attorney of the strength of its case, it must reveal significant facts. If the session does not end in a negotiated plea of guilty, the accused may go to trial aided by a defense attorney who has the advantage of having previewed the prosecution's case and having had the time to prepare against it.

The American Bar Association has proposed certain standards for establishing three major areas of plea negotiation:

1. Acceptance of a plea to a lesser offense.
2. Dismissal of pending charges.
3. Type of sentence to be imposed.

Trials

Should that least likely possibility, a not guilty plea, be entered, arraignment will be followed by a trial. The trial may take place with or without a jury, the choice being the defendant's. Constitutionally, he is entitled to trial by jury, but sometimes, especially in cases where the defense attorney would rather trust to the restraint, impartiality and legal expertise of a judge, the dedefendant may forego it. If he chooses a trial by jury, he will face trial by twelve of his peers, and two alternates, who are citizens of the location within which the trial is held. He won't come to trial, though, until he and his defense counsel have had sufficient time to prepare his defense.

Because the court calendars are crowded, a priority of trials has been established:

1. Criminal cases precede civil cases.
2. Felonies in which the accused is in custody are tried first.
3. Misdemeanors in which the accused is in custody are next.
4. Felonies in which the accused is on bail are next.
5. Misdemeanors in which the accused is on bail are last.

The Prosecution

The state's case will be presented by the prosecuting attorney, who may be known variously as district attorney, county attorney, county solicitor, state's attorney, public prosecutor. By whatever name he is known, he is usually a member of the bar and has obtained his position by appointment or election. As an attorney, he is constrained to follow Canon 7 of the American Bar Association's *Code of Professional Responsibility,* which imposes on him the primary duty not to convict, but to see that justice is done.

The prosecuting attorney is an American innovation. A Connecticut statute of 1704 declared:

> . . . Henceforth there shall be in every countie a sober, discreet and religious person appointed by the countie courts to be attorney for the Queen to prosecute and implead in the laws all criminals and to do all other things necessary or convenient as an attorney to suppress vice and immoralitie. . . . [1]

The prosecuting attorney, who is in many respects the chief law enforcement officer in the area in which he has jurisdiction, has certain specified duties: *1*) to see that the laws are faithfully executed and enforced, and to act when the laws are broken; *2*) to serve as the state's and the public's chief advocate and attorney in court proceedings; *3*) to observe the established codes of professional conduct; and *4*) to seek justice, not convictions, per the requirements of Canon 7.

The prosecuting attorney has a great deal of latitude in the performance of his duties. By the power to charge, or not to charge, a person with a crime he has initial control of which cases come to trial. In determining his action in any prospective trial, he must ascertain whether a crime has been committed, under what statutes the person may be charged, whether he has jurisdiction in the area in which the crime is alleged to have been committed, whether the suspect has been connected to the crime, and whether the evidence and witnesses are sufficient to allow for successful prosecution of the crime.

The Defense

The constitutional right of every defendant to counsel was a major advance in the 18th century. Prior to 1836, in England, the accused was not allowed legal counsel in felony cases, even when the possible penalty upon conviction was death. It was only in 1850 that Parliament enacted legislation that allowed defendants in capital cases to be represented by counsel. As indicated previously, Supreme Court decisions have extended the scope of the Sixth Amendment guarantees to counsel to the earliest phases of citizen-police encounters which place the citizen in jeopardy of being charged with a crime.

The defense counsel, the adversary of the prosecuting attorney, is the professional representative of the accused in all proceedings, and his responsibilities, within the bounds of decency, honor and professional standards of conduct, are to his client.

His major obligation to his client is to serve him at every stage of judicial proceedings in a manner that protects all his rights as enumerated in the Bill of Rights and federal and state statute. The defense attorney is not, however, his client's agent; he, and not the client, is supposed to be in control of every aspect of the defendant's case. Since the defendant is presumed innocent until proved guilty, placing the burden of proof on the prosecution, the defense counsel's actions, including examination of jurors, cross-examination of witnesses, challenges and motions in court, and so forth, are to be made not in the interest of impeding justice or confusing the facts of the case, but for the purpose of presenting in court as complete a record of events, motivation and extenuating circumstances as he can. His actions, however, do not extend to colluding with his client to present false or perjured testimony by the client or witnesses for his defense.

The defense attorney must establish with his client a relationship of mutual trust and understanding, which has as its core the attorney's obligation to see that justice is done by presenting in court every shred of evidence that indicates his client did not commit the crime for which he is charged, or that the crime with which he is charged is statutorily more severe than is required by the conduct of the accused, or that the client had overriding motives in extenuation of his conduct. Just like the prosecuting attorney, the defense counsel is obliged to seek justice, not merely acquittal for his client.

The Judge

The judge is *primus inter pares,* first among equals, in any court proceeding, in that he is also a lawyer. Appointment or election and, hopefully, long experience and suitable temperament have elevated him to a position as the central figure in court.

It is he who regulates the conduct and tempo of the trial, supervising the actions of the prosecution and defense, judging the motions raised by both, determining the admissibility of evidence, instructing the jury as to the nature of the crime and the basis on which they are to render judgment. In some cases the trial judge will, at the request of the defendant and his counsel, render judgment without a jury trial. The judge's role is underscored, of course, by the fact that all the decisions of superior courts in the state and federal government will be based upon evaluation of the trial as it has been conducted by the judge.

The Jury

The jury, as it is currently in use in United States court trials, consists usually of twelve persons, with two alternates, who hear the case and remain ready to render judgment if any of the regular jurors becomes ill or otherwise incapable when the case is given to the jury to render its verdict. Jurors are selected from among the tax rolls or voting registers of the city, town, or county in which they reside. A person accused of a crime is supposed to be tried by a jury of his peers, that is, persons who are substantially like him in education, economic and social status, attitudes, and general beliefs. There are numerous exclusions from service on a jury. Persons who have been convicted of misdemeanors or felonies, persons who are of notably bad character or alcoholics or addicts, persons who are not literate, persons who are under 25 or over 65—all these may be excluded. Many other eligible persons may choose to be excluded, including mothers, attorneys, doctors, teachers, clergymen, public officials, and a host of others. In addition, during the pre-trial examination of the jury both the prosecution and the defense will narrow selection to a core group that each feels is most likely to render a fair and impartial verdict. The defendant, therefore, is being tried before a group of his fellow citizens who may or may not turn out to be his peers. There are times when a defendant or his counsel may request a change of *venue*—location of the trial proceeding—or a verdict may be overturned by a superior court because of a judgment that the jury that rendered verdict in the case was not the defendant's peers.

THE TRIAL PROCESS

The trial itself follows an established and precise order, and it is one of the main functions of the judge to see that this order is adhered to.

The first phase of the trial consists of the opening statements by the prosecution and the defense. The prosecution's statement gives a broad outline of the facts of the case, the crime with which the defendant has been charged, and the method by which the defendant's guilt will be proved. The defense's statement will review the same facts, introduce other facts, and indicate the method by which the defendant will be proved innocent. These statements are actually not the first indication the jurors have had of the facts in the case. During the pre-trial impanelling process, both the prosecution and defense will have revealed some of the basic elements during the examination of prospective jurors. The opening statements are made because it is usual that the defendant is in jeopardy only after the jury has been sworn in or when the first witness has been sworn.

After the opening statements, the prosecutor presents his case using one or more witnesses to testify to the facts. Testimony is elicited by *direct examination*. The prosecutor asks the witness a series of simple questions, the answers to which should set forth the essential facts the prosecution wants the jury to consider. The defense now engages in *cross examination*. Again a series of simple questions is asked, the answers to which should reveal how much of the facts the witness does not know or how much of what the witness knows may be mitigating or unharmful to the defendant.

If the prosecution wishes to, it may engage the witness in *redirect examination*, questioning essentially those facts that have been brought out in the cross examination.

If the defense then wishes to, it may engage the witness in *recross examination*, questioning only those facts brought out in redirect examination.

The witness may then be dismissed and one or more other witnesses may be sworn in. Each witness may be subjected to the process outlined above. After the prosecution has brought forth all its witnesses, it rests its case.

The defense now begins to present its case. However, before bringing forth any witnesses for the defense, it may petition the trial judge for a dismissal, contending that the case as presented by the prosecutor is insufficient to prove the defendant's guilt. If the trial judge rules in his favor, the case is dismissed and the defendant is released. If the trial judge denies the motion for dismissal, the defense proceeds to present its case, calling as many witnesses as it deems necessary to prove the defendant's innocence. The procedure is the same as described above, but now it is the defense counsel who engages in direct examination and redirect examination, and the prosecution which engages in cross examination and recross examination.

After the defense rests its case, the prosecutor may choose to engage in *rebuttal,* in which, using the procedure described above, he calls forth witnesses who have already testified or introduces new witnesses to amplify or clarify his case. The defense counsel may, at the end of rebuttal, engage in *surrebuttal,* which serves the same purpose for his case and is conducted in the same manner. At the end of surrebuttal, he will most likely once again ask for dismissal of the case, contending that the prosecution has failed to prove its case. The judge may grant this request and release the defendant from custody, or he may deny it, in which case both prosecution and defense proceed to their *summations.*

The summations, obviously, are extended statements by both the prosecution and defense of the facts of the case as they have been brought forth. The prosecution will try to show how through his array of witnesses and experts he has proved the facts of the case as he had promised to in his opening statement. The defense will try to show how it has disproved these facts or presented compelling extenuating evidence that proves the defendant not guilty.

After the summations, the judge instructs and charges the jury. Before allowing them to retire to their deliberations, he reviews the legal principles involved in the case, indicating the amount and type of evidence that must have been presented for the jury to properly render a guilty verdict, or indicating which of a number of offenses the defendant may be guilty of on the basis of the testimony presented, or indicating those conditions under which the defendant ought to be declared not guilty. He then charges the jury to render a "true and just verdict."

The jury retires to its deliberations in private. It may take several hours or several days to reach a verdict. During this time the jury is sequestered under the care of the bailiff, who sees to it that the jurors are fed, housed and transported without coming into contact with outsiders. The verdict is reached by majority or unanimous opinion, usually unanimous.

When it has reached a verdict, the jury informs the court through the bailiff. The jury is returned to the courtroom and in the presence of the judge, prosecution, defense, and defendant renders its verdict through its foreman. If the defendant is found not guilty, he is released from custody. If the defendant is found guilty, the defense may poll the jurors, in which case each juror will be questioned as to his verdict. If the poll verifies the guilty verdict, the defense may make a motion for a new trial or a mistrial on the grounds of irregularities or errors in the trial proceedings. If the motion is granted, the defendant will be placed on bail or remanded to custody. If the motion is denied, the defendant will be held over for sentencing.

Sentencing usually follows within twenty days, a period during which a presentencing investigation may review the defendant's personal history, the nature of his crime, his need for counseling, rehabilitation or punishment, and society's need for a person convicted of a particular crime to be treated in a particular way. During this time the judge will review the trial record and evaluate his own feelings about the crime, the defendant, proper punishment, and so on.

Sentence will depend on the recommendations of the persons who conduct the presentencing investigation, the judge's feelings, and, not least importantly, the statutory requirements related to the particular crime. In all of this there is a great deal of discretion, and the sentence for any crime may be mild or severe. This discretion, with its attendant inequities, has led to sharp and incisive debate and contention. The Supreme Court's last decision against capital punishment was based on the capriciousness and randomness of its imposition.

Depending upon the crime, the offender may be sentenced to a number of different penalties: imprisonment, commitment to a state hospital or medical correctional facility, a fine payable to the state, damages payable to the injured party, forfeiture of public office, forfeiture of public property through confiscation.

The sentence can be suspended, that is, have its execution delayed. This can be done in two ways: the defendant can be released on his own recognizance with the expectation that he will conduct himself in a manner that will not involve him with the law again, or he may be placed on probation, a period of supervised conduct during which time he must report to a probation officer and give evidence of his ability to function in society successfully without committing the offense for which he was first arrested.

Whatever the sentence decided upon, it is imposed because, to quote Plato, "When anyone commits any injustice, small or great, the law will admonish and compel him either never at all to do the like again, or never voluntarily."

SUMMARY

Although there is evidence of judicial activity in ancient Egypt, Greece and Rome, America's judicial system is most directly affected by the development of the English system. The evidence indicates that the earliest settlement of disputes was personal, in the form of trial by oath, trial by combat, or trial by ordeal. Only in the 12th century was the judgment of disputes entrusted to the states, with the Assize of Clarendon. During the next several centuries, the English system introduced vicecomes (circuit judges), justiciars, and justices of the peace.

America's judicial system is divided into federal and state organizations. Though the various state court systems are arranged along similar lines, having courts of limited jurisdiction, major trial courts, and appellate courts, there are differences from state to state, especially in nomenclature.

A person involved in the criminal justice system passes through a set pattern of arrest, booking and arraignment. If he goes to trial, he passes through a trial procedure that is carefully maintained to see that his rights are protected and justice is done. The major participants in the trial are the judge, the prosecutor, the defense counsel and the jury. The trial itself is conducted in a carefully set pattern that passes from examination and cross examination to redirect examination and recross examination to rebuttal and surrebuttal and, finally, to summations by both prosecution and defense.

Should a defendant be found guilty of the offense charged, he will be held over for sentencing, which will come within several weeks, during which time the trial judge will study the offense, the defendant's history, the record of the trial and the recommendations of court personnel who have conducted a pre-sentencing investigation. The defendant may be sentenced to incarceration, fine, probation, or may be released in his own recognizance under a suspended sentence.

NOTES

1. Quoted in A. C. Germann, Frank D. Day, and Robert R. J. Gallati, *Introduction to Law Enforcement and Criminal Justice,* Springfield, Ill.: Charles C. Thomas, Publisher, 1973, p. 202.

STUDY QUESTIONS

1. Discuss the pros and cons of plea bargaining. Who is the chief beneficiary of plea negotiation?
2. Why does the prosecuting attorney control the court calendar?
3. What are the reasonable limits to a defense counsel's responsibilities to his client?
4. How does the jury system serve the cause of justice?
5. What are some of the qualifications for serving on a jury?
6. What does the presiding judge cover in his charge to the jury?
7. What are the advantages and disadvantages of having justices of the peace who are not lawyers?
8. What is the function of the character witness in a trial?
9. What are the limits to points brought up in summation?
10. What are the major influences on the determining of sentences?

4

Corrections: Treating the Convicted Offender

What's in a name? asked Shakespeare. In the disposition we make of persons convicted of violating the law, apparently everything. By common assumption and agreement, when we speak or write, we use words to describe and define acceptable facts; we do not use words to hide, mask or cloud facts. In numerous ways, from the stylist's advice to "say what you mean and mean what you say," to the contemporary admonition to "tell it like it is," we show our constant concern for the accuracy and truthfulness of words.

What judgment shall we make then of the use of the word "corrections" in the title of this chapter? Is the system in general use in the United States a "corrections" system? Does it take the people entrusted to its care and, by a program of academic education, psychological counseling, emotional support and even stern admonition, correct the errors of their ways and return them to society with a determination not to do wrong? In most cases, apparently not. Is the word then a sham? A euphemism? Or does it merely express the philosophy, the intention and motivation of the system, the direction in which it is moving?

This chapter might instead have been headed "Penology." A look through the dictionary will show a disproportionate number of words that indicate the historic fate of persons who were convicted of violating the law. They were sent to *prison,* to *jail,* to the *can,* the *clink,* the *lock-up,* to *stir,* or to a *house of detention,* and they were confined there in *cells* or *dungeons.* All of these words indicate an incarceration that served little purpose but to punish prisoners for their transgressions and an eventual release that found them as little prepared to cope with the demands of society as they were at the time they were committed. Occasionally, we come upon words like *penitentiary* or *reformatory,* which, while still denoting physical confinement, at least indicate a positive program or intention of returning the prisoner to society no longer a threat to it.

Would "penology," then, have been a more accurate heading? The distinction is critical, as it indicates the use to which we put the system. Penology denotes punishment, and as Robert Wicks points out, "Recognition is now widespread that punishment, much less punishment by itself, is useless as a corrective measure."[1]

Still, words have enormous power, and if the word "corrections" denotes not the actuality but the aim of our present system of prison, probation and parole, it is fair to use it. Furthermore in using it we can hope that it will serve as a reminder to every law enforcement officer of the goals and aims of the system.

In this chapter we will examine the treatment accorded convicted violators of the law, concentrating attention on prisons, probation and parole. The first part presents a brief history of jails and prisons, focusing especially on those institutions which have been most influential in setting future patterns. The second part of the chapter looks at the conflicting correctional philosophies: retribution versus rehabilitation, giving the main arguments of the proponents of each approach. The chapter then surveys the nation's jails and prisons and examines their inmates, discussing salient features of facilities, services, and programs of representative institutions and sociological and educational profiles of the inmates. Attention is given also to the phenomenon of recidivism and the problems it creates.

Finally, the two major alternatives to incarceration—probation and parole—are discussed. The standards upon which probation is granted are set forth and the rules by which probationers must abide are presented. Parole boards are described and the standards by which parole is granted and the rules under which the parolee must live are set forth.

PRISONS: A SHORT HISTORY

Incarceration as a punishment for violating the law is a rather recent development. Throughout history the more usual forms of punishment included flogging, branding, exile and death. Under the Greeks, persons convicted of violating the law were compelled to make restitution to their victims either by payment to them of a sum of money or by a period of labor in their service.

The American view of criminal penalties stems from three main sources: English common law, the Puritan moral code and the practical requirements for an orderly Western settlement of the frontier. The Puritans of New England employed the lash, the stocks or fines as punishment. It is worth noting that the penalty imposed depended not upon the crime committed but upon the social or financial standing of the person to be punished. There is substantial evidence and documentation to show that this bias has been practiced throughout American history to present times.

Prisons as we know them today originated as workhouses in

Conditions in a typical 18th century, London prison.
The Granger Collection, New York

which paupers, vagrants and debtors were incarcerated. In the early 1700's these workhouses began to be used to confine prisoners awaiting trial. Because the usual sentence upon conviction was either banishment or death, these workhouses were not prisons in the sense we know them today, since they were used only for pre-trial, not post-trial, detention. In the middle of the 18th century, in response to the rising clamor against it, the death penalty began to be used less and less as a punishment for the broad range of crimes for which it was once imposed. The sentence was more likely to be banishment, service in ship's galleys, or corporal punishment. About this time, in response to an outcry against the cruelties of corporal punishment, a sentence of confinement in prison for a specified period began to be imposed as punishment for a specific crime.

The first prisons built expressly to serve the purpose of detention after conviction of violating the law were the papal prison erected in Rome in 1700 by Pope Clement XI and the Belgian

A cell block in a modern U.S. prison.
Magnum Photos

prison erected in 1773 by order of Hippolyte Vilian XIII. Each prisoner confined to these prisons was given a cell. He worked during the day, and the stated objective of his incarceration was rehabilitation.

As humanitarian considerations worked against the use of the death penalty and corporal punishment, more and more convicted felons were remanded to jail to serve specified terms. Because local jails proved inadequate or insecure for the confinement of dangerous long-term felons, larger state prisons began to be built. New York erected a state prison in 1796, New Jersey in 1798, Virginia in 1800, Massachusetts in 1803, Vermont in 1808, Maryland and New Hampshire in 1812, and Ohio in 1816. Most of these state prisons were ill-equipped, overcrowded, unsanitary institutions in which prisoners, often chained, or confined to cells day and night, with poor food and clothing, and little or no fresh air, languished in misery.

The Quakers led the way in the reform of the operation of prisons in the United States. In 1787, before the large state prisons had begun to be built, they organized the Philadelphia Society for Alleviating the Miseries of Public Prisons. The Pennsylvania legislature, influenced by the society, allocated funds for the conversion of the Walnut Street jail into a prison with 30 cells set aside for implementation of the Quaker plan. Each prisoner was placed in a cell and remained there for the duration of his term. He could be visited only by the chaplain and other prison officials. He was allowed to do no work. His only reading material was the Bible. The Quakers' rationale was as follows: A prisoner, isolated from other prisoners and from the rest of society, with no work to distract his mind and only the Bible to read, could spend all his time in contemplation of his misdeeds and so would truly repent. This system, which came to be known as the Pennsylvania system, was followed for years in many states.

With the erection of the Auburn Prison in New York in 1816, a new system was introduced in American penology. Prisoners were first divided into groups of ten men, but discipline proved too difficult to maintain, so the warden divided the prisoners into three groups. Those considered most incorrigible were placed in solitary confinement. A second group, considered less difficult, was kept in confinement only three days a week. A third group, made up of first offenders, was housed together and given work to do. The first group presented serious problems; the prisoners in solitary, denied all contact with the outside world, often went insane. Prisoners in the second and third groups, living together as they did, began to practice sexual perversion and became unmanageable. Because of this, a new plan was worked out. The prisoners were allowed to eat and work together during the day *in silence,* but were locked into separate cells at night.

For decades both these systems found their outspoken advocates, but gradually the Auburn system gained favor, because, the state soon discovered, by putting prisoners to work it could gather substantial revenues.

Nineteenth-century prisons were brutal institutions generally. Prisoners were confined to disease-breeding cells. They were allowed no exercise, and were given a change of clothing but once a month. Their food was scarcely fit for animals, and sometimes so scarce that prisoners died of starvation. Poor hospital and medical facilities resulted in frequent outbreaks of epidemic and a soaring death rate. Recreation and education were unheard of; newspapers were forbidden; visits and correspondence were rare. In addition, the prisoners were literally worked to death by prison officials or outside contractors who took them from their cells at dawn and returned them at night after many hours of back-breaking labor enforced by the liberal use of the club or the whip. Corporal punishment, usually ten lashes at a minimum, was meted out for even the slightest infraction of harsh rules.

Attempts to reform these institutions met with little public support, so reformers turned their attention to juvenile delinquents, supposing that society would be more sympathetic to the plight of minors. They succeeded in having the first reformatory for minors built in New York in 1825, with similar institutions built in Boston and Philadelphia in 1826. Reformatories for adults were established in Europe in 1840 and the idea spread to America, where, in 1867, the New York State legislature passed a statute establishing a reformatory for first offenders between the ages of 16 and 30. This reformatory, at Elmira, received its first prisoners in 1876. In 1870 the American Prison Association was formed, and promulgated a set of principles so advanced that they have never been fully implemented. Elmira's first superintendent was Zebulon Brockway, who induced the legislature to establish the indeterminate sentence now used in many jurisdictions.

Elmira's program was characterized by vocational training, education of illiterates, and the use of recreation and athletics to maintain and improve prisoner health. The program was promoted as the answer to the failures of the severe system of most other American prisons. After many years, however, it was discovered that many persons who had been confined to Elmira and released turned up as inmates at other prisons. Some people, disregarding Elmira's positive reforms, pressed for a return to stricter discipline and regimentation. Well into the middle of this century most reformatories were operated on the basis of repressive prison principles.

THE CONFLICTING PHILOSOPHIES

Punishment may serve one or more purposes. It may be *deterrent,* in that it convinces both the person being punished and those who observe or learn of the punishment never to commit a particular offense. Some present-day critics, with perhaps something more than tongue in cheek, taunt advocates of capital punishment with the proposal for a revival of public executions. It may be *preventive,* in that by confining a person who has committed a crime society keeps him from committing that crime again, at least as long as the confinement is in effect. Proponents of tougher treatment for offenders point vehemently to the number of crimes committed by persons with long criminal records who have been released from detention by bail, probation or parole as an argument in favor of longer prison sentences. It may be *retributive,* in that it may gratify the feelings of the victims or assuage the outrage of society in general. It may be *reparative,* in that, particularly in grievous crimes that upset the fabric of society, the apprehension and proper punishment of the offender allows for a healing in the fabric of society.

Current progressive thinking introduces another aspect of punishment, that of reformation or rehabilitation. Proponents of this ideal indicate that either incidentally or innately this aspect of punishment, coupled as it may be with incarceration, includes all the other aspects of punishment, but adds to it a new dimension that focuses positively upon the needs of the criminal and not upon his crime.

The puzzlement expressed earlier over the accuracy of the term "corrections" to describe the system in which we segregate convicted violators of the law stems essentially from the continuing battle over their proper treatment. As long ago as the Babylonian empire, the fate of criminals was ordained by the *jus talionis;* the Bible prescribed punishment that likewise echoed the theme of "an eye for an eye." During the Roman empire, Seneca (4 B.C.–65 A.D.) declared, "Punishment is designed to protect society by removing the offender, to reform its subjects and to render others more obedient."[2]

A more recent observer notes:

> Traditionally, the threat of punishment has been held to perform three major functions: (1) to permit the expression of retaliatory, retributive motives; (2) to prevent crime by rehabilitating, incapacitating or executing offenders; and (3) to avert crime by deterring offenders from repeating their crimes and deterring others from engaging in similar acts.[3]

The conviction is deeply ingrained in most citizens that every person who violates the law must be punished and that the punishment should be commensurate with the crime. As Koko pointed out in Gilbert and Sullivan's *The Mikado,* "Let the punishment fit the crime." This universal, almost innate, regard for punishment is accepted as normal by sociologists such as Emile Durkheim, who declares, "There is no society where the rule does not exist that the punishment must be proportional to the offense."[4]

Two schools of thought have long been in contention over what to do with persons confined in prisons. One school advocates retribution: The person who has violated the laws of society must be punished, both to pay him back for the wrong he has done to a fellow citizen and to society and to impress upon other, would-be or potential, offenders the fate that awaits them. The other school advocates rehabilitation: The person who has violated the laws of society must be treated, like anyone else suffering from an illness, through a combination of education, vocational training, social and psychological counseling.

The first school contends that a person who has once committed a crime will, unless he is caught and punished, commit that or another crime again. He must be confined for a fixed period to prevent that second and subsequent crimes from occurring. The purpose of incarcerating the convicted criminal is not only to provide him with an object lesson in the fruits of his action, but also to provide the same lesson to all others who may contemplate engaging in similar behavior. This first school believes adamantly in the right of society to collect a debt from the person who has violated the law, and that the debt should be some portion of that person's time and freedom.

The second school, less vengeful and more hopeful in its thinking, believes that while punishment in the form of confinement may be necessary, confinement itself is not an end in and of itself, but should be used in conjunction with a well-planned program of rehabilitation designed to return the prisoner to society fully capable of functioning in it without violating its rules again. This school is not emotionally or philosophically tied to the idea of incarceration and tends as much as possible to accomplish the reformation it seeks under programs of probation and parole.

Because of this conflict, no clear-cut program or consistent philosophy has ever been worked out. Even when proponents of a more forward-looking rehabilitative approach have held sway they have not been completely successful, because whatever program they have been able to implement has of necessity been within the unnatural confines of a prison. When these programs prove ineffective, proponents of the first, "tough" policy are quick to point to whatever failures are evident to push for more stringent treatment.

Proponents of rehabilitation place the blame for whatever failures exist not on their programs but on the environment of the prison system in which they are carried out. They point out the following:

1. For the most part convicts are grouped together without any sorting or discrimination; young and old, educated and unschooled, first-time offenders and multiple repeaters—all are grouped together in an unnatural, tension-filled situation.

2. Men and women are confined to all-male or all-female institutions, and normal sexual relations are necessarily forbidden for a number of years.

3. Normal relations between prisoners and their families are restricted. Incoming and outgoing mail is censored, visits are limited and strictly regulated, and all contact takes place within the confines of the prison, usually under the scrutiny of prison guards.

4. Too little of the prisoner's time is spent in useful education, vocational training, recreation, or work, and too much time is spent in idle tedium.

5. Prisons are an unnatural environment. Prisoners are segregated from society and spend their time alone or in contact with other prisoners or guards. Their routines are unchanging and there is little demand for or inspiration of initiative. If prisoners are to be trained to be able to return to society and to lead normal, law-abiding lives there, prison is the least likely place in which to provide that training.

In recent years, attempts have been made to answer some of these complaints. Some states which have adequate facilities segregate their prisoners into minimum, medium and maximum security facilities. They separate first-time offenders into reformatories rather than prisons. Mentally defective or sociopathic prisoners are confined to medical facilities.

More normal personal relations are afforded trustworthy prisoners through programs of conjugal visiting (which is still quite rare), or short furloughs home, or confinement to half-way homes.

The silent system has been all but abolished and personal contact between prisoner and prisoner and prisoner and guard have been made more normal and less menacing. Visits by family, including children, have been made freer, and instead of a visit marked by separation by a wire screen, the prisoner and his family may be allowed to enjoy time together in privacy.

More numerous and effective educational programs, sometimes in schools with regular programs, have been put into effect. Prisoners have been allowed to enroll in correspondence school courses and in some jurisdictions have even been granted education release, a program under which they are allowed to attend regular college classes during the day and return to prison at night. Much of the emphasis has been on vocational training designed to equip the prisoner with a trade, and this has even been wedded in some cases to a work-release program under which the prisoner is allowed off the prison ground during daylight hours to work at a regular job and returns to prison at night. A great proportion of the prison population comes from that part of American society that is poor, underprivileged, undereducated and underemployed. The supposition is that with a proper education, sometimes including a college degree, or with a trade, released prisoners will be able to find jobs and careers and lead useful and productive lives. The record is mixed. In many jurisdictions a prison record denies a person the right to engage in certain occupations, such as hack, chauffeur, plumber, or other trades for which a license is required. In practically all areas citizen fear and discomfort disqualify any person with a prison record from being hired for many jobs. In the United States in the mid 1970's the economic downturn, resulting as it has in the highest unemployment rates since the Great Depression, has aggravated the situation.

JAILS, PRISONS, AND INMATES

Only in recent years has there been a concerted effort to tabulate the nation's jails and prisons and to survey the persons confined to them. The distinction between jails and prisons should be borne in mind; the terms are not synonymous. A jail is a locally administered facility that is authorized to retain adults for 48 hours or longer. It is the intake point for the entire criminal justice system, housing those accused of having committed crimes. It is also a correctional facility for those convicted of criminal charges, but usually of misdemeanor-level offenses. A prison, on the other hand, is a state or federal institution used almost exclusively for the detention of persons convicted of serious offenses. While jails number their inmates in the hundreds or fewer, prisons number them in the thousands.

Local Jails and their Populations

America's jails hold both the accused and the convicted, the felon and the misdemeanant, the first-time offender and the repeater. Inmates are typically male, young, poor and uneducated. At any one time, a survey will reveal that almost 75% of sentenced inmates have served a prior sentence. Along with the sentenced inmates, however, the jail population comprises those being held for arraignment, for transfer to other authorities, for trial or for final sentencing.

A 1972 survey[5] of the nearly 4,000 jails in the United States revealed that they housed almost 150,000 inmates. Approximately 95% were male and almost 60% were under 30 years of age. Almost 40% were unemployed at the time of admission, and of those who were employed 20% worked on a part-time basis only and 50% earned incomes below that considered poverty level by the U.S. Government. About half the inmates had never been married. Blacks, though 11% of the U.S. population, constituted about 42% of the jail population.

Half of all inmates were between 19 and 29 years of age. About one-fourth of the inmates had only an eighth-grade education; two-fifths had entered high school but had not been graduated; one-fourth had completed high school but had not gone on to college.

Offenses

One of the most striking differences found among the inmates awaiting trial was in the nature of the offense with which they were charged. Of the black inmates awaiting trial, 47% had been charged with murder, kidnapping, rape, aggravated assault or robbery. Only 22% of the white inmates were awaiting trial on similar charges. Far more than blacks, whites were charged with such offenses as forgery, fraud, possession of drugs, public drunkenness and vagrancy.

These marked differences held among the portion of the jail population serving time after conviction. Whites were usually serving time for misdemeanor-type offenses, blacks for felony-type offenses. While 20% of white inmates had been convicted of one of the seven FBI-labeled "index" crimes, 36% of blacks had been so convicted. About 40% of the white inmates had been convicted of one of the three most common misdemeanor type offenses—drunkenness or vagrancy, drug possession, and traffic violations.

Jail Facilities

Three-fifths of all jails are located in courthouses and/or police stations. One-third of all jails occupy separate buildings, and these are usually designed to accommodate a few hundred inmates. In most jails, each cell holds one inmate, but many jails contain dormitory-type lodgings and drunk-tanks.

Inmates are usually segregated by type but without any particular or prescribed pattern, except for the general separation of juvenile and adult inmates. While 9 out of 10 jails segregate inmates with known or suspected mental disabilities, three out of five do not separate pretrial defendants from convicted offenders and three out of four do not separate first-time offenders from repeat offenders.

Social and Rehabilitative Services

The same 1972 survey, conducted by the National Criminal Justice Information and Statistics Service, found that only a small percentage of inmates benefited from the social and rehabilitative services offered in the nation's jails. Approximately six out of ten jails offered facilities for religious services. Despite the large numbers of inmates held on alcohol- and drug-related charges, only one-third of the jails offered alcoholic treatment services and only one-fourth maintained drug addiction treatment programs. Counseling, remedial education, vocational training and job placement programs were found in fewer than one out of five jails. More than two out of five jails, however, sponsored work-release programs, but only 8% of all sentenced inmates participated.

State and Federal Prisons

At the end of 1973, the nation's state and federal prisons held more than 200,000 inmates, adult and youthful offenders who had been sentenced to terms of a maximum of a year and a day or longer. The bulk of these inmates were held in state prisons, almost 175,000; the federal prisons held almost 23,000.

The characteristics of the inmate population outlined in the survey of the nation's jails held generally true in the prisons. Prison facilities and services showed improvement over those in jails, in part because they were usually larger and in part because their inmate populations were generally serving longer sentences. Therefore, prisons more regularly had staff medical practitioners, clinics, and hospitals; educational and vocational training centers, including classrooms, labs, and workshops; staff psychological and counseling services.

Recidivism

The continuing debate between proponents of the retributive and rehabilitative schools of thought on corrections policy is fueled by a thoroughly well-noted phenomenon—*recidivism*. Recidivism refers to the repetition of crime, conviction and incarceration of persons who have already been prison inmates one or more times. According to reliable estimates, at least three-quarters of all crime is committed by recidivists. The phenomenon is most prevalent in crimes against property—burglary, auto theft, forgery, and larceny; it is least common in crimes of violence. That, having spent a shorter or longer period of time in prison, many persons violate the law again upon their release says something about the ineffectiveness of the program they underwent in prison.

The two schools of thought divide sharply. Old-line, hard-line, "lock-em-up-and-throw-away-the-key" advocates see recidivism as pointed proof that current trends in corrections mean coddling prisoners. Criminals cannot be remolded, they contend, they can only be punished and can be prevented from committing additional crimes once they are allowed to return to society only by a fear of being committed once more to the confines of a harsh any unyielding prison regimen. The way to reduce the rate of recidivism is to make prisons more prisonlike. The newer, more optimistic thinkers declare that the rate of recidivism does not reflect any failure of progressive programs, but a failure to implement such programs more fully and wholeheartedly. A program of corrections, they contend, is working under a serious handicap to begin with by having to be conducted within the confines of a prison. The answer, they say, is to make prisons less prisonlike. Besides, they say, a former inmate's failure to abide by the rules of society, evidenced by repeated violation of the law, does not indicate the failure of the rehabilitative program he may have undergone in prison; it reflects the failure of society to find an appropriate niche for the returned prisoner. The vast majority of persons committed to prison in the first place are society's outcasts and misfits—the poor, the uneducated, the unskilled, in short, the have-nots whose acts are actual and symbolic revenge against a society that has denied them the fruits it has allowed so many other of its citizens to gather. These fruits have been paid for, to a considerable extent, by lives lived in accordance with the rules of society, but also by the money received from jobs in the shops, factories and offices of the land. Prisoners, still poor, perhaps a little better educated, perhaps skilled or semiskilled in a trade, return to this society and find that they still have difficulty in finding and keeping jobs, and are often condemned to a return to the barren, hopeless social milieu which may have led them to crime in the first place.

Prison Administration

The chief administrator of any house of detention is referred to as the warden or superintendent. Depending upon the size of the facility, he usually has one or more deputies to assist him. The warden is presently most often a professional specialist in the field of corrections, but he may also be a nonprofessional political appointee. In either case, he is not always entirely a free agent, but someone who must cope with and adjust to the dictates of the state administration of which he is an officer, general public attitudes toward prison policy, and the practical problems of any complicated managerial situation. He must deal not only with a large and mixed prison population, but with a professional staff of administrators, educators, psychologists, sociologists, doctors and nurses, and a working staff of corrections officers. He is concerned with the practicalities of recruitment, personnel training, safety and security, medical care and hospitalization, engineering, educational and recreational and vocational programs, food facilities, laundry and cleaning, clerical assistance and a host of other problems.

PROBATION

A general recognition of the failure of prisons to reform the men and women entrusted to their care has led over the years to a steady increase in the use of probation as the appropriate sentence for many convicted persons.

Probation is essentially an American development. It began with the efforts of a Bostonian named John Augustus in 1841 to have men released to his care rather than to be confined to prison. Augustus handled and kept records, which exist to this day, on more than 1,500 convicted offenders. Because of the success of his efforts, the city of Boston wrote the first probation statute in

1878. In 1891 Massachusetts became the first state to allow probation. In 1925 federal laws allowed probation to be granted.

Of course, probation is granted with a great deal of circumscription. It is granted only to those who are considered capable of fulfilling its obligations, who can live in society without being a threat to it, and who can be counted on not to commit further crime while on probation. It is important to keep in mind that probation is an open-ended treatment for the convicted person; he or she must abide by a series of stringent rules of conduct or be remanded to jail. Probation, therefore, is conditional upon good conduct, and adherence to the terms of probation is in some measure guaranteed by the threat of imprisonment for failure to do so.

Probation is usually granted to a person who can reasonably be assumed to be ready to abide by the following conditions:

1. Be capable of rehabilitating himself without the need for incarceration.
2. Be capable of observing all the laws of society.
3. Be capable of maintaining a good work or school record.
4. Be willing to associate only with approved persons and avoid contact with known or suspected criminals.
5. Be willing to abide by the conditions of probation set down by the sentencing judge.
6. Be willing to not marry or divorce without the approval of the probation officer.

The granting of probation is not entirely discretionary. Most state laws define the conditions under which probation can be granted, and these laws usually forbid probation to felons convicted of serious crimes such as robbery, assault with a deadly weapon, forcible rape and selling drugs to juveniles. Felons convicted of lesser crimes, especially those that did not involve physical violence, are likely to be placed under probation with professional supervision. Most misdemeanants will be placed under probation without professional supervision by virtue of a suspended sentence. Both felons and misdemeanants are well aware, though, that probation is merely a substitute for the prison sentence that has been set, which can be reimposed and even added to if during the time they are on probation they violate the law again.

During the presentencing investigation various factors that might indicate the value and validity of probation are looked into. Among these factors are the following:

1. Was the crime relatively minor and did it cause minimal harm to the victim?
2. Was the crime committed deliberately and by premeditation, or did it result from circumstance, provocation or pressing economic need?
3. Has the offender already been punished sufficiently by the accusation, arrest, trial, and conviction; by time spent in jail; by loss of income resulting both from inability to work at his regular job and by having to pay attorney's fees?
4. Is the offender for the most part a law-abiding citizen who has not previously been in trouble?
5. Does the offender come from a solid, respectable family who are ready and willing to help him through the period of probation?
6. Does the offender respect the legitimacy of the criminal justice procedure through which he has passed? Does he indicate his willingness to abide by the program of treatment and supervision to which he will be subjected? Does he show any sign of animosity towards the agents of the system with whom he has or will come into contact?
7. Is the offender willing to make amends or restitution to his victim?

Probation as an alternative to imprisonment is on the rise not only because of a general recognition that it is a more successful instrument of rehabilitation than are prisons, but also because it is less expensive. Imprisonment costs the state a great deal of money; it removes from society a significant number of earners of money and turns them into consumers of money. Probation, on the other hand, allows the probationer to work and earn a living, thus keeping himself and his family off the welfare rolls. Imprisonment generally is five times as expensive as probation.

In addition, the records indicate that persons who have been on probation are much less likely to be recidivists than persons who have been in prison and this too is an economically beneficial phenomenon.

Improvement of the probation process lies largely in improving and providing increasing professionalization of the probation officer. Because probation as a system of dealing with convicted offenders is still relatively new, there has not been time to develop and organize any systematized standard for probation officers. They are often poorly screened before selection, ill-trained after selection, underpaid and overworked by their case loads. Qualifications for probation officers vary. Some jurisdictions require a high school diploma; others require a bachelor's or even master's degree. The probation officer may be employed by a city, county, state, or federal agency and may or may not be a member of a labor union.

PAROLE

Parole differs from probation in that it is granted to a person who has spent some part of his sentence in prison and who is being released early, partly on the basis of a good record within prison and partly because of the promise of good behavior outside of prison. Parole is also being resorted to increasingly in recognition of the inadequacy of confinement as a means of rehabilitating prisoners.

The use of parole dates from the middle of the 19th century, when it was introduced in 1840 by Sir Walter Crofton in England. In 1846 it was introduced in France by the penologist deMarsangy. He advocated that prisoners be handled in a series of stages of confinement, with passage from one stage to the next contingent on good conduct and meritorious labor. First a prisoner was to be kept in strict confinement; then he was to be placed at labor on a chain gang; then he was to be granted freedom within a restricted area; then he was to get a "ticket on leave." Finally, upon the successful passage through all of these stages, he was to be given his full freedom.

Rules governing eligibility for parole vary from state to state; the one apparently standard rule being that the offender spend some minimum period in confinement before being eligible. Certain offenders are sentenced to prison with specific instructions that parole not be granted. Offenders convicted of serious crimes, murder, rape, kidnapping, and multiple felony offenders stand little chance of obtaining parole except after long years of incarceration.

There are generally three types of boards sitting in judgment upon parole applications:

1. *Institutional Board.* Members are recruited from among the staff of the prison and will usually consist of the warden, chaplain, educational director, psychologist, social worker and other trained professionals.

2. *Central Board.* Members are not part of the staff of any single institution but have responsibility for parole decisions at each institution within its appointive jurisdiction. Members are usually professionals with relevant training and background, but may also be prominent interested citizens.

3. *Public Officials.* Members are usually appointed by the governor of the state. Selection may be haphazard, linked to political connections, and members will usually devote much of their time to other interests, giving only part of their time to parole.

Parole is granted by a parole board sitting within prison upon application by the prisoner. The parole board studies all the relevant data about the prisoner: the record of his crime and conviction, the conclusions of the presentencing investigation, the reports of interviewers and counselors who have dealt with the convict in prison. In addition, they interview the prospective parolee. Their decision is necessarily made on the basis of objective analysis of all the known facts and the subjective impressions they gather from their meeting with the parolee.

Their decision will be based on a combination of the following factors:

1. How well the offender has adjusted to his life in prison.

2. How well he has responded to the educational, vocational and counseling services offered him in prison.

3. How well these programs and the educational and vocational skills he possessed before he was committed to prison prepare him for a return to civilian life.

4. How positively and affirmatively he views his experiences in prison and in the outside world and how he perceives his own chances of success upon a return to the outside world.

5. How positively reinforcing this outside world is. That is, will he be returning to a job, to friends and family that care for him, and to a stable social environment? Or will he be returning to a society and a criminal subculture that will program him once more for a return to crime?

Once a person is granted parole, he is not merely set free to fend for himself. Like the probationer, he is enlisted in a program of professional supervision under the care of a parole officer. He must conduct himself in a peaceful, law-abiding manner, get a job, report his experiences regularly, and make no change in residence or marital status without notifying his parole officer. The parolee agrees to abide by certain conditions:

1. He will meet periodically with his parole officer.
2. He will not fraternize with known criminals.
3. He will not partake of alcoholic beverages.
4. He will not break any law.
5. He will not leave the jurisdiction without permission.

These conditions may be needlessly restrictive and are probably observed only in the breach. It requires the parolee to walk a delicate tightrope and the parole officer to blink at infractions, such as the taking of a cocktail, that may be absolutely inconsequential in the average citizen but threaten a parolee with revocation of his parole and a return to prison.

Parole officers, like probation officers, are often poorly trained, underpaid and overworked. As dedicated and selfless as they may be, as devoted as they may be to their charges and to the assignment which they have received, they can cope only fitfully and sporadically.

> The parole officer to whom the prisoner reports is supposed to act as a sort of social case worker, but this is in theory only. The Crime Commission found that parole officers are so pressed with an overload of cases and so concerned with trying to be a policeman that they have little time to help on matters that count like finding jobs and solving family problems.[6]

Parole Effectiveness

Both probation and parole entail risks. The probationer and the parolee risk their freedom upon their ability and willingness to "stay clean." Correctional authorities risk their reputations and positions upon the good conduct of released offenders. Should they commit crimes while on probation and parole, public confidence in and sympathy for the programs are shaken, legislative and administrative anger is aroused, and hopes for the offender's rehabilitation are dashed.

To provide accurate information on the success of parole, and to contribute to better parole decision-making, the Uniform Parole Reports Project has gathered and interpreted data reported by 55 agencies in fifty states, the federal government, and Puerto Rico.[7] The data pertain to more than 100,000 parolees from 1965 to 1970, with one-year follow-up studies.

Their data indicate that a large proportion of the offenders released on parole have no major offense convictions or allegations during the first year after parole. Of 79,322 parolees reported, 7,159 showed new major offense convictions or allegations, and of these 5,238 showed new major offense convictions, a rate of less than 7%. Studies of the parole records of persons convicted of willful homicide show even better results. Of 6,908 such parolees, 122 showed new major offense convictions or allegations during the first year after parole, and of these only 82 showed convictions, a rate slightly more than one percent. Of these 82 convictions, 15 were for another willful homicide, a rate of about one-fifth of one percent.

FUTURE TRENDS

One important objective is coordination and integration of police, probation and parole officers. Historically, and in many jurisdictions presently, there has been little contact between the various practitioners, and it is likely that police officers generally are opposed to cooperative programs. Police in general guard their status jealously. Their uniform sets them apart and gives them a special status which they are not ready to extend to others. They think of their work as the valuable part of the criminal justice system, protecting the law-abiding citizen from the depredations of criminal elements. They think of probation and parole officers as persons concerned not so much with the law-abiding citizen as with the law-defying citizen. They fail too often to understand the value of the work that the probation and parole officers perform in keeping persons who have once violated the law from doing so again. No little consideration must be given, too, to the factor of salary as an aspect of status. Police officers are anxious to maintain their exclusivity to maintain a favorable salary and benefits structure. Unfortunately, city, town and state administrators do not press for any advancement in status for probation and parole officers, partly to maintain the lower salary and benefits structures under which they function.

Law enforcement officers, the general public and legislators at all governmental levels need to give serious consideration to the evaluation of prisons, probation and parole. In the midst of increasing crime and decreasing law enforcement manpower, all must rethink how best to prevent crime from occurring, how to treat offenders once it has occurred, and how to prevent any recurrence of it. Some reallocation of priorities among prisons, probation and parole is probably inevitable, with more money, manpower and programs being invested in probation and parole.

The 1970's have seen a series of prison riots as revolts against old-line prisons. (And old, too. At least 25 facilities are more than 100 years old and more than 60 facilities are more than 75 years old.) These facilities are marked by poor food, lack of meaningful work, inadequate education and recreation, harsh regulations and brutality. Perhaps more clearly than the prison administrators themselves or their staffs the inmates were able to see and declare in the form of revolt that these institutions were improper instruments for returning to society offenders who would no longer be threats to society.

As Germann, Day, and Gallati point out:

> The public should soon come to understand that they own the prisons and that their business is failing—both the 70% recidivism rate and the increasing severity of crimes committed by prison graduates are clear evidence that current prisons fail to rehabilitate in any positive way. Instead, they become breeding grounds for hatred and violence. Prisons are a bad investment for citizen-taxpayers.[8]

SUMMARY

Persons convicted of crimes in the United States may be punished by fines, by forfeiture of office, or by loss of their freedom. By far the most common punishment is loss of freedom, absolutely in case of confinement to prison, conditionally in the cases of probation or parole.

The use of prisons as punishment for crimes is a fairly recent development. In former times punishment more often consisted of fines, flogging, branding, exile or death. By one of the common paradoxes of history, imprisonment was introduced as a reform measure against the cruelties of corporal or capital punishment. Despite an attempt by early prison administrators to reform their prisoners, prisons soon came to be harsh and cruel institutions and confinement to their harsh regimen became almost the worst of all punishments.

Two conflicting corrections philosophies may be discerned which have prevented the adoption of a uniform program of prison administration. One philosophy feels that persons who violate the law must be punished and that prisons, besides confining them, should be tough and unpleasant institutions whose very regimen will punish the prisoner and instill in him a determination never to commit a crime and risk being confined again. The other philosophy holds that persons who violate the law are sociologically ill just as other people are physically or mentally ill, and that confinement in prison, if it is necessary, must be accompanied by a professional program of education and vocational training, social and psychological counseling, and recreational activity. The conflict between these philosophies remains unresolved.

The nation's jails and prisons are marked by several distinctive features. Jails are smaller, local institutions, housing mainly inmates who have not yet been convicted in the courts, and housing among those inmates who have been convicted primarily those with misdemeanor-type offenses. Prisons are larger, state or federal institutions, housing primarily long-term felons. Because of the differences in their populations, jails usually have few rehabilitation services or facilities, while prisons usually have many, with the professional staffs to maintain and administer them.

To an increasing extent, most persons in the criminal justice system have come to recognize incarceration as a sterile form of correction. Rather than reforming persons committed to them, prisons more likely confirm them in lives of crime. As much as is consistent with funds and personnel available, convicted offenders are placed on probation. This depends on several factors: the nature of the crime they committed, their past record, the probability that probation is the proper treatment for them and their willingness to abide by certain fixed rules. Those persons who are sent to prison may find an increasing tendency for release on parole as early as possible in their sentences. Parole is granted largely on the basis of standards similar to probation, the essential element being the parolee's ability to conform to the requirements of parole without committing any further violation of the law.

NOTES

1. Robert J. Wicks, *Applied Psychology for Law Enforcement and Correction Officers*. New York: McGraw-Hill Book Company, 1974, p. 151.
2. Quoted in Germann, Day and Gallati, *op. cit.*, p. 45.
3. Stuart L. Hills, *Crime, Power, and Morality*. Scranton, Pa.; Chandler Publishing Co., 1971, p. 43.
4. Emile Durkheim, *The Rules of Sociological Method*, translated by Sarah A. Solovay and John H. Mueller. New York: Free Press, 1938, p. 73.
5. National Criminal Justice Information and Statistics Service, "Survey of Inmates of Local Jails." Washington, D.C., Department of Justice, Law Enforcement Assistance Administration, 1972.
6. Robert M. Cipes, *The Crime War*. New York: The New American Library, 1968, p. 165.
7. National Council on Crime and Delinquency Research Center, "Parole Risk of Convicted Murderers." Davis, Cal.: *Newsletter*, Uniform Parole Reports of the National Probation and Parole Institutes, Dec., 1972.
8. Germann, Day and Gallati, *op. cit.*, p. 213.

STUDY QUESTIONS

1. How successfully do prisons reform or rehabilitate?
2. Are prisons today better equipped to help their inmates than prisons in the nineteenth century?
3. What are the various philosophies of punishment? With which do you most agree?
4. What are some differences between the black and white prison populations? What are some of the reasons for these differences?
5. Is there any solution to the problem of recidivism?
6. Is probation a useful means of reforming or rehabilitating convicted felons?
7. What circumstances influence the placing of a convicted felon or misdemeanant on probation?
8. What are some of the determining factors in the granting of parole to an incarcerated felon?

Part II
OPERATIONS

5

Crime and Criminality

It is likely that every American citizen who reads the daily paper, listens to the radio or watches television will agree with this familiar complaint:

> We all know that at present the police seem powerless for good; and that bold and dangerous criminals were never so bold and dangerous; and life and property were never so insecure; that gambling and prostitution and illegal trade were never so open and shameless; that public danger from violence was never so acute, nor with so much reason.[1]

It may surprise that American citizen to learn that this is a quotation not out of a recent newspaper, magazine or book, but out of the *New York Tribune* of February 5, 1857. Quotations similar to it from earlier times, centuries and even millennia earlier, could likely be found, all of which would underscore the citizen's eternal concern for peace and personal safety, his fear that these are constantly in jeopardy, and his belief that earlier times were less troubled and more tranquil. Those of us who are now living through a period characterized in part by a general apprehension that it is a period of unprecedented criminal activity need to focus clearly on the matter of crime and criminality and the interrelationships of both with society.

In this chapter we will examine crime from the legal, sociological and typological points of view. After the discussion of major crime categories such as violent crime, professional crime, organized crime and white collar crime, special attention is given to violent crime, its perpetrators, its victims, its causes.

The second part of the chapter examines the criminal and presents various ideas of who the criminal is. Much of this is linked to the crime categories of the previous section. The most troublesome of criminals, the social psychopath, is analyzed as a model for much other criminal behavior.

The last parts of this chapter study the causes of crime, concentrating on current theory and the most conspicuous studies of the past. Among contemporary factors analyzed are the victims of crime and the role they play, social and economic conditions, the distribution of wealth in American society, and the effectiveness of law enforcement agencies. Our discussion of past studies of the causes of crime will touch the works of Bentham, Beccaria, Lombroso and Ferri; and then we will look at more recent studies by Kretschmer, Sutherland, Shaw, Taft and England, and Sheldon.

CRIME

Basically, a crime is an act in violation of the law. It may be a crime of commission, doing something which is forbidden by law, or be a crime of omission, failing to do something which is demanded by law. Typically, the law provides that a person who is convicted of a crime is to be punished in a prescribed manner.

An Anatomy of Crime

There are several ways of categorizing crimes. Already alluded to in Chapter 1 are the labels *mala in se,* for those acts which are evil by their very nature (murder, rape, arson, burglary, larceny, and forgery) and *mala prohibita,* for those acts which are crimes only because they violate legislative statute. Crimes that can be labeled as *mala prohibita* are a very clear indication of society's attitudes, for only those actions which become offensive to a majority of the people in a society or to a powerful and influential segment of society become the subject of criminal sanction.

Two examples may illustrate the relationship of society's attitudes and the criminalization of conduct that is not innately criminal. One has to do with the consumption of alcohol. Except in some states or portions of some states, and except for regulations controlling the manufacture, distribution, and sale of alcohol, the consumption of alcohol is currently legal in the United States. Yet, under pressure of the temperance movement, the United States, by constitutional amendment, decreed the manufacture, distribution, sale, and consumption of alcohol to be illegal. One day in 1920 an act commonly engaged in by the broad masses of the people in every age and in every part of the world became a crime and remained a crime for more than a dozen years, until another constitutional amendment repealed the previous one. The other has to do with the use of marijuana, which was not subject to restriction under federal law until 1937 and was restricted under state laws that were generally loosely enforced. Over the years the laws became ever more restrictive as the use of marijuana emerged from the slums and barrios of the nation, became more common among white, middle-class America, and became increasingly identified with a counterculture in open social, cultural and political conflict with the mainstream of America. Year by year state legislatures increased the penalties for the sale, possession or use of marijuana until in some states these became capital crimes and in others the penalties were generally more severe than those for any other crimes but murder or rape. Some relaxations of the penalties have been enacted in recent years, but only under considerable pressure and the growing realization that the legislative response was out of all proportion to the "menace" that marijuana represented.

In more legalistic terminology, crimes are categorized according to the punishment which may be meted out upon conviction. The major categories are:

Capital Crime. Murder, kidnapping, rape, or any other action which by legislation becomes punishable by death. Depending, of course, upon a pending Supreme Court decision, there may in the future be no such thing as a capital crime.

Felony Crime. Robbery, burglary, larceny, arson, or any other action which may lead upon conviction to a sentence of one year or more in prison.

Misdemeanor. Lesser crimes which may be punishable by imprisonment for less than one year and/or by the imposition of fines.

Infractions. The least serious offenses, usually vehicular, which are usually punishable by fines only, although repeated offenses could result in the suspension or revocation of licenses.

It is also possible to categorize crime not by the nature of the act and the legal definition of the crime committed but by the identity of the offender. Such categorization establishes such labels as street crime, professional crime, organized crime, and white collar crime, among others.

It is possible that street crime, because it so directly affects the citizen and disrupts the even tenor of his life and because it has become the subject of political controversy, may be most typical of our times. Nonetheless, in terms of the number of offenses committed and the losses it inflicts upon its victims and society in general street crime is much overdrawn.

Professional crime is a label given to a series of acts such as robbery, burglary, forgery, larceny and confidences that are engaged in by a criminal subculture inhabited largely by persons who choose to maintain their lives outside the law in spite of repeated arrest and imprisonment. Crimes committed by professionals often involve consenting victims or victims who neither know nor see the perpetrator, so that if he is apprehended the victim will find it difficult to recognize or identify him.

Organized crime is a series of acts initiated, maintained and controlled by several large groups, typically gambling, prostitution, pornography, narcotics, loansharking, hijacking, bootlegging and numbers. Of all these activities, gambling, Ahern indicates, is the major source of illicit income; ". . . it provides a predictable volume of income whose source is so widely based that it cannot dry up."[2] While the people who are involved in organized crime may be thought of as professional criminals, some important distinctions are evident. First, the crimes committed by those referred to as professionals are by nature intermittent, while those committed by those in the organized crime category are largely continuous. Second, the crimes engaged in by those labeled as professional criminals are committed largely without the knowledge, consent or cooperation of the victim; the crimes engaged in by organized crime often contain an element of cooperation between criminal and victim. People who play the numbers, place bets with bookmakers, purchase "hot" merchandise, deal in narcotics or consort with prostitutes know the criminality of the acts committed by the people they are dealing with and the corrupt uses to which the enormous flow of money is put. Yet they enter into these acts freely and voluntarily, largely because they expect some gain for themselves.

White collar crime may be the great unknown. While persons eminently qualified to make such judgments, Ramsey Clark among them, declare that the financial losses it inflicts upon its victims and society in general are staggering, the public at large is generally oblivious to it, because it consists essentially of quiet crimes. It is marked by the shopkeeper short-weighting his customer, the merchant raising his prices to take advantage of shortages of goods, the worker taking materials home from his job or working fewer hours than he is obliged to, the banker embezzling funds, the politician accepting kickbacks of goods or services and a host of other acts. The entire range of municipal, state and federal regulatory agencies has been established over the years in part to prevent actions that might be categorized as white collar crime. In a book entitled *White Collar Crime,*[3] Edwin H. Sutherland studied the records of 70 large corporations in regard to decisions by the courts and the regulatory agencies concerning allegations of false advertising and violations of antitrust, patent, copyright and labor laws. He discovered these corporations to be the subjects of 980 adverse decisions. In spite of almost a century of activity by some of these agencies, white collar crime is so widespread and pervasive that the Attorney General has only recently proposed the establishment of a new federal strike force to make fresh efforts to root it out.

Why is the public generally so unaware of or seemingly unconcerned about white collar crime? In part because it doesn't understand the nature of the crimes committed; often only accountants or lawyers can recognize a series of actions as violations of the law. In part apparently, because it accepts such crime as a normal element in the business sector of American life. In part because it engages in or would engage in the same activities. The law enforcement officer, uniformed or plainclothes, often shares the public attitude toward white collar crime, since it involves him so infrequently in his performance of his duties.

Clinard and Quinney offer an eight-point typology of crime:[4]

1. Violent crime (murder, rape, aggravated assault).
2. Conventional crime (robbery, burglary, theft).

3. Professional crime (swindling, shoplifting, counterfeiting, forgery, pickpocketing).
4. Organized crime (gambling, prostitution, drugs).
5. Occupational crime (embezzlement, fee splitting, price fixing).
6. Property crime (auto theft, shoplifting, vandalism).
7. Political crime (treason, sedition, criminal protest).
8. Public crime (drunkenness, traffic violations, homosexuality).

James F. Ahern, former Police Commissioner of New Haven, Connecticut, divides crime into four broad categories: consensual crime, street crime, organized crime, and white-collar crime.[5]

VIOLENT CRIME

The man in the street who has been the victim of a mugging or is a relative or friend of someone who has been a victim, the radio or television commentator who stridently decries the city streets as a jungle unsafe for ordinary passage, the politician who vows to take the streets away from the criminals and those who are soft on crime and return it to the forces of law and order—all these concentrate on a narrow but frightening aspect of the crime problem: violent crime. They forget the illegal activities of gamblers, bookmakers, loansharks, drug dealers, pickpockets, auto thieves, embezzlers, price fixers and fee splitters, apparently on the assumption that they can be free of their depredations if they choose to be. It is the gut issue of violent crime, the atavistic fear of sudden, incomprehensible assault that moves them and their public.

Statistically, only a small fraction of all crime is violent.[6] According to the FBI's index of reported crimes, major crimes of violence—homicide, rape, robbery, and assault—represent only 13 percent of recorded crime. The average American citizen is five times as likely to die in an auto accident as in a murderous attack by a stranger. He is 100 times more likely to be injured in an accident in his own home than in a mugging.

Again speaking statistically, however, the rates of violent crimes of all sorts have increased dramatically, providing fodder for the political campaigns of office-seekers and legitimate bases of fear for the man in the street. Between 1960 and 1968 the national rate of criminal homicide rose 36%, that of forcible rape 65%, aggravated assault 67%, and robbery 119%.[7] Any review of the figures since 1968 will show a continuing increase in these figures.

Figures on the identities of perpetrators and victims of these crimes offer some perspectives and may allay some fears. In cases of homicide, where the offender is male, his victim is usually male; where the offender is black, his victim is usually black; and where the offender is 20 years old or older, so is his victim. In most cases, the murder occurs outside a person's premises, on the street. The same personae and settings characterize most recorded cases of aggravated assault. In cases of forcible rape, the victim, of course, is female and the occurrence is usually indoors, but the characteristics of race and age hold true. Cases of armed robbery show a slightly different pattern. While the male perpetrator usually acts against a male victim, the black perpetrator usually acts against a white victim, and if the perpetrator is under 25 years of age, his victim is usually over 25 years of age.[8]

Violent crime is primarily a phenomenon of large cities. Twenty-six cities with populations of 500,000 or more represent 17% of the nation's population, but 45% of its recorded major crimes. Six larger cities of 1,000,000 or more citizens represent 10% of the nation's population, but 30% of its recorded major crimes.[9]

Violent crime is also predominantly a phenomenon of the ghettos and slums in which most of the blacks in these larger cities live. The rate of rape and aggravated assault in these ghettos is 10 to 11 times higher than the national average, and the rate of robbery and homicide 16 to 17 times higher.[10] These slums are marked by significant and easily identifiable signs of social disintegration and physical decay:

1. Low income.
2. Physical deterioration of homes, schools, and shops.
3. A high degree of welfare dependency.
4. Almost total racial or ethnic concentration.
5. A high proportion of broken homes, with absent fathers and working mothers.
6. Low educational and vocational skills.
7. High unemployment.

8. High proportion of single males.
9. Overcrowded, substandard housing.
10. High infant mortality.
11. Low rate of home ownership.
12. Mixed land use.
13. High population density.
14. High rate of tuberculosis.[11]

Violent crime in the city is also predominantly a product of young males between the ages of 15 and 19. In recent years it has increasingly been the product also of youths between the ages of 10 and 14. Between 1957 and 1968, recorded cases of assault by these youngsters soared a startling 300% and recorded cases of robbery by 200%.[12] Studies were made in Philadelphia of 10,000 boys born in 1945, 3,000 of whom were black and 7,000 white. By the time these boys had reached the age of 18, 50% of the blacks and 20% of the whites had had some recorded police contact. Fourteen of these youths had been involved in murder, all black; forty-four had been involved in rape, 80% black; 193 had been involved in robbery, 90% black; and 220 had been involved in cases of aggravated assault, 82% black.[13]

As James A. Ahern points out in his recent book *Police in Trouble:*

> Street crime is largely the activity of alienated young men—a relatively small proportion of the criminal population, usually derived from the urban poor, with histories of employment problems, narcotics use, and with backgrounds of exposure to racial or ethnic discrimination. They have not had the support of a responsive educational system, or of positive community or peer groups, and have often succumbed to a pattern of crime as teenagers.[14]

Lest anyone interpret the figures cited as proofs of a contention that equates blackness with criminality, let it be emphasized that most blacks live in the deteriorating urban slums marked by the characteristics cited above, and it is these that breed crime, not blackness itself.

The reasons for the rise in violent crime in the United States are outlined with clarity in the book *Violent Crime,* issued in 1969 by the National Commission on the Causes and Prevention of Crime.

1. The U.S. has been changing with a bewildering rapidity—scientifically, technologically, socially, and politically—and these rapid changes have caused a considerable amount of physical and psychological dislocation.

2. Law enforcement agencies have not been strengthened sufficiently to contain the violence that accompanies these changes, and have not been sufficiently trained to understand the violence as a result of these changes rather than willful or unreasoning desires to violate the law.

3. Public order in a free society cannot rest solely on the application of force or threats of force by authorities. Public order must rest essentially on the people's acceptance of the legitimacy of the rule-making institutions.[15]

THE CRIMINAL

The question "Who is a criminal?" can be answered in a variety of ways. A most strict and cynical assertion would be that everyone is. Given the multiplicity of statutes on the lawbooks regulating every aspect of social, commercial and personal life, everyone is a criminal because at one time or other he has violated the law, even though he has not been discovered or apprehended (or is even aware of having done so). A most loose, indiscriminate, and meaningless assertion would be that no one is. Given the harshness of social and economic conditions, the overreach of the law into personal affairs and the unfairness of police enforcement, no one is a criminal, but everyone is a victim. The truth, by any valid standard of definition, lies somewhere between these two extremes.

Police and others involved in the criminal justice process divide criminals into two broad general types: professional criminals and accidental or occasional offenders. This division plays its part in the criminal justice system, as it affects the police apprehension process, concepts of arraignment, indictment, trial and sentencing, and decisions on corrections, probation and parole.

The criminal is represented in all walks of life, all age groups and social classes. The criminal may be old or young, man or woman, black or white, blue collar, white collar or professional. The nature of the crimes committed may vary, and society's reaction to these crimes and to the nature of the punishment to be meted out may vary, but each of these types finds its representatives in police custody, on trial or in prison.

Concepts of who is the criminal are as varied as the criminals themselves. To some, he is the average man gone wrong. To others he is a weak or morally deficient person. Still others think of the criminal a person who is biologically or mentally deficient. A fourth class of criminals is the shrewd, intelligent adversary, one discovered occasionally in real life and found often in fiction's guise of the master criminal.

One type of criminal deserves special attention, the criminal psychopath: first, because quite mistakenly the public thinks of him as the quintessential criminal—or, more accurately, thinks of all criminals as essentially psychopathic—and second, because this is the type of criminal the criminal justice system is least able to cope with. The criminal psychopath, unlike all other criminals so far discussed, can be examined in terms of psychological analysis. He suffers essentially from a "sociopathic personality disorder," which manifests itself in antisocial behavior, sexual deviation and drug or alcohol addiction. He is the person most people have in mind when they think of crime, and he is the cause of most people's fear of crime, since they sense the violence that manifests itself in the sociopath's reactions. Yet only a small percentage of criminals are social psychopaths. Most criminal justice systems fail because they are built around a concept of punishment as a deterrence to crime. Deterrence has no effect on the social psychopath and has a negative effect on the vast numbers of persons who have committed criminal acts but who are not social psychopaths.[16]

The social psychopath exhibits several characteristics which may be discovered in part by examining his behavior and in part by interview. Most notable are:

1. Absence of guilt or tension.
2. Undeveloped conscience.
3. Inadequate personal relations.
4. Impulsive, irresponsible nature.
5. Inability to profit from experience.
6. No goal in life and lives only for the gratification of the moment.[17]

In addition, the social psychopath is usually bright and has learned to manipulate most people to his own ends. Since he does not have a well-developed conscience, is self-centered and has neither sympathy nor feeling for others, he will adopt almost any means to arrive at his goals. Not only the ordinary citizen, but everyone in the criminal justice system, including law enforcement and correction officers, attorneys and judges, and even consulting psychologists and psychiatrists, must be alert to the machinations of the social psychopath.

In his everyday activities, the law enforcement officer must be especially alert to the dangers of dealing with social psychopaths. Since they have no sense of guilt or tension over the acts they may have committed, they may remain absolutely calm while being questioned about a crime, lulling the officer out of any sense of apprehension or danger. This same lack of guilt may lead them into sudden outbursts of violence, especially if this is necessary to escape arrest and confinement. The law enforcement officer should be especially alert if he encounters the social psychopath while he is committing a crime, for he is impulsive enough to try almost anything to avoid being apprehended.[18]

CAUSES OF CRIME

Shorn of all political controversy, emotional appeals and primitive fears, solid data indicate that crime has been on the increase for many years. Politicians, social scientists, members of the criminal justice system and the ordinary citizen are united in puzzlement over this increase, and have begun to look with greater scrutiny at the causes of crime. Some are readily apparent:

1. Availability of victims and their activities. While some victims of crime are objects of assault (rape, muggings, auto theft), others sometimes fall victim for failing to exercise necessary precautions. Other victims of crime are to some extent participants in the crime (abortion, prostitution, homosexual encounters, gambling) and as often as not will not want the crime to be discovered or reported.

2. Social and economic conditions. Slums, urban crowding, poverty and racial discrimination breed crime, especially crimes of violence in which residents are most often victims of their neighbors.

3. Unequal distribution of wealth. Since the end of World War II, the United States has been an "affluent society" and this affluence has been promoted and publicized in all the mass media. Happiness is having the autos, clothes, TV's, appliances and other appurtenances of affluence, and those who don't have them will often put aside moral and ethical scruples to obtain them.

4. Ineffectiveness of law enforcement agencies. Most police agencies simply lack the men, equipment, and technique necessary to prevent or control all the crime that is committed within their jurisdiction. Of necessity, they concentrate on controlling those crimes which are most conspicuous, those which most often breach the public peace.

Certain other factors have been established by the examination of crime statistics.

1. *Age*. There is a significant correlation between age and crime, with an inordinate amount of crime committed by young persons. Of all age categories, that from 15 to 24 accounts for the greatest number of crimes. Many factors account for this. Crime is in many cases the folly of youth. Crime is also related to the physical condition, leisure time and economic dependence of youth.

2. *Sex*. Far more males than females commit crime, the ratio being about 10 to 1, but the increase in crime among women has grown rapidly in recent years.

3. *Race*. The data show a disproportionate rate of crime among blacks. The highest arrest rate is among blacks, but so also is the number of victims who are black. There is no apparent correlation between color and crime; other factors are probably more important as causative agents. Blacks are, in general, poorer than whites, with low-income blacks being generally poorer than low-income whites. The rate of unemployment among blacks is markedly higher than the rate among whites. Blacks, more often than whites, are confined to the teeming urban slum. Black areas show more social disorganization than white areas. Hot spells, with little or no means of escaping the confines of the area for relief, add to the number of crimes.[19]

The rise in crime can be easily assigned to many factors, without resort to partisan political appeals, racial or ethnic attacks, or emotional outcries that forces which are soft on crime must be replaced by staunch advocates of law and order. These factors are the growth of population: as the population grows, crime grows; the growth of the youth population: as the proportion of the population under the age of 25 grows, crime grows; the growth of cities: as the urbanization of America increases, crime grows; the growth of affluence: as more and more people accumulate money, there is an increasing split between the haves and the have–nots.[20]

HISTORIC SEARCH FOR CRIME CAUSATION

The search for the causes of crime has engaged some of the best minds for several centuries and has resulted in a variety of fascinating theories.

The French philosopher René Descartes (1596–1650) introduced a theory of crime based on the doctrine of free will. The Cartesian Dichotomy was based on the thesis that the powers of reason and will were divine gifts that set man apart from all other forms of life.

Cesare Bonesana, the Marchese de Beccaria (1738–1794), postulated the theory that crime was based on "pain avoidance." He believed that a potential violator of the law weighed the pain of the punishment he might receive against the pleasure of his gains from the crime. He was the first of a group of theorists known as the classical school of criminology to attempt to modify the severe sentences often meted out for minor offenses. He thought that legislatures should assign punishments for crimes that were sufficient to counteract the motives that impel a person to the crime, but not unnecessarily severe.

In 1765 Beccaria published his treatise on crime and punishment under the title *Dei delitti e elle pene*. Among the points he makes in this treatise are the following:

1. People who commit crime do so of their own free will.
2. People seek pleasure and try to avoid pain.
3. Punishment is useful both as deterrent and as punishment.
4. Criminal law, including the punishments prescribed, must be publicized to have its effect.
5. Punishments should be fixed in law and applied uniformly.

6. Children and the mentally incompetent are not to be charged as criminals.

Many of these points are still active elements in the administration of criminal justice in the United States.

The English philosopher Jeremy Bentham (1742–1832) had a mathematical concept of the motives for crime and believed that an ascending scale of punishments could serve as a deterrent to crime. Like Beccaria, he stressed the need for humanitarianism. Punishment, he felt, should never be more severe than is necessary to deter men from committing a particular crime. The amount of punishment meted out should be governed by the need to prevent crime, not by the moral transgression or the intensity of public indignation. Other points in Bentham's thoughts on crime were:

1. The seriousness of the crime should be judged by the social harm it causes rather than by concepts of its sinfulness.
2. Crime is caused by man's rational effort to increase pleasure and decrease pain.
3. Each crime should be punished by inflicting as punishment pain that is greater than any pleasure gained or expected to be gained from the crime.

An Italian doctor, Cesare Lombroso (1836–1909), concentrated in his early medical practice on treatment of the mentally ill and from this arose an interest in the relationship between insanity and crime. He postulated a theory of the "born criminal." He believed that the criminal was an atavistic throwback to a more primitive and more savage man. He divided criminals into three essential types: the born criminal, the insane criminal and the criminaloid, a person with a tendency toward crime.

Lombroso's most important work, *L'Uomo Delinquente,* was published in 1876. He theorized in it upon common, observable anthropological characteristics of the criminal. Although in his later writings Lombroso concentrated more heavily on the social forces that determined criminal behavior, even as late as 1909 he was writing of the born criminal and linked certain physical characteristics to savage races. These characteristics included, among others, low cranial capacity, skull thickness and lack of sensitivity.

One of Lombroso's students, Enrico Ferri (1856–1929), was educated for the legal profession and became professor of law in several universities. While he accepted Lombroso's concept of an anthropological criminal type, he stressed in addition the application of sociology. While modern studies lend some support to the validity of the link between a person's physique, physiognomy, psychological temperament, and chromosomal makeup and pathological criminality, Ferri's emphasis on sociological factors foreshadowed many current concepts of the causalty of crime.

In the United States, research efforts have tended to follow this dichotomy between biological and physical determinants of crime and social and psychological causes.

An American anthropologist, Ernst Kretschmer, divided the people he studied into three types of physiques: the *asthenic,* the *athletic* and the *pyknic*. The male asthenic was lean (all skin and bones) and though not necessarily tall he gave the appearance of being tall. The female asthenic was also lean, but was usually very short. The male athletic was of medium height to tall, had a muscular physique and a V-shaped trunk that tapered from large chest to trim, firm stomach. The female athletic shared these characteristics, but was usually fatter. The male pyknic was of middle height and had a soft, rounded figure. The female pyknic was similar, and was notable for deposits of fat in breasts and hips. Kretschmer found a distinct correlation between body makeup and two major forms of mental illness or emotional instability. The pyknic body type was often represented in manic-depressive illnesses, the asthenic body type in schizophrenic illnesses.[21]

William H. Sheldon developed a system of somatotypes and a theory of behavior based on these types. Sheldon's three types were: *endomorphic*—round, soft, visceral development, marked by comfort and sociability; *mesomorphic*—heavy, hard, muscular development, marked by assertiveness and competitiveness; *ectomorphic*—thin, marked by sensitivity and restraint. Of the three types, the mesomorphic was, by his nature, most likely to be represented among the ranks of criminals.[22]

Sociological examinations of the causation of crime have been just as prolific and marked by sensitivity and insight.

Clifford K. Shaw of the University of Chicago made a long-term study of crime. Using pin maps, he located the residences of

56,000 juvenile and adult delinquents. Certain neighborhoods, he found, housed a disproportionate percentage of delinquent children and criminal adults. Upon closer examination, he found these neighborhoods to be disorganized, congested, and demonstrated a marked absence of social influences or controls.[23]

Taft and England examined neighborhoods with high crime rates and noted a number of marked characteristics:

1. Poverty areas with fairly normal family organization.
2. Slum areas characterized by poverty, anomie and a mixed population.
3. No man's land between slum and conventional society.
4. Rooming house area with transient, impersonal population.
5. Ghetto, occupied by a single minority group.
6. Vice area, where gambling, prostitution, and other crimes flourished unimpeded by any police interference.
7. Deteriorated rural area that served as a hideout or rest area for urban criminals.[24]

The major theory of the "American school of criminology" was advanced in 1939 by Edwin H. Sutherland. Sutherland's theory of "differential association" states that persons become criminals because they are constantly exposed to criminal behavior patterns. "Criminal behavior," said Sutherland, "is learned through interaction with others by means of the same mechanisms that are involved in any other learning process."

In more expanded form, Sutherland's theory makes the following assertions:

1. Criminal behavior is learned.
2. This learning is acquired in interaction and communication with others.
3. Person-to-person contacts are more important elements than mass communication and media.
4. Learning involves tutoring in techniques plus reorientation of attitudes, motives, and rationales.
5. Behavior becomes criminal because of an abundance of definitions favorable to criminal action.
6. Differential associations vary in priority, frequency, duration and intensity.

7. Criminal behavior is an expression of general needs and values.[25]

Other theories of the origins of crime vary widely and are marked more by singular instances than by broad-based proof of their importance or validity. From a hereditary standpoint, much is often made of the Jukes family in England, who through several generations displayed an inordinate involvement with crime, marked by mental defects, insanity and illegitimacy. More recently, attention has centered on the XYY chromosome syndrome. The typical chromosomal makeup of the male is XY. It has been found that on rare occasions a person has inherited an extra male chromosome, making him XYY. This extra male chromosome has been asserted to be the underlying cause of some male aggressiveness and hostility and has even been used as the basis of a defense made in a murder trial. Most recently, J. I. Rodale has called attention to a prevalence of a blood sugar imbalance among persons convicted of crimes.

CRIME'S VICTIMS

In recent years increasing attention has been given to the victims of crime. Advocates of "law and order" who decry the decisions of the the Warren Court and all other jurists who are "soft on crime" complain vociferously that while everybody's attention is on the perpetrator of the crime, no one is concerned for the victim. In part because of this outcry, and in part because enlightened members of the criminal justice system recognize the legitimacy of aiding the victim of a crime, some constructive steps are being taken. Again, most often the crime we are talking about is violent crime. In our humanity and compassion we are concerned for the victims of rape or assault and the families of murder victims.

In legal parlance, the victim of a crime is an aggrieved party, a complainant, a person whose legal rights have been invaded by a criminal act. The entire machinery of the criminal justice system is put into gear to redress his grievances.

Surprisingly, vast numbers of crimes go unreported. In 1965, research indicated that more than 50% of all crimes and 38% of all Uniform Crime Records Index Crimes went unreported.

The figures were higher in the high-crime areas of Boston, Chicago, and Washington, D.C., indicating that wherever there is a greater number of crimes, a greater proportion of them goes unreported.[26] Many nonviolent crimes also go unreported. In the area of business crimes, this is especially true in cases of shoplifting, employee theft, passing bad checks.[27]

Why do so many crime victims fail to report crimes? The reasons are varied.

1. They feel a closer identity with the offender (who is quite often friend, relative or neighbor) than with the police.
2. They do not recognize the act as a crime.
3. They fear reprisal.
4. They fear increased insurance rates.
5. They are unwilling to get involved.
6. They have little faith in the ability of the police to apprehend the offender.
7. They have little faith that the offender, if he is apprehended, will be convicted or punished.[28]

DECRIMINALIZATION

It is generally accepted that the problem of crime cannot be solved by increasing the size, scope and personnel of the criminal justice apparatus. There are not and cannot be enough policemen, attorneys, judges, courthouses, jails and prisons to handle the load. If every person who commits a crime were arrested, booked, arraigned and brought to trial, the system would collapse. "Placing more, better trained and better-equipped police officers on the street may be necessary, but it results in more arrests, which in turn increase caseloads in the courts to the choking point."[29] The answer is not to apprehend every person who has committed a crime, but to prevent crime from occurring.

One proposal has attracted increasing attention: decriminalization. Simply stated, this is the proposal that many acts now considered crimes should no longer be so considered; reduce the crime rate by making fewer acts crimes.

Morris and Hawkins, of the University of Chicago, propose the following:

> The first principle of our cure for crime is this: we must strip off

> the moral excrescences on our criminal justice system so that it may concentrate on the essential. The prime function of the criminal law is to protect our persons and our property; these purposes are now engulfed in a mass of other distracting, inefficiently performed, legislative duties. When the criminal law invades the spheres of private morality and social welfare, it exceeds its proper limits at the cost of neglecting its primary tasks.[30]

Accordingly, they would make the following actions legal and not subject to criminal sanction:

1. Drunkenness.
2. Narcotics and drug abuse.
3. Gambling.
4. Disorderly conduct and vagrancy.
5. Abortion.
6. Sexual activities.
7. Juvenile delinquency.[31]

SUMMARY

Though many Americans may feel that criminal activity is greater today than ever before, the concern with crime has long been a major concern of the average citizen and many serious thinkers.

There are several ways of categorizing crime. Activities that are by law criminal can be divided into the categories of crimes that are *mala in se* or those that are *mala prohibita.* Crimes may be divided according to the penalties incurred upon conviction: capital crimes, for those punishable by death; felony crimes, for those punishable by a prison sentence of at least one year and a day; misdemeanors, for those punishable by a shorter incarceration; and infractions, for those lesser offenses usually punishable by fines.

Crime can also be categorized into several broad areas that focus both on the nature of the activities and the identities of the perpetrators. Some of these are street crime, violent crime, professional crime, organized crime, and white collar crime. Of these various activities, the greatest toll is taken by organized crime and white collar crime, but the greatest attention has been given to street crime, both for the violence that accompanies it and because of the attention it has been given by politicians and the media. An examination of street crime indicates that it is essentially the product of young men, of large cities, of ghetto areas within large cities.

Studying the criminal finds him essentially representative of society in general or of his own educational, professional, working class, or social subculture. There is no typical criminal. One, however, deserves special attention, the sociopathic criminal, who represents a special threat to all involved in the criminal justice system. The social psychopath shows no sign of guilt, tension, conscience, or goal in life; he has an impulsive, irresponsible nature; and he is willing, often without warning, to do almost anything to avoid capture or incarceration.

The causes of crime are multitudinous. One is the role that victims themselves play, either by being unwary or incautious, or by participating in various criminal activities. Another is the social conditions and upheavals of American society. A third is the uneven distribution of wealth between the haves and have nots. The rise in crime is partially attributable to these factors and partially to statistical factors: the growth of the population, the increasing proportion of the population that is under 25 years of age, increasing urbanization, and the increasing impoverishment of those who have not shared in America's affluence.

Many men have searched for the causes of crime. Descartes introduced a theory of crime based on the doctrine of free will. Beccaria postulated several notions based upon his thesis that persons who consider committing a crime weigh the pleasure to be gained from it against the pain inflicted as punishment. Both he and Bentham felt that punishments should be commensurate with the crimes they are invoked against and should be severe enough to deter a person from committing the crime. Lombroso formulated the theory of the born criminal and studied the physical characteristics of criminals to support his views. His student Ferri added an emphasis on sociological factors.

In the United States numerous studies have resulted in many meaningful formulations. Kretschmer examined male and female physiques and found a significant correlation between two types of physique and mental illness. Sheldon developed a famous theory of body types. Shaw used pin maps to study delinquent children and deviant adults and found that the neighborhoods from which they came were marked by distinct sociological characteristics. Taft and England also found that neighborhoods with high crime rates shared easily recognizable characteristics. Sutherland formulated the major theory of "differential association," whose major theses are that criminality is a learned behavior, that it is acquired from one's peers, and that it reflects the needs or values of the criminal.

Oddly enough, with all the emphasis on crime, evidence indicates that a significant number of crimes go unreported; the higher the rate of reported crime, in fact, the higher the rate of unreported crime. The reasons for this are varied. Crime's victims may fear reprisal, may be unwilling to get involved, may have little faith in the ability of the criminal justice system to apprehend, convict and incarcerate the perpetrator, or may, indeed, feel closer kinship to the criminal than to the police.

One recent proposal to reduce crime is to make fewer activities crimes. This idea, called decriminalization, has engaged the attention of several serious thinkers.

NOTES

1. Quoted in William A. Westley, *Violence and the Police,* 2nd ed. Cambridge, Mass.: The MIT Press, 1970, p. 3.
2. James F. Ahern, *Police in Trouble*. New York: Hawthorn Books, 1971, p. 106.
3. Edwin H. Sutherland, *White Collar Crime*. New York: Holt, Rinehart and Winston, 1949.
4. Marshall B. Clinard and Richard Quinney, *Criminal Behavior Systems —A Typology*. New York: Holt, Rinehart and Winston, 1967, pp. 12–19.
5. Ahern, *op. cit.*, p. 143.
6. *Violent Crime*. The Report of the National Commission on the Causes and Prevention of Violence. New York: George Braziller, 1969, pp. 33–34.
7. *Ibid.*, p. 35.
8. *Ibid.*, pp. 42–43.
9. *Ibid.*, p. 37.
10. *Ibid.*, p. 41.
11. *Ibid.*, p. 48.
12. *Ibid.*, p. 39.
13. *Ibid.*, p. 42.
14. Ahern, *op. cit.*, p. 156.
15. *Violent Crime,* p. 66.
16. Robert J. Wicks, *Applied Psychology for Law Enforcement and Correction Officers*. New York: McGraw-Hill Book Company, 1971, p. 60.
17. *Ibid.*, p. 61.
18. *Ibid.*, p. 76.

19. Thomas F. Adams, *Law Enforcement*, 2nd ed. Englewood Cliffs, N. J.: Prentice-Hall, Inc., 1973, p. 22ff.
20. Norval Morris and Gordon Hawkins, *The Honest Politician's Guide to Crime Control*. Chicago: University of Chicago Press, 1970, p. 36.
21. Ernst Kretschmer, *Physique and Character—An Investigation of the Nature of Constitution and the Theory of Temperament*, 2nd ed. New York: Humanities Press, 1951, pp. 17–35.
22. William H. Sheldon, *Varieties of Human Physique*. New York: Harper and Row, 1949, pp. 234–239.
23. Clifford K. Shaw, et al., *Delinquent Areas*, 1927; *The Jack-Roller*, 1930; *Natural History of a Delinquent Career*, 1931; *Brothers in Crime*, 1938; *Juvenile Delinquency and Urban Areas*, 1942. Chicago: University of Chicago Press.
24. Donald R. Taft and Ralph W. England, Jr., *Criminology*, 4th ed. New York: Macmillan Publishing Co., 1964, pp. 165–168.
25. Edwin H. Sutherland and Donald R. Cressey, *Criminology*, 8th ed. Philadelphia: J. B. Lippincott Co., 1970, pp. 78–79.
26. Albert J. Reiss, Jr., *The Police and the Public*. New Haven: Yale University Press, 1971, p. 66.
27. *Ibid.*, p. 68.
28. *Ibid.*, pp. 68–69.
29. Bernard Botein, *Our Cities Burn*. New York: Simon and Schuster, 1972, p. 24.
30. Morris and Hawkins, *op. cit.*, pp. 1–2.
31. *Ibid.*, p. 3.

STUDY QUESTIONS

1. Discuss the reasons for the belief that the United States is in the midst of a crime wave.
2. Which type of crime—professional, organized, white collar, or violent—represents the greatest threat to American democracy?
3. What are some of the causes of the rise in violent crime?
4. What are the social conditions typical of areas in which violent crime occurs?
5. Is there such a thing as "the criminal type"? If so, what are some of the characteristics?
6. Is there a relationship between body type and criminality?
7. What are the major elements of the theory of "differential association"?
8. What role does the victim play in contributing to crime?
9. Why do some crime victims not report crimes perpetrated against them?
10. What are the pros and cons of decriminalization?

6

Juvenile Crime and Juvenile Delinquency

Amid the general public outcry against the rising tide of crime in the past two decades, one strand has become of increasing, and perhaps central, concern: the phenomenal rise in crime by the young. The 1967 report of the Task Force on Delinquency of the President's Commission on Law Enforcement and Administration of Justice called juvenile crime "the single most pressing and threatening aspect of the crime problem in the United States."[1] Now, almost ten years later, the problem is even more critical. Over the years this rise has been marked by several noteworthy characteristics: increasing frequency, increasing violence and the decreasing ages of the perpetrators. In 1972, according to FBI figures, 7,000,000 persons were arrested in the United States. More than one-quarter of these were juveniles, and they were responsible for 44% of the violent crimes that were committed. This number of arrests marked a 10% rise over 1971 and a 60% rise over 1967. Earlier in this text we mentioned that crime is essentially a phenomenon of the young, the poor, the uneducated, the member of a racial or ethnic minority. Recently it has become increasingly clear that while all of these characteristics hold true, the age of the perpetrators has gradually gone down from mid to late teens to the early teens and the pre-teens, and the incidence of aggravated assault, forcible rape, and murder has skyrocketed. Statistics gathered in New York State may be considered representative. In slightly less than ten years (1964–1972) the number of violent crimes committed by children between the ages of 7 and 15 increased 650%. In New York City, in 1971, 59,000 crimes by juveniles were recorded, 9,000 of which were felonies (44 murders, 117 rapes, 3,417 robberies, 692 felonious assaults among them).

In this chapter we will examine the perplexing and increasingly acute problem of juvenile crime and juvenile delinquency. The introduction presents pertinent statistics on the dimension of the problem. The first section defines juvenile delinquency, outlines the relationship of juveniles to the law and calls attention to the status of "youthful offender." The second section discusses the relationship of juveniles to the police and the various courses open to the police in handling youngsters.

Next we will look at the juvenile court system: its origin, jurisdiction and modus operandi, and discuss the difficulties the court faces in finding meaningful treatment methods for delinquents. This section also reviews Supreme Court decisions that have had significant bearing on the law as it relates to juveniles. After a review of correctional facilities for juveniles, we move into a discussion of the causes of juvenile delinquency: educational, psychological, emotional, and sociological.

JUVENILES AND THE LAW

Once again we must, before proceeding, clarify the terms involved, because the terms have been loosely defined, and the conformance of the terms with the actions and concepts involved can be troublesome. We have spoken above of crimes committed by young people: assault, rape, murder. However, in legal parlance, these are not crimes but incidences of juvenile delinquency, and the persons who have committed these acts are not criminals but juvenile delinquents. The President's Commission has presented what may be the most succinct and satisfactory definition:

> "Juvenile delinquent" means a person over 7 and less than 16 years of age who does any act which, if done by an adult, would constitute a crime.[2]

What this means essentially is that whether an act is considered a criminal offense is determined not by the nature of the act but by the age of the offender. A ten-year-old who takes the life of another person cannot be tried for murder or manslaughter in any degree; depending upon the jurisdiction within which the act is committed, he cannot be charged with the crime unless he is 16 or 18 or 21. He is a juvenile delinquent and his case is adjudicated on this basis. (Not all offenses charged to juveniles that constitute delinquency, however, are crimes in the adult criminal justice system. A youngster may be involved with the juvenile justice system for having committed an offense, such as truancy, consumption of alcoholic beverages, or violations of curfew, which is applicable only to juveniles, not to adults.)

This basic definition of juvenile delinquency, which determines that the acts committed are not criminal acts, leads to a central aspect of the problems of juvenile delinquency: all processing of juveniles takes place within the civil rather than the criminal system. All the trappings of the criminal justice system are brought into play: commission of an act that might be considered a criminal act were it committed by an adult, apprehension by a police officer, investigation by social case workers and probation officers, hearings before a justice, detention before or after the hearing, sentencing to a correctional facility after the hearing. Yet the processing remains a civil action. The focus of the proceedings is not accusation or adjudication, but investigation, diagnosis and prescription. This is largely in keeping with the basic philosophy of the juvenile court that decisions should be based not on the offense but upon the character of the juvenile offender, the circumstances of his life and the prospects for guiding him to a peaceful, law-abiding adulthood.

The concept of separating children from adults and treating them differently in the criminal justice system has a long history. English common law long held that no child under the age of seven could be held criminally responsible for his actions. American law has incorporated this concept. In the 10th century, England's King Athelstan enacted a law that declared "man shall not slay none younger than a fifteen winters' man." In 1290, Edward I had legislation enacted which required that the state was to be responsible for any person under the age of 21, if his parents were dead or seriously neglectful of him.

In the American legal system, as in many others, therefore, criminal responsibility is determined in part by the age of the offender. Children under the age of seven are free of criminal liability. Children over the age of seven, but under the age of 16 (or 18 or 21, depending upon the state of jurisdiction) are adjudged juvenile delinquents. The first comprehensive juvenile court law in the United States was enacted by the Illinois legislature in 1899. By the end of the first decade of the 20th century 35 other states had passed such laws.

Certain states such as New York and California have enacted legislation which allows the granting of "youthful offender" status to persons who are still relatively young but beyond the age of jurisdiction of the juvenile courts. The concept of the "youthful offender" permits greater flexibility in the judicial processing and in the treatment-oriented sentencing of youngsters who might be harmed rather than helped in the usual adult prison environment. Persons granted this status are often separated from other adults from pre-trial detention on and may spend their confinement, when necessary, in a juvenile facility.

By way of example, the Domestic Relations Court Act of New York City defines a juvenile delinquent as any child between the ages of seven and sixteen who

1. Violates any federal, state or local ordinance.
2. Is incorrigible, uncontrollable, habitually disobedient and beyond the control of parent, guardian or custodian.
3. Is habitually truant.
4. Deserts home or residence without permission or just cause.
5. Engages in an illegal occupation.
6. Begs or solicits alms or money in public places.
7. Associates with immoral or vicious persons.

Because of the general legal definitions, our discussion has concentrated entirely on the age of the child. This must focus attention on a critical aspect of the problem, especially important to the law enforcement officer: the size and physical attributes of the juvenile delinquent. There is no longer as distinctive a physical difference as there once was between youngsters and adults. Teenagers and sometimes even pre-teeners may range up to six feet in height, with the girth and strength to be a menace to many adults and a match for many police officers. Attitudes have changed, too, so that age and sex no longer command the respect or sympathy they once did. Restraints against physical violence have gradually been dissolved in the adult as well as the juvenile population.

JUVENILES AND THE POLICE

Most youngsters who achieve some record of juvenile delinquency do so initially through the intervention of the police. Almost one-half of the incidents in which juveniles are taken into custody originate with the police screening process in which the police do not acknowledge the juvenile's right to privacy, silence or representation by counsel. As part of their general law enforcement activities, police note young people who gather on street corners or on premises that have a local reputation for disorderly or criminal activities. The problem becomes especially acute in urban areas where large numbers of juveniles may be idle after school or without work and with no recreational activity to occupy them.[3]

Police encounters with juveniles are essentially negative and arise mostly from the need, expressed or implied, to admonish them or take them into custody. Whereas police encounters with adults most often arise out of citizen initiation, as indicated in Chapter 7, police encounters with juveniles tend more often to be police initiated.

Police encounters with youths are often negative and arise from a need to admonish them or take them into custody.
Magnum Photos

Most police-juvenile encounters result quite early in a character assessment by the police, and these assessments are usually more influential on the treatment accorded the juvenile than any alleged offense. Basically, the police officer will make a determination, on the basis of the juvenile's action, speech and demeanor, whether he is a serious delinquent, a misguided youth or a good boy in a scrape. Both the police and the courts will often base their judgment of a youth and their subsequent decisions concerning the treatment he is to receive on such an initial character assessment. A juvenile can expect good treatment, no matter the nature of the act he is alleged to have committed, if he is contrite about the offense, is respectful to police and court officers, shows respect for and fear of authority, and is genuinely alarmed by the offense and its consequences. A juvenile can expect poor treatment if he is disrespectful to or not fearful of police and court officers, is unconcerned by authority, is argumentative and is unchastened by the offense with which he is charged.

For the police, the juvenile presents troublesome problems of control. While the juvenile is capable of committing acts that in adults might result upon conviction in long prison sentences, he is essentially free of the sanction of criminal law. If he is unawed by his involvement with the legal system, he makes an especially difficult problem for the police.

> Patrol officers commonly regard juveniles as the most difficult class of citizens to police and the most leniently handled in the system of justice. . . . They show less respect for law and authority, are more aggressive and defiant, and rebellious, are more aware of restrictions on police conduct.[4]

The police officer involved with juvenile misconduct has significant discretionary power. In fact, the opportunities afforded him in this area result in a considerable reduction of the court's case load. These powers are ". . . release with reprimand . . . referral to a social service or similar community resource, or referral to court."[5] There are others, such as taking the juvenile directly home to his parents or referring the juvenile (by formal application) to the police department's juvenile division for further evaluation and/or processing. The fact the officer has these discretionary powers, has considered them, and gone on to arrest the offender only leads to his further frustration when he appears in court and finds his actions and his judgment questioned.

Discussions in other chapters acknowledge that the law enforcement officer has prejudices and biases, and it might be presumed that he will act on the basis of these. It could then be rather easily concluded that he will act most alertly and harshly toward blacks and Hispanics, and least harshly to white youths, treating the former more often to the finality of arrest and the latter to the ease of a reprimand. Statistics, however, show that the officer applies the same standards to all he comes into contact with and that arrests of minority youths are no more prevalent than arrests of white youths.

Actually, the police officer's actions do not stem from his prejudices or lack of them, but from a sense of practicality. As often as possible he will utilize his discretionary powers to avoid involvement with interminable court processes such as booking, preliminary appearances, trials, etc. He rationalizes his action on the presumption that the final result for him will be the same in any event—frustration and disillusion.

There is, however, some limit to the exercise of his discretionary power based largely on the nature of the offense with which he has become involved. When the offenses are minor, he will exercise his discretion; when they constitute what would be serious misdemeanors or felonies in adults, he will usually make an arrest. The "Task Force Report" encourages this philosophy, but imposes guidelines specifying the extent of the officer's discretionary powers. They do not, however, vary much from the qualifications already noted.

THE JUVENILE COURT

The discussion in Chapter 3 of the United States court system indicated that it was based upon an "adversary system." Juvenile and adolescent courts operate from another concept, which to some extent disregards this theory. These courts are informal in their deliberations and in many cases are unconcerned with the formal judicial procedures by which adults are tried. They are more concerned with rehabilitation than with punishment; indeed, they were set up with this purpose in mind, and are staffed with judges who could operate successfully from the presumptions inherent in the establishment of such courts.

The juvenile court is a division of the state's supreme court and its jurisdiction is defined by age. Its judgments in this area are final. In various states the courts have been given different names: Family Court, Children's Court, Adolescent Court. Nevertheless, their authority and duties are basically similar. Generally, their powers are as follows:

1. Granting outright dismissal of the charges.
2. Giving suspended sentences.
3. Reprimanding the alleged offender.
4. Levying and collecting nominal fines.
5. Placing the offender on probation.
6. Referring offenders to other agencies for social, emotional and psychological counseling.
7. Releasing offenders to the care of parents or guardians.
8. Committing offenders to training school, work camp or youth house.

For the victim of an offense committed by a juvenile and for the police officer the proceedings in the juvenile court are sources of great frustration and exasperation. The victim need not attend the proceedings to see that the offender is tried and convicted of the offense with which he is charged. The proceeding is held in acknowledgment of the offense and is concerned entirely with the proper disposition of the offender. The police officer views these proceedings with a jaundiced eye. He finds that he is rarely, if ever, called to testify and that when he is, he will usually find his actions and his testimony challenged, as if he had to defend and justify the actions he took that brought the juvenile to these proceedings in the first place.

The basic presumptions are that every child is redeemable and that the proper wisdom, succor and treatment will redeem him. The tendency, therefore, is to remand juveniles to those facilities where they may receive the necessary discipline, education and psychological counseling, or to release them to probation or to the custody of their parents.

Each of these solutions is seriously handicapped in its chances of success, except in those rare cases where the offense is minor and the offender is essentially a good child gone momentarily off the track. The preponderance of cases that find their way to juvenile court are for more serious offenses, committed by children with already serious educational, psychological, emotional and economic handicaps. The most serious offenders may go to training school or to a youth house, but for no longer than eighteen months to two years, far too little time in which to effect any significant change in their problems. This is compounded by the fact that many of the facilities to which they may be sent are overcrowded and understaffed and only a rudimentary attempt at rehabilitation can be expected. In far too many cases the end of incarceration finds the youths back on the streets as ill-prepared to cope with their problems and as ready as before (and even better equipped) to act out their frustrations in some offensive act. Placing youthful offenders on probation is handicapped by the excessive workloads of the probation officers and their consequent inability to offer more than cursory attention to the youths placed in their charge. Placing them in the custody of their parents presents most of the problems alluded to below: the parents are either neglectful of them, have rejected them, are poor role models for them, or have such serious problems of their own, either psychologically or emotionally or under the weight of caring for other children, that they cannot take proper care of these youthful offenders.

Many people can recognize the inadequacies of the juvenile justice system. "From their enlightened origins several decades ago, the juvenile courts and detention facilities have deteriorated to the point where they promote rather than combat juvenile delinquency," Ahern asserts in a common complaint.[6] Few have come forth with suggestions for reform that would meet the objections raised. The tendency, as might be expected, is to roll back the maximum age of coverage by the juvenile laws and subject juveniles who have committed serious offenses to the penalties of the criminal justice system. "If they're old enough and big enough to mug, and rape, and kill, they are big enough and old enough to suffer the penalties usually handed out to persons convicted of those crimes," goes the argument.

The United States Supreme Court has played as significant a role in the evolution of the law as it affects juveniles as it has in the sphere of the adult criminal justice system. Several landmark decisions are worthy of note.

The first is *Haley v. Ohio* (332 U.S. 596), a decision handed down in 1948. John Haley, a fifteen-year-old, was arrested by the police and charged with murder. He was taken to police headquarters and questioned there from midnight to 5 A.M., at which time the police emerged with a signed confession. Haley was tried in an adult court and convicted. The Supreme Court, in reversing the verdict, held that Haley's rights under the due process clause of the Fourteenth Amendment had been violated. During the entire late-night interrogation Haley was alone with his police captors and was without legal counsel. No fifteen-year-old, the court held, can be thought capable of withstanding the pressures of a professional police interrogation or of making a valid confession, voluntarily, without coercion, and in full knowledge of the charges against him and the consequences of his response to those charges.

The second is *Gallegos v. Colorado* (370 U.S. 49), which centered around an informal confession of murder by 14-year-old Robert Gallegos. The Supreme Court nullified the confession on the grounds that it had been secured illegally because of the following violations of the youth's rights: he was detained in a juvenile detention center for five days, two days longer than required by state law; his parents were not summoned; he was not given any hearing; and he was not advised of his right to counsel.

The most momentous decision of all, *In re Gault* (387 U.S. 1), came in 1967, in a case which began one night five years earlier. In 1962 Gerald Gault, 15, was accused by a neighbor, Mrs. Cook, of having telephoned her and making remarks of an "offensive, adolescent, sex variety." Gault was arrested and, without notification to his parents, was placed in a Children's Detention Center. Several days later a hearing on the charge was held. Mrs. Cook, the neighbor who made the complaint, was absent. Gault was accompanied to the hearing by his mother and a brother. He was not advised of his right to counsel. There was no sworn testimony, and no recording or transcript of the proceedings was made. Gault alleged at this hearing that not he but a friend, Ronald Lewis, had made the offensive remarks. The presiding judge took the case under advisement and Gault was remanded to the Detention Center to await the decision. At a second hearing, Mrs. Cook was again absent. The judge found Gault guilty and sentenced him to the Arizona State Industrial School "for the period of his minority unless sooner discharged by due process of law." Because Gault was only fifteen at the time, this constituted a sentence of imprisonment for six years.

A petition appealing the conviction was heard in Superior Court but was rejected, even though it was demonstrated at this hearing that an adult convicted of the same offense would have received as penalty a fine no greater than $50 or imprisonment for no longer than two months.

A petition to the Arizona Supreme Court was also rejected in spite of the fact that the court discerned six violations of due process during the initial trial proceedings.

In 1967 the case came before the United States Supreme Court and the Court, in an 8–1 decision, overturned the original conviction and ordered Gault released. The Court declared that the initial hearings had violated four constitutional rights: the right of notice of a charge of delinquency, the right to counsel, the right to confront and cross-examine witnesses, and the privilege against self-incrimination. In addition to the tally, the decision was far-reaching because each of the justices delivered opinions commenting on various aspects of the case and its relationship to constitutional law. The major thrust of these several opinions was that a juvenile in a delinquency proceeding is entitled to all the constitutional safeguards commonly afforded an adult in a criminal proceeding.

By the time Gerald Gault was released, he had already served more than three years of his sentence, far longer than the two months he might have served had he been an adult when convicted.

CORRECTIONAL FACILITIES FOR JUVENILES

In spite of the long-standing legal separation of children and adults, for many years there was no separation in prison. Children incarcerated for violations of the law were routinely committed to prison with adults and suffered untold hardship at the hands of their guards and their fellow prisoners. After a while there was recognition that such children were not being reformed but were being confirmed in their criminal ways. The first attempt to provide special care came with the founding by Pope Clement XI of a center in Rome for the correction of "profligate youth." In 1756 the Marine Society of England established a special institution for the reformation of juvenile offenders.

Table 6-1—**Detention Status of Children in Juvenile Facilities by Type of Facility, June 30, 1971**

All types of facilities	Total population			Adjudicated delinquents			Juveniles held pending court action			Dependent and neglected children			Juveniles awaiting transfer to another jurisdiction		
	Total	Male	Female	Total	Male	Female	Total	Male	Female	Total	Male	Female	Total	Male	Female
NUMBER															
All facilities	57,239	44,140	13,099	48,050	38,075	9,975	7,717	5,178	2,539	942	520	422	530	367	163
Detention centers	11,748	7,912	3,836	3,449	2,382	1,067	7,300	4,908	2,392	489	271	218	510	351	159
Shelters	363	237	126	36	23	13	164	106	58	153	101	52	10	7	3
Reception or diagnostic centers	2,486	1,988	498	2,462	1,973	489	4	3	1	18	11	7	2	1	1
Training schools	35,931	27,839	8,092	35,498	27,590	7,908	248	160	88	177	81	96	8	8	—
Ranches, forestry camps and farms	5,666	5,376	290	5,647	5,367	280	1	1	—	18	8	10	—	—	—
Halfway houses and group homes	1,045	788	257	958	740	218	—	—	—	87	48	39	—	—	—
PERCENT															
All facilities	100	77	23	83	66	17	14	9	4	2	1	1	1	1	*
Detention centers	100	67	33	29	20	9	62	42	20	4	2	2	4	3	1
Shelters	100	65	35	10	6	4	45	29	16	42	28	14	3	2	1
Reception or diagnostic centers	100	80	20	99	79	20	*	*	*	1	*	*	*	*	*
Training schools	100	78	22	99	77	22	1	*	*	*	*	*	*	*	—
Ranches, forestry camps and farms	100	95	5	100	95	5	*	*	—	*	*	*	—	—	—
Halfway houses and group homes	100	75	25	92	71	21	—	—	—	8	5	4	—	—	—

*0.5% or less. (Detail may not add to totals because of rounding.)

Table 1. Source: U.S. Department of Justice, Law Enforcement Assistance Administration, National Criminal Justice Information and Statistics Service.

Table 6-2—**Number and Percent of Juvenile Facilities With Medical and Recreational Services by Type of Facility—Fiscal Year 1971**

Type of facility	Total number of facilities	Medical services[1]				Recreational services[2]			
		None	Infirmary without beds	Infirmary with beds	Other	None	Radio, movies or TV	Library	Gymnasium or athletic field	Other
NUMBER										
All types of facilities	722	289	162	169	102	6	707	588	595	361
Detention centers	303	128	89	24	62	6	294	234	225	133
Shelters	18	11	—	3	4	—	17	11	12	10
Diagnostic or reception centers	17	1	5	10	1	—	17	16	16	7
Training schools	192	21	45	111	15	—	191	184	190	103
Ranches, forestry camps and farms	114	57	23	18	16	—	113	99	108	66
Halfway houses and group homes	78	71	—	3	4	—	75	44	44	42
PERCENT										
All types of facilities	100	40	22	23	14	1	98	81	82	50
Detention centers	100	42	29	8	20	2	97	77	74	44
Shelters	100	61	—	17	22	—	94	61	67	56
Diagnostic or reception centers	100	6	29	59	6	—	94	94	94	41
Training schools	100	11	23	58	8	—	99	96	99	54
Ranches, forestry camps and farms	100	50	20	16	14	—	99	87	95	58
Halfway houses and group homes	100	91	—	4	5	—	96	56	56	54

1. Detail may not add to totals because of rounding.
2. Percentages add to more than 100 because many institutions provide more than one type of recreational service.

Table 2. Source: U.S. Department of Justice, Law Enforcement Assistance Administration, National Criminal Justice Information and Statistics Service.

Table 6-3—**Number and Percent of Juvenile Facilities With Educational, Counseling and Job Placement Services by Type of Facility—Fiscal Year 1971**

Type of facility	Total number of facilities	Educational services[1]				Counseling services[2]				
		None	Academic only	Vocational only	Both academic and vocational	None	Individual counseling	Group counseling	Couunseling with juvenile and his family	Correctional facilities with job placement programs
NUMBER										
All types of facilities	722	65	256	4	397	29	679	558	413	164
Detention centers	303	57	164	—	82	26	268	172	151	†
Shelters	18	2	5	1	10	3	15	9	10	†
Diagnostic or reception centers	17	—	11	—	6	—	17	16	10	†
Training schools	192	—	23	1	168	—	190	176	124	88
Ranches, forestry camps and farms	114	2	40	2	70	—	114	109	73	47
Halfway houses and group homes	78	4	13	—	61	—	75	76	45	29
PERCENT										
All types of facilities	100	9	36	6	55	4	94	77	57	100
Detention centers	100	19	54	—	27	9	88	57	50	†
Shelters	100	11	28	6	56	17	83	50	56	†
Diagnostic or reception centers	100	—	65	—	35	—	100	94	59	†
Training schools	100	—	12	*	88	—	99	92	64	46
Ranches, forestry camps and farms	100	2	35	2	61	—	100	96	64	16
Halfway houses and group homes	100	5	17	—	78	—	96	97	58	37

*0.5% or less.
†Not applicable.

[1]Detail may not add to totals because of rounding.
[2]Percentages add to more than 100 because many institutions provide more than one type of counseling service.

Table 3. Source: U.S. Department of Justice, Law Enforcement Assistance Administration, National Criminal Justice Information and Statistics Service.

The first institution in the United States to provide children confinement separated from adults was The House of Refuge, established in New York City in 1825. Philadelphia established a separate facility for children in 1826.

Massachusetts pioneered the concept of remanding delinquents to a reform school, opening the first such institution in 1847. It housed boys only. In 1855 Chicago established a reform school that housed boys and girls.

Juveniles taken into custody are held in a variety of facilities. A 1971 census[7] found more than 57,000 persons housed in 722 juvenile detention and correctional facilities. The most common of these, numbering 303, was the detention center which, like the local jail, its counterpart in the adult criminal justice system, was usually small, modestly equipped and locally administered. Less common were shelters and reception or diagnostic centers. Shelters were also locally administered and were used for dependent and neglected children as well as for suspected delinquents. Therefore, they imposed little physical restraint upon their residents and offered a broad range of child welfare services: education, recreation and counseling. Reception or diagnostic centers handled adjudicated delinquents only and were state administered.

Adjudicated delinquents, defined as juveniles who have been found guilty of a criminal offense or in need of supervision of the court, are most commonly remanded to one of three types of facility: *a*) training school, *b*) ranch, farm or forestry camp, and *c*) halfway house or group home.

The training school offers the most secure form of incarceration. It is usually a large, state administered facility; 60% of the training schools in the 1971 census accommodated 150 or more juveniles. In 1971 training schools housed 75% of adjudicated delinquents. Youngsters who are judged to present milder correctional problems may be sent to ranches, farms or forestry camps. These are usually far from the legal residences of the youngsters housed there and this distance, plus the hoped-for benefits of hard and useful work in the open air, allow for less strict confinement. Still other adjudicated delinquents are remanded to halfway houses or group homes, which are usually located in urban areas. These are small facilities, often housing 25 persons or fewer, and are the least physically restrictive of all facilities. They allow for community contact; in most instances the residents are allowed to leave during the day to work or go to school.

All of the facilities offer a broad range of services. Almost all offer educational and counseling services, though detention centers, because their populations are often short-term and transient, offer little in the way of formal programs. Fully 96% of the training schools are equipped with libraries and at least 90% of them administer a regular program designed to allow their residents to continue their formal education.

CAUSES OF DELINQUENCY

A number of behavioral scientists and investigators have presented theories on the causation of deviancy and crime and these have been examined in previous chapters. It is essential to keep these in mind when considering juvenile delinquency, for the root causes of deviancy are the root causes of delinquency. While the entire apparatus of the law enforcement and criminal justice systems separates juveniles and youthful offenders from adult offenders—and properly so, since there is so much more hope of redeeming an offender when he is treated early—it is essential to keep in mind that there is a distinct relationship between delinquency and adult deviancy; they are two sides of the same coin. The relationship is so distinct that investigation will show a heavy incidence of adult deviants who have a history of prior juvenile delinquency and a very light incidence of adult criminals who have had no juvenile involvement. This is why the need to find a workable and practical method of rehabilitating youthful offenders is so essential; it is probably the only way to prevent them from becoming adult criminals.

Sociologists have come to recognize four general types among the thousands of youngsters accused of juvenile delinquency.

1. Those who suffer from organic physiological damage: includes children with evidence of brain damage, early birth trauma, hyperkineticism, poor muscle coordination and developmental retardation.
2. Those who are from grossly deprived backgrounds: includes children who have been raised under disadvantaged conditions, who may be illegitimate, suffer from parental rejection or cruelty,

or are raised without parents in foster homes. Such children generally exhibit poor impulse control, low threshold of frustration and a need for gratification.

3. Those who suffer from emotional disturbance: neurotic reactions may stem from deprivation, rejection or parental discord; psychotic reactions may exhibit themselves in early schizophrenic behavior or irrational, motiveless behavior.

4. Those who have severe family problems: disjointed family life often evident in mother approving of and encouraging antisocial behavior of delinquent, strict father subconsciously liking delinquency, or conflicts between mother and daughter resulting in delinquency.[8]

The inadequate family background discernible in many juvenile delinquents forms several distinct patterns.

1. Mother and father are divorced or separated.
2. Mother and father, even when still married, are usually absent from home.
3. Mother or father rejects the child and takes little or no interest in his physical, mental or emotional development.
4. Mother or father is an inadequate role model for the child.

Of drug addicts in New York City examined by Wicks, 80% came from such inadequate home and family backgrounds.[9]

The juvenile delinquent is usually a person raised in one of several backgrounds that tend to make him dyssocial. He may have been raised in a section where the only apparently successful person was a criminal or someone who obviously lived beyond or outside the law. Or he may have been raised in a society where people made their own laws. And he may even have been raised in a family environment that made him oblivious to or insensitive to the laws of society outside his own closely structured society.[10]

Here again the power of words to shape people's concepts or affect the actions they take based upon these concepts plays a vital role. To a certain extent, some members of society prefer to consider a wide range of behavior as "delinquency" rather than "deviancy," as though this makes the behavior less reprehensible and more acceptable. To a certain extent, this kind of labeling allows some toleration for the juvenile's behavior that varies from the norm. Provided that the equilibrium of society is not unduly altered, a wide range of youthful peccadillos—shoplifting, drag racing, association with prostitutes, gambling, and truancy—are blinked at as minor transgressions. These are often referred to as examples of "underconformity" (another semantic equivocation). The implication is that although these acts may be frowned upon, they should not place the juvenile beyond the pale. An opposite type of behavior, suggested by Dr. Ruth Cavan as a more serious aberration, is "over-conformity," defined as ". . . an exaggeration of the strict observance of formal social norms."[11] Oddly enough, the overconformer is viewed with distaste by society and may be cast as the villain in film, stage or television drama or may be the butt of the jokes in comedy.

Many factors enter into the causes of juvenile delinquency and adult deviancy: socioeconomic, psychological, biological, and anthropological. We will revert here, however, to the fundamentals considered as the major contributors to the problem—family, school and religion.

Family

The family, the first of the elements in our constellation of values, has always been the major element that has given our society and culture its essential shape. Our folkways and mores are founded upon the Judaeo-Christian philosophy that emphasizes the commandment "Thou shalt honor thy father and thy mother." This has been impressed upon our culture from time immemorial. Mother and father were the center of family life, raising their children, guiding them, assisting them with their problems.

Until recently, all of us were brought up with this concept deeply rooted in our minds; unfortunately, the commandment which furnished the basis of a stable family structure has now become a debatable issue with the younger generation, which declares that a blood relationship stemming from biological happenstance is no longer a valid basis for unquestioning allegiance and affection.

Society has become mobile, with families moving from place to place because of economic and social necessity. Ties beyond the nuclear family have become tenuous. Where families once lived in close proximity to each other—sometimes two or more generations within the same household and often brothers, sisters, aunts and uncles within the same neighborhood or area—many of today's rootless families live away from other members of their family and have little contact with them except at such special occasions as birth, marriage and death. Both father and mother are involved in the middle-class status seeking so prevalent in this upwardly mobile society. For the father this status is attainable by working long hours in search of raises or promotions, or by taking a second job for additional income, or by being involved with local social, political or fraternal organizations. For the mother it is attainable by involvement with parent-teacher associations, garden and hobby clubs, political organizations, women's liberation and consciousness-raising groups. Whatever the manifestations of this parental seeking after success, it leads inevitably to a lowering of the importance of the family, a loosening of family ties and a growing rootlessness and aimlessness among the young.

Even where the nuclear family remains together, the young are exposed constantly, through experiences reported to them or through exposure to radio, television, newspapers and magazines, to an ever increasing awareness of infidelity, domestic unhappiness and divorce. The values of the family structure have changed radically in our contemporary society and have created conflicts in the minds of juveniles, leaving them confused, rootless and in search of solid substitutes for the close-knit and supportive family.

The popularity of *The Godfather* may, in fact, be based not upon the savagery of the blood-spilling action or upon the casual, machismo sexual involvements, but rather upon the solidity of the family depicted. In almost a subliminal way the book and the film remind us of the power of the family that stays together under the guidance and direction of an all-wise, all-powerful papa who knows the answers, who can tell us what to do, who can solve our problems, who is beloved by family and friends alike, and whose advice is sought by all. It does not matter that he is the "Don" or that he is a criminal who rose to power and maintains his power by the threat or use of violence. He is a hero because he is the wise, solid and powerful father of us all.

Religion

Religion and the family have been interrelated for so long that it is commonplace to declare the vital support each institution gives the other. Like the family, established religious institutions have suffered increasingly from either attack by youth or by a growing indifference and alienation. While many youths demonstrate their revolt against family, society and religion by refusing to participate in any formal religious structure, and may actively espouse a belief that "there is no God" or that "God is dead," many others display what may be an innate religious impulse by participating in new religious groupings. Once youths are old enough to declare their freedom from the need to participate in any formal religion, they may discontinue such participation; they may spout anti-religious philosophy; they may utter absolute blasphemy that will shock family and friends alike. Or they may almost simultaneously seek the answers to their religious cravings by joining a sect completely new to them. The Jew who hasn't stepped into temple or synagogue since Bar Mitzvah may prance about in the robes of Hare Krishna. The Protestant who hasn't been to church since he sang in the choir as a boy may busy himself handing out leaflets or giving street-corner lectures explaining the doctrines of the Reverend Sun Myung Moon. The Catholic who hasn't been to confession in a dozen or more years may find himself experimenting with one of the growing Pentecostal churches.

Denigrating religion and faith has always found voice among the young, but any deeper look at the impulses that impel this denigration will usually reveal not a lack of religion or faith, but a disenchantment with the desire or ability of an established religious institution to involve itself with the problems of contemporary society. When an established institution becomes actively and seriously involved with social reform, with problems of drug addiction, family counseling, relief and aid to the poor and dispossessed, it maintains the interest and allegiance of its members, especially its younger members.

School

Because children spend so much of their time in school, with their usual completion of compulsory schooling coinciding with the age of majority and the maximum age at which youngsters are considered juveniles for the purposes of judicial determination of legal offenses, a considerable amount of the search for the causes of failures in today's youth focuses on schools. In many instances, schools and teachers have become convenient scapegoats for the failures of others. In some strange fashion, teachers have become surrogate fathers and mothers to today's youngsters. No longer are teachers charged merely with educating the young. Now they are also expected to guide them, counsel them, succor their emotional and psychological needs.

The socially acceptable doctrine of "overpermissiveness" on the part of parents overlooks the important factor of discipline. The impression has taken hold that discipline and punishment are concomitant and that, therefore, both are wrong. It is forgotten that punishment does not always involve physical means. Various other methods are available for enforcing discipline.

The concept of teachers and schools as the surrogate for the parents stems from the deep respect our forebears had for ministers, physicians and teachers. In times gone by, the teacher had the same authority over a child that the parent did. However, this authority has been taken from the teacher, and his position, once highly esteemed, has eroded to the extent that the title now bears with it little respect. In spite of this, the teacher is expected to exercise the duties of the parent without the authority to enforce his decisions concerning those duties.

DRUGS AND DRUG ABUSE

One major manifestation of the breakdown of certain social observances among the young is the problem of drugs. There is no need to stress the horrors of addiction; society has become increasingly aware of the affliction. What is important is to recognize drug use and drug abuse as the most severe manifestation among today's youth of its disenchantment with society.

Addiction to "hard" drugs such as heroin, cocaine and morphine and the heartbreak attendant upon such use are common knowledge. Although there is a keen awareness of the use of drugs such as LSD, barbiturates, amphetamines and others, they have not been given the same overwhelming attention. Various law enforcement agencies, federal, state and municipal, have cooperated as never before in attempting to eradicate this evil. Their combined efforts have proved to be extremely effective. The result is that heroin has become increasingly difficult to secure. Furthermore, the exposure given by various media to the dangers of addiction and the creation of agencies that assist the addict have had significant results. In fact, among large portions of the young, it is no longer considered "fashionable" or "in" to be on drugs.

Attention has turned recently to the problem of methadone and its addictiveness. Proponents of methadone say that it is useful because it allows the addict to function in society and that since it is dispensed free of charge, it is an effective weapon against crime. One theory has proposed that instead of methadone, the addict be given heroin, since both are drugs, the expense of administering methadone is greater because of the need for various centers of control and medical supervision, and the necessity to commit crime in order to pay for heroin will be eliminated. This is a debatable issue.

Government agencies maintain facilities for the rehabilitation of drug addicts. These leave something to be desired, since psychological and psychiatric counseling and job availability services are limited.

Private agencies seek the approach known as "cold turkey." They attempt to have the addict rid himself of his habit completely without the substitution of any other habit. The Pentecostal churches offer faith and belief in God and Jesus to assist the unfortunates. They have instituted a program in depth, offering counseling and guidance. Other institutions, such as Phoenix House in New York City, offer living quarters, counseling and the advice and encouragement of ex-addicts in their program of "cold turkey." One must understand that the choice of methadone or "cold turkey" is not quite that simple. When one becomes an addict, he is known to have "a monkey on his back." In spite of all his efforts, he will not shake it loose. Methadone is an acceptable substitute for heroin. "Cold turkey" is a horrifying experience, exacting a mental and physical toll on the addict that is beyond the comprehension of the ordinary citizen. Agencies that prefer a cure by complete abstinence are well aware of the tortures that await the unfortunate and attempt to assist him in any way they can.

Probably the most troublesome drug in common use today is marijuana. It is estimated that perhaps as many as 20 million persons have used marijuana at least once in recent years, that among high school and college students as many as 35% have used it, and that among college students more than 50% have.

Marijuana is the center of an on-going debate among users, medical experts and law enforcement agencies. The sale, use and possession of marijuana are crimes in all the states of the Union, but the differences in the penalties are extremely vast. The problem is compounded by the fact that marijuana has been used for many years and only fairly recently did it become the subject of severe criminal penalties. For many years marijuana was used largely by minority groups in the ghetto, largely by Spanish and Chicano youths in the Southwest and Far West. Only when its use spread to white, middle-class youths were laws passed in an effort to eliminate such use. The more marijuana came to be part of the youth scene, the stiffer became the penalties. Thus, judgment about a drug with a specific set of properties has been colored by myriad political considerations.

Before the early 1930's marijuana use was not considered a serious problem either by the public or the police and the few state laws banning marijuana were loosely enforced. Under pressure from the Federal Bureau of Narcotics, Congress passed the Marijuana Tax Act in 1937, which made the unauthorized sale, purchase or possession of marijuana a serious crime. After a widely publicized upsurge in the use of narcotics following World War II, Congress passed the Boggs Act in 1951. This provided for mandatory-minimum sentences for all drug offenses. Congress enacted still tougher legislation with the passage of the Narcotics Drug Control Act of 1956. This law allowed a sentence of two to ten years imprisonment for a first offense of possessing marijuana, five to 20 years for a second offense and ten to 40 years for a third offense. Selling marijuana called for a mandatory sentence upon conviction for a first offense of five to 20 years. State laws during this period underwent a similar stiffening of penalties. In Georgia conviction of a second offense of selling marijuana to a minor carries the death penalty. In Virginia possession of more than 25 grains carries a minimum penalty of 20 years; the penalty is the same for first-degree murder. In Ohio the sale of marijuana subjects the seller to a possible sentence of life imprisonment. In Massachusetts merely being found in a house in which marijuana is being used or is present brings a penalty of up to five years in prison. In North Dakota conviction of a first offense of possession of marijuana brings a penalty of 99 years at hard labor.

Much is known about the properties of marijuana, and one

thing that is known is that it is not addictive. The user is not hooked; he has no physiological need for marijuana. Rather his use of it is a sociocultural phenomenon, although it may be asserted that long-term use may result in a psychological dependence. We are, therefore, confronted by the question as to whether marijuana should be made an illegal drug, like heroin, cocaine or hashish, or whether it should be treated like alcohol. Those who favor changing the laws to decriminalize the use, sale or possession of marijuana emphasize its nonaddictive properties and liken its use among youth to the use of alcohol by adults. The effects of marijuana are similar to those of alcohol, and though the effects may last for three to five hours its aftereffects are minimal. It is no more dangerous, probably less dangerous, than alcohol, its advocates contend, and much cheaper.

Nevertheless, despite minor changes in various state laws which have lightened the penalties for use or possession, marijuana is still subject to criminal sanction in most states, and sale brings the harshest penalties. The marijuana user must be aware that he is breaking the law when he uses it and the law enforcement officer, no matter what his personal feelings are, must enforce the law.

THE JUVENILE AID OFFICER

An important supportive unit of the police department is the Juvenile Aid Division. At one time it was a preferred unit, because it served as an escape from the chores of uniformed patrol. Assignment was once based on "connections," and it was a sinecure for those not capable enough for duty in the other specialized divisions. The chief, under pressure to "take care" of such individuals, would make an assignment to the unit to keep them out of harm's way. Members of the unit would be assigned to such innocuous tasks as visiting playgrounds, making talks before school assemblies, speaking to various community organizations and writing reports.

Women seeking positions with the police department could assume that they would be assigned to the juvenile division. Few of them realized that they would be matrons in the women's section of detention centers, law officers assigned to searching female prisoners, and confidential secretaries to the higher echelons (since they could be more trusted than civilian secretaries).

The magnitude of the problems of juvenile delinquency has changed the requirements for the Juvenile Aid Officer. It is now expected that the Juvenile Aid Officer have a knowledgeable background concerning the problems of the juvenile. The chief has become exceedingly selective in assigning personnel to the division. The usual former standards, such as an officer having children of his own or that he like kids, no longer apply. As often as possible these assignments will go to officers with college education or degrees in psychology, sociology, or some other liberal arts discipline.

The further involvement of law enforcement in the areas of juvenile delinquency and assistance has had the effect of creating another surrogate family, with the individual juvenile aid officer as the surrogate for family, church and school.

The police department is acutely aware that its responsibilities very often extend beyond the primary duties of crime prevention and the apprehension of criminals. It has, nevertheless, accepted this program as it has accepted others. Police departments have instituted definitive prevention programs in conjunction with those offered by the schools. As a result of this participation, a new specialist has evolved: the "School Liaison Officer." He may be given other titles or be referred to in another fashion, but his duties are basically the same.

One Midwest police department instituted such a program and outlined the specific duties of the liaison officer. In essence, they are as follows:

1. To organize group counseling sessions for both children and parents.
2. To provide for individual counseling to both children and parents.
3. To seek prospective employers to provide for parttime jobs.
4. To assist the probation officer in his work with juveniles.
5. To recommend referrals to the school psychologist, speech therapist, nurse and other professionals.
6. To arrange for tutoring services.
7. To provide for the utilization of recreation facilities beyond those furnished by the school.
8. To arrange for foster-home placement.

9. To create a mentor-student relationship.
10. To foster a parent education program in the area of parent-child relationships.

Other police departments have not only included the aforementioned duties but added others as well. The assignment as a liaison officer is no longer a sinecure, but extremely demanding work, requiring additional hours beyond the usual eight-hour tour of duty, without additional compensation.

Early reports as to the efficacy of the program are optimistic. We may assume that it will eventually be highly successful and a regular feature of police departments throughout the country.

PREVENTING JUVENILE DELINQUENCY

Life would be simple if it were possible to predict the future conduct and behavior of the young. This has been attempted by sociologists for many years with varying degrees of success. They have evolved two distinct methodologies: the first known as the "statistical" or "actuarial" and the second as the "clinical." The statistical method is coldly numerical. Statistics are used based on the results of various testings of certain groups. The resulting conclusions are then incorporated into various classifications. Charts of probabilities are drawn from these figures.

The clinical method is concerned with the knowledge gained by direct personal contact with the individual or group. The theories of future causalities are then formulated based upon the information so gained. This system was first employed and used by Auguste Comte, a founder of the science of sociology. A sociologist thus involved is referred to as a "participant-observer."

As a result, innumerable analytical studies have been made as to the predictability of future behavior. The inference appears to be that something must be done to reinforce the tripartite base. The family must once more become the tightly knit unit it once was. This depends upon parents being made aware of their primary responsibilities—forgetting or forsaking social status and their quest for success. They should determine to concentrate on raising their children, being readily available to them. The decision will have to be made as to whether status, personal drives and desires should have first priority or whether their children's needs shall have first claim on parents. The churches must make an even greater effort to attract cynical and disaffected young. They must become, once again, houses of refuge—gathering places that offer more than the sophisticated popular methods of escape. Many churches are aware of their responsibilities and are actively engaged in serious efforts to overcome past deficiencies. In numerous instances, they are further along on the road to recovery than many critics give them credit for. Schools, the surrogate family, should be recognized as performing in this capacity, and government on all levels should make it possible for them to fulfill this capacity.

SUMMARY

One of the most disturbing aspects of the rise in crime is the rise in crime by the young. In addition to the rapid escalation in crime rates, the phenomenon is marked by increasing violence and decreasing age of the perpetrator.

Juveniles have a special place in the law enforcement and criminal justice systems. By law they are separated from the adult system and are generally exempt from the sanctions of adult criminal law, in spite of the fact that the offenses they commit might, if committed by adults, be labeled murder, rape, robbery, aggravated assault. This separation from the adult criminal justice system carries through the court and correctional systems. In the former their cases are adjudicated as matters of civil law, and the thrust of the court proceedings is not conviction on a charge of having violated the law but treatment-centered mediation of the juvenile's problems and needs. In the latter the institutions they may be remanded to are designed to rehabilitate youths through a combination of education, psychological and vocational counseling and training.

Because of the separation of juveniles from the adult criminal justice system, youngsters present a special problem to the police officer. Most youngsters who achieve any sort of record do so initially through police intervention, but police as a rule prefer to handle youngsters without involving them in the juvenile justice system. They do so not out of any consideration for the youngsters but as an expedient to keep themselves free of the frustrations and tribulations of the system. Like the victim of a juvenile offense, the police officer too often feels that he is being tried in the system, not the juvenile he brings into it.

The Supreme Court has played a significant role in the formulation of juvenile law, notably in three cases: *Haley v. Ohio, Gallegos v. Colorado,* and *In re Gault,* the last of which did most to establish the principle that any juvenile in a delinquency proceeding is entitled to the full range of constitutional protections given to any adult in a criminal proceeding.

Correctional facilities for youngsters vary. Most youths in custody are held in detention centers, which are analogous to local jails in the adult system. Some are held in shelters and diagnostic or reception centers. Most adjudicated youngsters are remanded to training schools, large, well-equipped, state-administered facilities. A smaller number, who require less secure incarceration, are placed in ranches, farms or forestry camps. A still smaller number are housed in halfway homes or group homes, which are usually located in urban environments and allow a good deal of community contact.

The causes of juvenile delinquency are numerous. Certain patterns are obvious: youngsters who suffer organic physiological damage, who come from seriously deprived backgrounds, who suffer from neurotic or psychotic disturbance, or who come from a disturbed family background. The combination of deficient family background and socially deprived milieu appears in overwhelming proportions among delinquents who are involved with drugs.

Drugs represent the most serious manifestation of a general disillusion among youth with the established centers of American social life: family, religion and schools. Federal and state governments have mustered all their resources to combat drug addiction and abuse and have been successful to a considerable degree with addictive drugs and those others which have been proven damaging to mental and physical well-being. The most pervasive problem and the one which seems least soluble is that of marijuana. Marijuana use was once restricted to some urban ghettoes and slums and the few state laws barring such use were loosely enforced. When marijuana emerged from the ghettoes and swept through the ranks of white middle-class American youths, marijuana laws were enacted and enforced. As marijuana use became commonplace penalties escalated to the point where they were harsher than the penalties for crimes as serious as felonious assault, rape or homicide.

To combat juvenile delinquency, various police organizations are refining their approach by hiring and training personnel with specific duties with regard to youth. These are variously referred to as juvenile aid officers or school liaison officers.

NOTES

1. Willard A. Heaps, *Juvenile Justice*. New York: Seabury Press, 1974, p. ix.
2. *Task Force Report: Juvenile Delinquency*. President's Commission on Law Enforcement and the Administration of Justice. Washington, D. C., 1967, p. 26.
3. Paul B. Weston and Kenneth M. Wells, *Law Enforcement and Criminal Justice*. Pacific Palisades, Calif.: Goodyear Publishing Company, 1972, p. 220.
4. Albert J. Reiss, Jr., *The Police and the Public*. New Haven: Yale University Press, 1971, p. 137.
5. *Task Force Report,* p. 13.
6. James F. Ahern. *Police in Trouble*. New York: Hawthorn Books, Inc., 1971, p. 160.
7. *Children in Custody: A Report on the Juvenile Detention and Correctional Facility Census of 1971*. Law Enforcement Assistance Administration. National Criminal Justice Information and Statistical Service. Washington, D. C., 1971.
8. Robert J. Wicks, *Applied Psychology for Law Enforcement and Correction Officers*. New York: McGraw-Hill Book Company, 1974, Chap. 6.
9. *Ibid.,* p. 63.
10. *Ibid.,* p. 62.
11. Ruth Shonle Cavan, "The Concept of Tolerance and Contraculture as Applied to Delinquency," in *Readings in Juvenile Delinquency,* 2nd ed. Philadelphia: J. B. Lippincott Co., 1969, p. 9.

STUDY QUESTIONS

1. Discuss the causes of the rise in juvenile crime.
2. What are the reasons for separating juveniles out of the adult criminal justice system?
3. What is the difference between a juvenile delinquent and a youthful offender?
4. What options are open to the juvenile court in dealing with delinquents?
5. What are the advantages and disadvantages of each of these options?
6. What is the significance of *In re Gault?*

7. Is it valid to separate juveniles out of the adult criminal justice system and still accord them *all the Constitutional protections inherent in that system?*
8. What are the major causes of juvenile delinquency? What are the prospects for their successful elimination?
9. What roles do family, religion and schools play in juvenile delinquency?
10. Is marijuana more or less dangerous than alcohol?

7

The Police Role: Myth and Reality

Several years ago the New York City Police Department issued a brochure entitled "The Hundred Hats of Officer Jones" to indicate the multiplicity of roles played by the police officer. The title is apt, because in any tour of duty, the police officer is called upon to perform a wide variety of tasks: those he is sworn to do in his role as a law enforcement officer, those he is given each morning by his duty officer, and those he is asked to do during any part of his tour by any citizen who feels the need for his help.

In this chapter we examine the myth and reality of the role the police play in American society and the image of the police officer—how he is seen by the public and how he sees himself. First we outline the police officer's essential duties and demonstrate that the major proportion of an officer's time is taken up with order maintenance and public service functions, not with crime-related activities.

Then we will discuss the method by which the officer fulfills his assignments, concentrating on patrol, its varieties, its innovations, and its prescribed duties. We also discuss investigation, the role the police officer plays in it, and its importance in enhancing the officer's conception of his role.

Next we look at police training, emphasizing the requirements for recruits and the adjustments made for women and members of minority groups. And finally we analyze the ambivalent images the public has of the police officer and the effect that these images and the trying nature of police work have in creating both covert and overt police societies.

THE NATURE OF POLICE WORK

Generally speaking, the primary purpose of any governmental police agency and of the police officers who are members of that agency is the protection and security of the individual citizen and, through this, assuring the orderly functioning of society. All the duties of the individual officer and the administration of the police department are managed in accordance with this basic premise. The functions the police perform in the furtherance of this premise can be divided into five broad categories:

1. *Crime prevention.* A variety of activities designed to keep people from committing crimes, including public education programs, demonstrating and publicizing the ability and availability of police, working with young people to guide them in the right direction, and cooperating with probation and parole personnel in the management of persons entrusted to their care.
2. *Crime repression.* Investigating crimes that occur, identifying and apprehending offenders, recovering stolen property, assisting in prosecution and conviction of offenders.
3. *Regulation of noncriminal conduct.* Consists largely of managing the ordinary citizen in a variety of public activities—traffic control, crowd control and public safety at theatres, ball parks, parades, rallies and so forth.
4. *Provision of public services.* Such mundane matters as giving information, advice, directions, general assistance, licensing and registration.
5. *Protection of citizens.* Mediating domestic disputes, preventing or quieting arguments between citizens, evacuation of fire and disaster scenes, and so forth.

Of these five areas, the last three occupy by far the major portion of the police officer's working day. The police officer spends at least three-quarters of his day on noncriminal matters and not more than 25% of his time on crime-related matters. The current turmoil over rising crime in the United States links the prevention

The primary purpose of any governmental police agency is the protection and security of the individual citizen. This patrolman has just rescued a baby from a wrecked automobile.
Photo courtesy of the Nassau County Police Department.

of crime with increases in the numbers of police and, conversely, decreases in the numbers of police with a necessary further rise in crime. The facts belie the contention.

> Overall, 99 percent of the time in preventive patrol nets no criminal or noncriminal incidents, an indication that preventive patrol is markedly unproductive of police matters processed in the system of criminal justice. . . . Only two-tenths of 1 percent of the time spent on preventive patrol is occupied in handling criminal matters.[1]

The amount of time that police in all jurisdictions spend on non-criminal matters, however, and the number of arrests made by the police in the areas of public drunkenness, possession and use of drugs, gambling, prostitution and other "victimless" crimes contradicts the widespread belief that the police can have any noticeable effect on reducing the number of violent crimes that is at the heart of this current turmoil.

For many centuries, police work remained what it had originated as, a variety of guard duty, and the major responsibility of the police officer was to enforce the law and maintain public order. It is probably safe to assert that this was the primary nature of police work well into the twentieth century, when the combination of industrialization, urbanization and involvement in complex international struggles radically changed the nature of American life and led to the host of domestic problems that plague us today. For some strange reason solutions to the problems eluded the wisdom and the efforts of the experts in education, sociology, psychology; by default solutions came to be expected of a group of men singularly unprepared and ill-equipped to provide them—the average American cop, "who is underqualified or undereducated or undertrained, who is subject to all the warping influences that society brings to bear on him . . . ."[2]

Over the years, the prescribed duties have grown. The police officer now functions as the chief regulator of conduct in the cities. He is a major referee of essentially private matters, like disputes between spouses, and is the peacekeeper of relationships between adversary racial, religious, and ethnic groups.[3] All this essentially without any special education or training.

A significant portion of a policeman's duty may be taken up with settling domestic disputes, and for the policeman it is a harrowing experience. As Ahern indicates involvement in domestic disputes results in a "disproportionate percentage of police injuries."[4] In any case, domestic strife is "a problem to which there is no solution, in which the policeman is ill at ease, in which the public appears in a most unfavorable light."[5]

In many ways, the police officer faces an impossible task in fulfilling all the roles assigned to him. He may be presumed to know and be ready to enforce approximately 30,000 federal, state and municipal laws. At almost any time of the day, in any location, the patrolman is exposed to dozens of situations. He is expected to make an immediate judgment and act upon that judgment. The action he takes, if it concludes in an arrest, is subject to review at several steps along the way—by the prosecuting attorney, who must decide whether to seek arraignment and indictment; by a

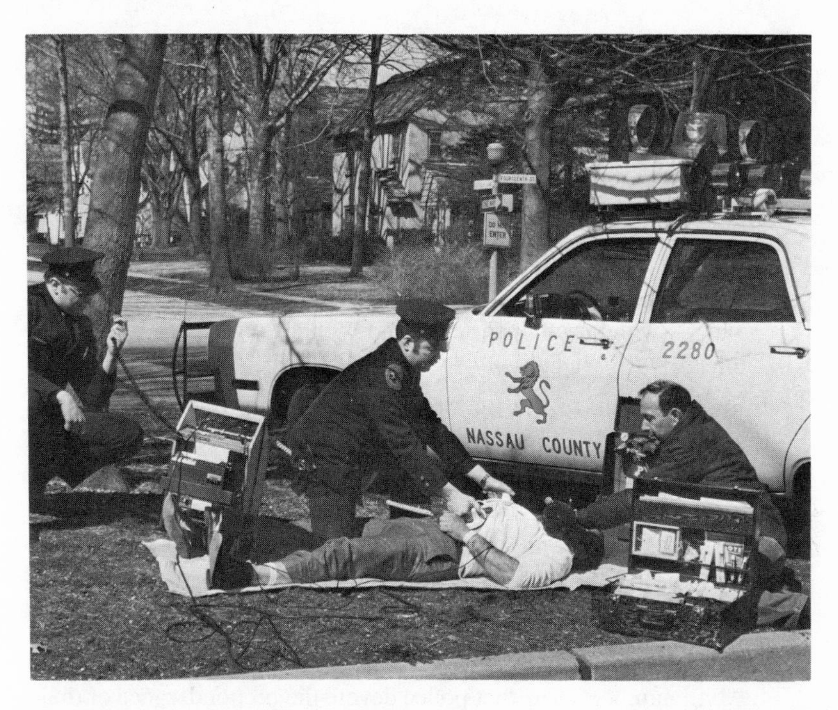

At almost any time of day, in any location the patrolman is exposed to dozens of situations.
Photo courtesy of the Nassau County Police Department.

defense attorney, who must attempt to prove his client free of guilt of the charge the police officer has made against him; by the trial judge, who by his conduct of the trial, his decisions regarding substantive matters of law, and his charge to the jury indicates his evaluation of the police officer's action; by justices at various levels of appeal up to and including the United States Supreme Court, who may overturn a conviction initiated by the police officer's action. Of course, his action is also reviewed immediately, though informally, by the citizens he comes in contact with, those who may have called him, those he may take into custody, and those bystanders who witness his performance of duty.

> Nothing is tougher than being a police officer in our democratic society. The policeman is supposed to mediate family disputes that would tax the wisdom of Solomon, maintain race relations in a ghetto with little knowledge of history, sociology, or psychology, enforce literally hundreds of laws without fear or favor, use great discretion; and identify and apprehend criminals who have left little or no trace of their activities.[6]

Yet he must not shirk his duties; when a situation arises that calls for him to act, act he must. In that very moment, he may become father-confessor, sociologist, psychologist, physician, attorney, and Supreme Court justice, but he must accept the role, come what may. The difficulty of the policeman's role is compounded by the requirement that he be available 24 hours a day.

> This is not an empty rule, but is frequently invoked. Police are called for emergencies, for court appearances, for the whim of the chief—without compensation and without regard for his private life or personal and family commitments.[7]

In essence, one of the major problems facing the police officer is that the public expects too much of him. He is supposed to solve the problems of society that have developed over hundreds of years, formed by forces of national consequence over which he has no control, and insoluble by politicians, professors and pundits. The public has many misconceptions of how the policeman spends his time, what he does with his time and the effectiveness of his efforts.

> Myth number one is that police devote the preponderance of their time and resources to combating serious crime. The second myth is that there is a fairly fixed, definable, and measurable thing called crime. The third is that good police work can somehow lower crime rates regardless of what other institutions do.[8]

Unfortunately, the police themselves, either individually or through their organizational or union spokesmen, distort the effectiveness of the police in the area of crime prevention. Any hint of, or actual implementation of, a reduction in the number of police personnel is greeted by a chorus of warnings that such action will lead to riot, looting, anarchy and crime run rampant. Such fears do not, however, prevent police from striking, often in violation of state law, to achieve certain contractual goals. On some occasions when police have gone on strike, their own dire predictions have not come to pass; indeed, statistics indicated that the incidence of crime went down.

PATROL

The heart of any local police operation is patrol, the stationing and circulating of uniformed officers in specified areas at specified times. Patrol performs many functions, some theoretical, some actual. From the standpoint of citizen psychology, the primary purpose of patrol may be crime prevention: the cop on the beat will prevent a crime from taking place or detect a crime in progress and apprehend the criminal in the act or shortly thereafter. This is far from an accurate perception. Only a very limited percentage of all the crime that takes place does so in the presence of or in proximity to the uniformed officer. Most activities that can be labeled violations of the law take place outside his presence and most often the policeman is summoned into action by a citizen request, not by his own discovery of the violation. Only massive police patrol, far beyond the capacity of any force, especially in times of stringent municipal budgets, could have any impact in the area of crime prevention. Routine police patrol can only repress those crimes that form a regular pattern, a numbers or bookmaking operation, prostitution, loansharking or bootlegging. These activities go on every day; they are known to the policeman and very often so are the persons engaged in them. Whenever social or political pressures call for a crackdown, the police can throw out their net and bring in their fish.

> In the absence of massive police manpower, proactive policing is a feasible method for discovery only when crime is routine and organized, and therefore predictable. From a sociological point of view, the patterned activity of vice, traffic, and organized groups such as gangs, lend themselves to proactive forms of policing.[9]

It is in the other four major police roles that patrol plays its most important part. The policeman on the beat is a symbol of municipal order and safety and by a wide variety of actions that may change kaleidoscopically each day—directing traffic, helping an elderly person across a street, caring for a lost child, giving first aid to someone stricken on the streets, checking stores to see that they are locked after hours—he does his part in seeing that society functions smoothly and peacefully.

The method by which this is accomplished is, of course, by patrol, the movement of police on foot or in vehicles around and within a preassigned area. Two distinguishing characteristics of patrol are that the police are in uniform and their cars are marked. Plainclothes officers and detectives in unmarked cars are not on patrol, except under very special conditions and only with very specific assignment. The purpose of patrol is to distribute the police in sufficient numbers and geographical spread to eliminate or reduce the opportunity for crime and to increase the likelihood that the police can apprehend and arrest an offender when a crime does take place.

The Beat

The fundamental patrol unit is the beat, a limited area that can be covered by a policeman on foot or in a motor vehicle. The

The fundamental patrol unit is the beat.
Magnum Photos

beat is flexible in size and may be smaller or larger depending on the frequency of crime in the area, the population density of the area, land use and the number and types of buildings in the area, and the flow of traffic in and around the area. The officer assigned has primary responsibility for the beat, must keep it under constant surveillance and must answer all calls.

Several beats may be joined together in a larger unit called a sector, usually headed by a police sergeant. Several sectors are joined together into a still larger unit called a precinct, usually commanded by a police captain and housed within a permanent location known as a precinct house. Especially in large urban areas, the precinct house is an important focus of social and civic affairs.

In large urban areas the foot policeman and the squad car are supplemented by a variety of other units: mounted police, motor scooter and motorcycle patrol, helicopter and harbor units. Yet it cannot be said often enough that it is the man on the beat who is at the heart of the police department and it is by the effectiveness of his efforts that the success of any police department may be measured.

Patrol Duty

During the time the patrolman is on duty, he will encounter a great variety of demands upon his time and he must be prepared for all of them. At the same time, he will find that he has to perform a certain number of fixed and regular duties, among them:

1. Checking his uniform.
2. Checking his equipment.
3. Listing alarms.
4. Following post assignments.
5. Doing escort duty.
6. Checking his vehicle.
7. Operating radio equipment.

The moment the patrolman arrives on his post, he must be constantly observant. This does not necessarily mean that he is aware of the things that "look right," but of the things that do not look right, such as open doors to houses or stores, loitering people, cars parked with their motors running, and many other items that should arouse his suspicion. When he does become aware of such matters, he is expected to take "proper police action." This would include informing residents or storekeepers of open doors, questioning loiterers, checking the position and intention of the driver of the running car. He must be aware of the need to inform his headquarters about what he is doing and must alert them to those incidents he thinks are significant. It is a good rule to inform a superior officer of all untoward incidents and let him decide on their importance and the action the patrolman should take.

The patrolman should also take another precaution in the performance of his duties and that is to enter everything in his memo book. This serves a twofold purpose: recording the patrolman's movements, actions and effectiveness, and serving as an aid to his memory whenever he is called upon to give evidence in court.

The patrolman's continual observation naturally involves him in situations in which he must take some kind of action. The patrolman who is constantly alert cannot help but be involved in many incidents. His dedication and, consequently, his activities, are related to the term *aggressive patrol,* which has several interpretations. The police administrator insists on strict enforcement of the laws and ordinances of the municipality he is operating in and he expects his men to be continually active as far as arrests, citations and so on are concerned. The general public insists on aggressive patrol, as it feels that it reduces the incidence of crime and maintains "law and order." It should be understood, however, that the public is ambivalent in this regard. While they insist in the abstract on the strict enforcement of the law, they will resist it when they find themselves on the receiving end of strict enforcement and will look askance at the patrolman enforcing the law in a situation they are unfamiliar with. Minority groups and civil liberties groups have attached another connotation to aggressive patrol; to them it is directed specifically toward minorities and they view it as repressive.

Stop and Frisk

The police officer will find himself, his actions and his motives being constantly questioned. But he should not be deterred from carrying out his duty and fulfilling the daily assignments he may have gotten. In order to do this in accordance with a policy of aggressive patrol, he has been given legislative and judicial authority to conduct what is known as a "stop and frisk." Whenever he has sufficient cause to investigate a person who is acting in a suspicious manner, he is permitted to stop that person and search him as a part of the field interrogation. This procedure was instituted by legislation in New York and Ohio. It was upheld by the United States Supreme Court in the Terry case (392 U.S. 1, 1968). Many police departments insist that certain procedures be followed in such situations. The patrolman who conducts a "stop and frisk" is always required to submit a report form known as a "field interrogation," which requires the listing of the following information:

1. Name and address of person.
2. Identification of person.
3. Location of incident.
4. Description of incident.
5. Reason for "stop and frisk."
6. Date, time, place, patrolman's post.
7. Disposition.

This form is kept on file by the department for future use, and is always available in case of complaint, review, or court trial.

Patrol Innovations

Police departments are aware of the job they have to do and honest in their appraisals of the success with which they do them. While they are proud of their successes, they are aware of their failures—stemming from inadequate budgets, lack of personnel, paucity of training and practice, poor public cooperation—and constantly seek methods of improving. Most of these efforts are concerned with improving patrol and response time, the critical time elapsed between the commission of a crime and of a police response to that crime.

One of the earliest attempts was Operation 25, which was put into operation in New York City in 1954. It was based on the theory of concentrating manpower in high-crime neighborhoods.

The theory worked; crime was reduced dramatically in the first four months of the program's operation. The successor to Operation 25 was the Tactical Patrol Force, an elite unit divided into squads of four to eight officers assigned to keep the peace in high-crime areas. While the Tactical Patrol Force is often kept as a reserve unit, to be used when a situation develops that is beyond the control of the regular police force within the area, members are sometimes assigned to regular patrol, working to prevent crime and to reduce tensions within troubled areas.

The *flexible unit* was instituted by the Pontiac, Michigan, police department. It consisted of a six-man squad whose assignment was mainly to complement the selective enforcement process.

The term "game theory" has been applied to *random patrol,* which is essentially an attempt to reduce response time, as well as underlining the preventive aspects of patrol by increasing the presence of the unit. Certain formulas must be applied in order to be able to predict assignments, but their applicability requires the services of an expert mathematician.

The concept of *team policing* was introduced in England in an attempt to rotate manpower. Team policing was characterized by the following:

1. There were no individual beats.
2. The beats became sections.
3. A sergeant and approximately six officers were responsible for the section.
4. The sergeant was responsible for changing assignments and redistributing his men according to anticipated needs.

Another English innovation is *unit beat policing,* which merely means that the officer is assigned to work in his home community and operates out of his home. A similar stateside experiment is functioning in various small Connecticut communities in which some of the residents are state police.

Selective distribution refers to the apportionment of personnel which reflects several factors, such as area, time, incidence of crime and community services. In other words, more attention is given where it is called for.

Selective enforcement involves dealing with a specific problem in a special area for a limited amount of time, usually until that problem has been cleared up or eliminated. Unfortunately, this phrase has been distorted by dissident groups, who imply that the law enforcement officer is selected according to his discretionary actions and powers as they pertain to minority groups.

Selective assignment encompasses all of the above methods of accomplishing the goals of the police department and is based primarily on the philosophy of preventive patrol, which presumes that the presence of a police officer plays its part in preventing the commission of a crime.

All of these experiments are based to some degree on the firmly established three-platoon system—three tours of duty in each 24 hours, with an equal number of men assigned to each tour, without regard to the needs or goals of the department. Thus, the difficulties facing the police administrator under this restriction force him to dilute his concentration of manpower during periods of high crime and in areas of high crime.

The New York City Transit Police Department instituted an imaginative program that cut the "Gordian knot" of this restriction—it created a fourth platoon that operated between the hours of 8:00 P.M. and 4:00 A.M., traditionally the period of highest crime. The city was saturated during this time with one patrolman at each subway station and one on each subway train. This resulted in a dramatic decrease in crime during this period and the system has been relied on whenever increases in crime have called for this response.

While all these methods of patrol are largely in the area of administrative responsibility, the patrolman must understand the purposes behind the methods the administrator chooses to respond to the problem of crime.

INVESTIGATION

All of the duties mentioned above still have not taken into account one other, investigation, which is most important in the repression of crime and in the police officer's feeling of fulfillment. In the former it serves as the first legal gathering of evidence that may be crucial in the solving of a crime. Because it is a truism, it is often forgotten that the patrolman is usually the first representative of the legal apparatus to appear at the scene of a crime. His first duty, of course, is to prevent the crime from being committed, if he arrives early enough. His second duty is to apprehend the offender, if that is possible. His third duty is to render whatever assistance he can to the victim of a crime. After that, his primary responsibility is to begin an investigation. This serves to bolster the patrolman's concept of the significance

Investigation serves as the first legal gathering of evidence that may be crucial in the solving of a crime.
Magnum Photos

of his job and his own importance. Within every police department there is a distinct rivalry between the patrolman on the beat and the detective, who is often jealous of his prerogatives and his rank and, perhaps, condescending to the patrolman, who is below him in the ranks. The media—whether radio, television, motion pictures and sometimes the press—underscore this rivalry with their heavy concentration upon the detective as the key figure in the solving of crime. When the patrolman can play a significant role in the solution of a crime by the keenness of his initial investigation, he feels proud of the role he is playing. He is no longer a traffic director, a mediator of minor scuffles, a temporary proprietor of lost property or a uniformed clerk, but an important contributor to the fight against crime.

When the patrolman is dispatched to the scene of a crime, he has a number of specific duties, and his effectiveness in fulfilling these duties has a significant effect on the eventual solution to the crime.

1. Make an arrest, if possible.
2. Assist the injured.
3. Seal off the area.
4. Inform headquarters and request specific help.
5. Question the complainant.
6. Gather witnesses.
7. Protect the evidence.
8. Submit a full and accurate report.

We are assuming here that the crime has occurred in a large urban area which has a police department with a separate detective division, with all the necessary equipment and special personnel. Most police departments do not fit into this category, and so they must depend on their patrolmen to assist in follow-up investigations, too. Most police departments cannot afford a crime lab specialist in photography, fingerprinting and so forth, so the patrolman must learn a number of specialties. A police department under these circumstances must make use of all the talent available. The police force becomes self-sustaining when every officer can ably conduct interrogations and interviews, take fingerprints, make moulages, take, develop and print photographs, and perform a variety of other special tasks. This is known as the

Because of the varied roles the police officer must play, persons selected for training in the police must display a number of talents.
Photo courtesy of the Nassau County Police Department.

"total police concept," and it is compatible with the President's Crime Commission Report, in which the emphasis is on the "police agent" and his duties.

POLICE TRAINING

Because of the varied roles that the police officer must play in the world about him, persons selected for training for the force must display a number of talents. They must demonstrate through a series of tests and interviews a certain minimum degree of physical, mental and emotional qualifications. Though the requirements vary from jurisdiction to jurisdiction, and though some of the physical requirements have been modified, the following may be considered fundamental:

1. *Physical.* Minimum height 5′7″ to 5′9″; minimum weight 150 to 160 lbs. (requirements for women officers differ); there are no maximum height and weight limitations; strength and

agility must be demonstrated by running, jumping and weight-lifting tests; vision should be 20/20 (but may sometimes be 20/40 or 20/50 if correctable with eyeglasses to 20/20); there may be no physical impairments.

2. *Mental.* Intelligence determined by written and oral tests designed to show good general knowledge, a high degree of common sense and a steady, well-controlled temperament.

3. *Education.* Minimum of a high-school diploma, though more and more departments are stressing college education, if not a degree.

4. *Age.* Usually a maximum of 29 years.

5. *Residency.* Varies, often on the basis of the need for recruitment, as to whether the candidate is or is not a resident of the locality whose police department he wants to join.

6. *Personal Background.* No prior record of misdemeanor or felony arrests; no association with subversive and/or anti-American groups.

In addition to the above, some departments require candidates to undergo polygraph testing.

Since 1973 the New York City Police Department has omitted height and sex requirements from its application forms. A U.S. district judge recently ruled that the height, weight and sex requirements usually required by a police department for admission were unconstitutional. "The court is unable to find rational support for the height and weight requirements and concludes that the requirements are based solely on the stereotype of the large male police officer."[10] An applicant who does not meet the posted requirements of the police department in his locality, however, should not assume that he can join the department in spite of his failure to meet its standards. Usually, the decision will have to be made by higher judicial authority.

Persons who wish to be appointed to state and federal law enforcement agencies should plan to receive a bachelor's degree from a college or university. The emphasis in these agencies is on education, and this emphasis is bound to filter down eventually to municipal agencies. Because work for state and federal agencies often does not center on patrol, physical and medical standards may be somewhat less stringent than on the municipal level, but general good health is a must.

The physical requirements noted above obviously cannot be met by most women. Since an increasing number of women are entering police service, these requirements are generally waived, though the women must demonstrate a certain degree of strength and agility. Where women were once restricted to certain specified duties as prison matrons, working with female and juvenile prisoners, acting as decoys, or working in confidential clerical assignments, they are taking their places besides male officers on foot patrol and in squad cars.

The restrictive physical requirements of the past have been lowered also in response to the demands of minority groups, among them the Hispanic. As it has become clear that the police force of any locality should have among its members representatives of every group in the general population, and as it has become apparent that the stereotypical brawny cop with the nightstick must give way to a more mechanized and technically sophisticated police officer, some of the height and weight requirements have been lowered.

There is an increasing emphasis on education in the training programs of most agencies.
Photo courtesy of the Nassau County Police Department.

IMAGE AND SELF-IMAGE

Everyone in this society has a certain set of notions about the police officer. Whether he knows a police officer or not, or has ever come into direct contact with one, he carries a number of assumptions about a police officer's intellect, intentions, attitudes and honesty. In one and the same breath a person may praise and denounce the police officer. On the one hand, he will chide the policeman for being inefficient, stupid and brutal. On the other, he will praise the police as the front-line citizen defense against crime and lawlessness, as the last bulwark keeping the nation from slipping into anarchy.

The police themselves are ambivalent in their feelings about themselves and their work. Like their fellows in every walk of life, they put forth a positive image, but this image is so constantly assaulted that the police are seduced into sometimes going overboard in their efforts to protect their image. An aggressive exterior protects a faint and uncertain interior.

> The police have such a poor image of themselves. They see themselves as the menial retainers of an authoritarian system, the paramilitary enforcers of an immutable criminal law. They talk as if they lack discretion; in fact, they have larger discretion than prosecutors, judges, and legislators. They see themselves as relatively powerless; yet the rawest police recruit when first on the beat disposes of a larger, immediate power than is accorded any other citizen.[11]

If it can be said that there is a typical civilian impression of the police officer, it is that of the policeman as an authoritarian personality. The great majority of police officers do not think of themselves in this way. Interviews with any number of policemen in any number of jurisdictions will reveal a striking similarity in the reasons they have become cops. Ahern reveals that when he was chief of the New Haven Police Department he requested incoming rookies to write short essays explaining why they had become policemen. "The essays were all the same. To a man, they had become cops to help people, to render obedient service to society, and to uphold the laws of the land."[12]

Only reluctantly and at the end of the list is one of the reasons given as the opportunity to give orders that will be responded to without question; in other words, to be authoritarian. Though it is not a significant motivation for joining the force, this authoritarian complex—or the F-scale syndrome—begins to make its appearance about three years after the patrolman has left the academy.

The average patrolman attended and was graduated from high school; he was a regular churchgoer. His social circle, his friends and acquaintances were usually limited to his own religious or ethnic background and he usually dated and married within this same limited circle. He never used objectionable language in the presence of women and would object to its use by others. In general, he tended to share the attitudes, biases and prejudices of his class, among which was a fear and mistrust of blacks and other minority groups.

He is appointed to his position, graduates from the police academy, completes his probationary period and is now inculcated with a new set of values, supposedly prepared to meet the world and its problems. These values consist of the secrecy of the police fraternity, distrust of anyone who may doubt his authority or interfere with it, the importance of his job and a patronizing attitude toward minorities.

He now also becomes aware that he is no longer a member of society as he once knew it, since his routine is not compatible with it. He finds himself working when others are playing. His social contacts grow fewer and his friends become those with similar jobs. He becomes sensitive to society's apparent lack of interest in him as a person; all the average citizen sees, he feels, is the uniform and its trappings, not the person within. Society's disinterest and disassociation hasten the process of authoritarianism; accordingly, he becomes dependent on conservative organizations, such as the John Birch Society, which make much of the police officer's valuable role. Arthur Niederhoffer, a former New York City police officer and the author of several books on the policeman, has pinpointed the reaction clearly. "The police feel that they deserve respect from the public. But the upper class looks down on them; the middle class seems to ignore them . . . with bitterness, therefore, they tend to think of themselves as a minority group in the society."[13]

In one respect, his behavior in relation to minorities is merely an extension or a sharpening of his relations with the public at large. For better or worse, the policeman has come to think of himself as a lonely soldier in the struggle against crime, a struggle he alone must wage without the help and support of the community.

> They huddle together, an anxious ingroup, battling the forces of wickedness, political corruption, citizen irresponsibility, and declining morals, particularly the immorality of youth. Their extra-corps contacts are cautious in the extreme. They are, they believe, insufficiently esteemed, inadequately rewarded, but gallantly carrying the burdens of society for a parsimonious and misguided citizenry.[14]

To some extent, the policeman even thinks of the public as the enemy, and this theme of an enemy public increases his isolation from the community and solidifies him as a member of the insular police subculture. Interviews with police officers will reveal that most of them feel that the public does not understand them or appreciate their efforts. The policeman's image of himself as reflected back from the mirror of society into which he peers every day is that of a brutal, stupid and inefficient person. As Westley aptly observes in his book *Violence and the Police,* the policeman sees "this public as a threat. He seldom meets it at its best and it seldom welcomes him. In spite of his ostensible function as protector, he usually meets only those he is protecting them from, and for him *they* have no love."[15] This theme of an enemy public that threatens and criticizes "binds the policeman's group to isolation and secrecy. It is an occupational directive, a rule of thumb, the sustenance and the core of meanings."[16]

As with any group, there are wide variations among its individual members, and it may be futile to ascribe one general feeling to all police officers, but the following is an apt summation:

> He sees man as ill-willed, exploitative, mean and dirty; himself a victim of injustice, misunderstood and defiled. Hungry for approval, uneasy as to his own worth, wrathful without dignity, he walks along—a pedestrian in Hell.[17]

Confronted with such realizations of what the cop feels about his job, we may wonder why anyone would wish to have such a job. In a very real sense because this realization is offset by his feeling that his job has value to society. There is a kinship between the police officer and the idealist who becomes a member of the Peace Corps; neither is probably aware of the similarities, and each may scorn the other, but in their dedication to their roles, they are one and the same. The policeman soon comes to feel that his efforts are unappreciated and perhaps that they have neither short-term nor long-term effect. Yet he is certain that without his efforts society as he knows and cherishes it may collapse. He believes further that he is one of the bulwarks of society, that the public and each individual citizen depend on him, that his daily duties consist mainly of helping people. His involvement with humanity, even one that does not always respect and acknowledge him, has become an obligation he cannot deny. There is nothing more important, he feels, than his chosen profession, none that renders greater, more useful service.

THE COVERT SOCIETY

In view of all of the confrontations and frustrations in their working lives, society's ambivalence or animosity, police officers have developed a deeply held and closely guarded defense mechanism —their own brotherhood. This is a covert culture—secretive to the extent that facts about it are hidden both consciously and subconsciously. An important factor of the covert society is its basic secretiveness. This particular phenomenon of police insularity has been described in many ways, but the central theme is that of a closed and secret fraternity.

> Policemen find that in order to endure their work they must relate to the public in ways that protect their self-esteem. Since they see the public as hostile to the police and feel that their work tends to aggravate this hostility, they separate themselves from the public, develop strong in-group attitudes, and control one another's conduct, making it conform to the interests of the group.[18]

> Secrecy among the police stands as a shield against the attacks of the outside world; against bad newspaper publicity, which would make the police lose respect; against public criticism, from which they feel they suffer too much; against the criminal, who is eager to know the moves of the police; against the law, which they too frequently abrogate.[19]

There are, of course, many closed and secretive subcultures, ranging from those based on race and culture and language (the

Chinese inhabiting various Chinatowns may be a good example) to those based on religion (the various Hasidic Jewish groupings) to those based on socioeconomic and fraternal considerations (the Masons, Elks, Oddfellows). What distinguishes the secret society of the police from these others, however, is that it is completely job-oriented, cutting across social, religious, political lines, and that it so completely pervades the thinking and controls the actions of all its members. "No one outside the policeman's closed fraternity knows the cop. Shrewdness and mistrust separate him from the people. He does not mix with them. They do not seek him out."[20]

The police officer, finding himself so often on the defensive among all strata of society, insulates himself.

It is difficult to determine whether the impenetrable wall between the general culture and the police subculture has been created by society or by the police—but it is there. This wall prevents the policeman from making any significant disclosures about his work to his friends or his immediate family. His credo is based on loyalty and honor; at times the police will refer to these qualities cynically, but the credo is very real nonetheless, and has a numbing effect.

> . . . the cop who is brutal—or even the cop who is blatantly corrupt—is never exposed by his fellows. He is protected, although perhaps uneasily, by the group. The sanctity of the group becomes more important to the cop than the often hypocritical views of outsiders. Even if a policeman wanted to expose a brutal or corrupt fellow officer, he would seldom know which of his superiors was "on the take," or the full extent of the brutal or corrupt cop's political connections.[21]

Indoctrination to the fraternity's secret begins at the training academy, with various comments and asides by the instructors outside of the approved curriculum. These comments range from impressing recruits with the importance of their new profession to pride in the department itself; to the responsibilities they must assume; and to their mandated duty to protect their partner and all other police officers. They are also made to understand their actions may be the subject of complaints by civilians and that this civilian society is irrational and does not appreciate the services it is being rendered by the police.

There are periods in the patrol officer's preliminary training when he is assigned to patrol duties with a senior officer. The themes introduced in the police academy are underscored by this senior officer, quite informally, but they have a profound effect on the recruit.

All of this comes sharply into focus when he is graduated and assumes normal patrol duties. By now he has a high degree of pride in the accomplishment of attaining his position. He feels that he has now earned a respected social status. The assault on this preconceived social status now begins. He finds himself unacceptable to both "right" and "left." The "right" looks upon him as inferior and subordinate; the "left" looks upon him as brutal and oppressive.

He also now discovers that he no longer can participate in his former social life, and that his friends now usually introduce him at social functions with such admonitions (supposedly in jest) as: "Be careful of what you say, he's a cop." He becomes a constant target for stories of the troubles people have had with the police, how some of them were unfairly tagged with traffic violations, how others have escaped by throwing some money their way, how complaints about robberies and burglaries are just filed and forgotten. Soon he comes to feel that he is being patronized and that he is no longer considered a member of normal society. He has no alternative but to react defensively. The defense mechanism is the creation of a wall of secrecy, a wall so solid and impregnable that although he himself does not condone incompetency, brutality or corruption, he will not reveal or discuss these matters outside of his own world. Thus, it becomes impossible for anyone in the department to publicly denigrate another officer, to make a statement damaging to the department or to have one member testify against another. It should be mentioned that such a situation exists also in the medical and legal professions, but for different reasons. There is an awareness on society's part that this code of secrecy exists, but it is only the police profession's code of secrecy that has become a matter of public contention.

The patrolman becomes increasingly aware of and sensitive to the encroachments on his "turf" by civilians; it becomes a matter of prime importance to his self-respect that his world is one "to have and to hold" against the rest of society. There have been some breaches in this wall of secrecy, but not many, and the wall has been repaired and closed as tightly as ever.

THE OVERT SOCIETY

An overt society really means that there is no secrecy involved in its practices—for example, the P.T.A., the Red Cross, and a host of other organizations. The term *secrecy* does not set well in our democratic society; it creates suspicion and distrust.

Consciously or not, this attitude is appreciated and understood by the members of the law enforcement establishment. Therefore, the methods by which the police society attempts to remain concealed and inviolate involve degrees of compromise which are at times ingenuous and ingenious. However, the efforts have succeeded in giving the fraternity the semblance of being open and aboveboard.

An individual patrolman, when given the opportunity, will discuss the following police matters, often at great length: the hardships of the job, the long and dangerous hours, the lack of normal family and social life, the daily confrontations with danger, the lack of pay commensurate with his position, the unfair and unfeeling demands of his superior officers, and the lack of understanding shown by everyone who is not a policeman—lawyers, judges, firemen, storekeepers. He will also discuss very freely his own cleverness, ingenuity and heroism (most frequently exaggerated).

The department itself, under constant scrutiny by innumerable private and public agencies and commissions, is not naive enough to believe that its world will be taken at face value—regardless of its honesty and sincerity. It cooperates fully and freely with all investigative efforts by these agencies and commissions, attempting as forcefully as possible at the same time to present the strongest case on its contributions to the community. There are, of course, many reasons why the department will be found wanting: insufficiency of patrol personnel, lack of modern equipment, inadequate training areas and facilities, too stringent budget and so forth. It will never be found wanting, however, in the dedication and effort of all its members.

SUMMARY

The range of duties of the uniformed police officer—those he has by virtue of the multiplicity of laws he is sworn to uphold, those he is given during each tour by his superiors, and those he takes upon himself during each tour of duty—is staggering.

Police work consists essentially of five major areas of responsibility: crime prevention, crime repression, regulating noncriminal conduct, providing public services, protecting citizens. Overall, the preponderance of an officer's time on duty is spent in the performance of the last three duties and only a small portion is given over to crime-related activities.

The major method by which the police fulfill their role is through patrol, the stationing and circulating of uniformed officers on foot or in squad cars within specified geographical limits. The fundamental unit in patrol is the beat; several beats become a sector headed by a sergeant; and several sectors comprise a precinct headed by a captain. Police organizations strive constantly to improve patrol and over the years numerous innovations have been instituted, including team policing, unit beat policing, the flexible unit and random patrol.

While patrol duty may often be uneventful or even tedious, the uniformed officer looks forward to playing his role in investigation. As the first officer usually on the scene of any incident, he has prescribed duties in conducting an investigation.

Police training is based on recruitment of qualified recruits. Major elements include size and strength, mental and emotional competence, solid education, and a good, untarnished personal history. Because more women and members of minority groups are entering police service, some of the physical requirements have been relaxed, but there is an increasing emphasis on educational attainment.

The police face a difficult situation in blending their roles with the demands and requirements of civilian society. Almost every citizen has a distinct set of impressions about the police officer and they may range within the same person from the positive to the negative. Police officers are esteemed as the prime fighters in the war against crime and the slide of American society into lawlessness and anarchy. They are also reviled as lazy, incompetent, brutal and stupid.

This inability to find a balanced place in society and the tribulations of police work combine to drive the police officer into his own closely knit society. Most police officers socialize only with other officers, and spend a considerable amount of their time exchanging data on the difficulties of their work, the insensitivity of their civilian critics and the uncaring demands of their superiors. Forming and maintaining their covert society requires that they keep a tight shield against the intrusion of outsiders, and so they refuse to discuss their work with others, speak ill of any fellow officer or report or testify against a brutal or corrupt fellow officer. What they do reveal, in what may be referred to as an overt society, is information designed essentially to elicit sympathy for the difficulties and hazards of their profession.

NOTES

1. Albert J. Reiss, Jr., *The Police and the Public.* New Haven: Yale University Press, 1971, pp. 95–96.
2. James F. Ahern, *Police in Trouble.* New York: Hawthorn Books, Inc., 1971, p. 2.
3. William A. Westley, *Violence and the Police.* Cambridge, Mass.: The MIT Press, 1970, p. 4.
4. Ahern, *op. cit.,* p. 118.
5. Westley, *op. cit.,* p. 60.
6. Vern L. Folley, *American Law Enforcement.* Boston: Holbrook Press, Inc., 1973, p. 192.
7. Westley, *op. cit.,* p. 28.
8. Ahern, *op. cit.,* p. 141.
9. Reiss, *op. cit.,* p. 102.
10. Cleveland *Plain Dealer,* Sept. 9, 1973, p. 4-D.
11. Norval Morris and Gordon Hawkins, *The Honest Politician's Guide to Crime Control.* Chicago: University of Chicago Press, 1970, p. 87.
12. Ahern, *op. cit.,* p. 4.
13. Arthur Niederhoffer, *Behind the Shield: The Police in Urban Society.* New York: Doubleday, 1967, p. 9.
14. Morris and Hawkins, *op. cit.,* p. 87.
15. Westley, *op. cit.,* p. 49.
16. *Ibid.*
17. *Ibid.,* p. iii.
18. *Ibid.,* p. 110.
19. *Ibid.,* p. 111.
20. Ahern, *op. cit.,* p. 2.
21. *Ibid.,* p. 24.

STUDY QUESTIONS

1. What is the difference between crime prevention and crime repression?
2. How can the police cope successfully with their many assignments?
3. What are the primary purposes of patrol?

4. What constitutes legitimate stop and frisk?
5. What are the differences between selective distribution, selective enforcement and selective assignment?
6. What are the main duties of the police officer in investigation?
7. What are the primary qualifications for police officers and how valid are they?
8. What are the differences between the way policemen see themselves and the way they are seen by society?
9. What differences are there between the police officers' overt society and covert society?
10. Can the police officer be more a member of society in general and less a member of his special police society?

8

The Police: Relationship to Society

In some ways the policeman is like the member of a religious order—he is both part of this world and not a part of it. As a working man, member of his community, husband and father, student, sportsman and consumer, he is indistinguishable from the vast majority of his fellow citizens. Yet, as a policeman, he is unlike them, for he is a policeman twenty-four hours a day, on call even when he is off duty. This colors and eventually controls every aspect of his behavior. While the vast majority of his fellow citizens can, if they wish, shed their working or professional roles after a specified period of the day, the policeman cannot. Even if he would and his commander allowed him to, his friends, family and neighbors will not. His identity inevitably controls their relationship.

Because of this ongoing involvement in his role, the police officer must constantly enlarge and deepen his understanding of the society in which he lives and in which he plays such a distinctive part. The police officer is inextricably involved with people. No matter to what extent his duties are specified with regard to machines, buildings, equipment and other inanimate objects or impersonal objectives, his primary obligation is personal service to society. Under these circumstances, it becomes necessary for him to understand people's behavior. This should give him greater objectivity in his daily work and make him less likely to become emotionally involved and less apt to be indiscreet. The police officer is more closely involved in a series of social interrelationships, interactions and controls than anyone else. He must, therefore, be concerned with understanding the behavioral sciences that explain the workings of society and the entire array of social, psychological, political, economic and religious forces that affect the way people in society behave.

In the following pages we will examine the several societies within which the police officer functions and his relationship with each of these societies.

The first part of the chapter studies interrelationships, interactions and controls, concentrating on those social controls that allow the police officer to exercise his authority. In this discussion we will look at the relationship between citizens and the police and the fluctuation of power between them.

The second part of the chapter differentiates among community relations, minority relations and public relations, indicating ways in which the police can make each of these more effective. And finally, we discuss sociological aspects of the police officer's relationship to his work, touching upon the hierarchy of basic needs, anomie and the new concept of anomic cynicism.

The police officer must constantly deepen and enlarge his understanding of the society in which he lives.
Magnum Photos

POLICE AND SOCIETY

To sharpen the definitions of the terminology used above, let *social interrelationships* refer to interpersonal relations, that is, anything that occurs between one individual and another; *social interaction* to intergroup relations, anything that occurs between two distinct groups or between one or more persons and a group; *social control* to the array of methods that society enlists to ensure that citizens conform to the basic rules. Social control depends to a great extent on the enlightened acquiescence of most citizens and only to a small extent on the efforts of the police or any other governmental authority. The peaceful functioning of society that is a general condition of all civilized nations is based not on police power or the threat of it but on the common agreement of the citizenry that such a peaceful functioning is most beneficial to all members of society. It is on this question that proponents of "law and order" and advocates of civil liberties divide. The former believe firmly in the value of increased police activity as an effective instrumentality of crime prevention. The latter believe just as firmly that preventive police action is a constant threat to personal freedom and that only massive police action that might border on establishing a police state can have any effect in crime prevention. The policeman himself must be careful in forming his attitudes on this issue. The more he supports the first group, the more he promotes his efforts as indispensable to public peace and safety, the greater the possibility that the public will be disappointed with his efforts and that he will become dissatisfied with his effectiveness.

It is in the area of social control that police must be most sensitive, for they often find themselves in paradoxical situations. By virtue of their role as policemen, they are invested with a certain authority. As Reiss points out in his study *The Police and The Public,* in modern democratic societies the police have a virtual monopoly on the *legitimate* use of force.

> Their *legitimate* right to intervene in the affairs of citizens, to enforce the law and keep the peace, also is unquestioned, provided it is done in legal ways. This monopoly and right to intervention in the affairs of citizens create a number of problems for the society. The principal problems involve the maintaining of the political neutrality of the police, the use of legal means in police behavior toward citizens, and the assurance that the police will use

universal criteria in their discretion to apply the law.[1]

The police must exercise their authority carefully. They are expected to invoke this authority whenever a situation arises which calls for their intervention, but they must often enlist the cooperation of the civilian population in order for this authority to be accepted. Often they must wait for a call from a member of this civilian population before invoking their authority, though they cannot wait so long that a situation gets out of hand. The proper guideline should be that the policeman will invoke his authority whenever the situation requires him to, especially when the action he takes elicits the support and respect of the civilian population. He should, however, be careful about invoking his authority when the situation is not clear-cut or when this exercise of authority arouses the resistance or animosity of the civilian population. Reiss indicates that the policeman is not automatically assured of the acceptance by the public of his authority; it must be established anew in every situation.

> The uniform, badge, truncheon, and arms all may play a role in asserting authority. Yet, it appears that the police exercise command in most situations simply by behaving as men in authority.[2]

In any situation that requires the police to arrest a citizen or to take him into custody, they must maintain both their firmness and their fairness. Half of all the people the police arrest, Reiss indicates, challenge police authority, arguing with them, insulting them or actually trying to escape from custody. Nine per cent of such persons, in one study, had to be handled with gross force (use of handcuffs or other physical restraints), 42% were handled with firm assertion of authority, and 50% were handled easily and were allowed freedom of movement.[3] When challenged, the police must assert authority. The police subculture holds several firm convictions in this regard: any failure to assert authority lessens respect for the police; many citizens, especially in the lower socioeconomic levels, understand and respect coercive authority; any backing down from a challenge makes future police tasks more difficult.[4] It is a fairly safe assumption that a significant portion of the populace holds similar convictions. Still, the exercise of authority must always be legitimate. The "unwarranted use of authority toward citizens includes a variety of charges relative to the employment of illegal means such as the undue use of force and threats, harassment, uncivil treatment through abusive language and demeaning epithets."[5]

POLICE AND PUBLIC

Police power has essentially two forms. One is positive. It involves coercion in the power to arrest and to use necessary force in making an arrest. The second is negative. It involves the power of the police to withdraw their protection. The legal privileges accorded to the policeman entitle him to use the first form of power but forbid him the second. In actual practice, however, both forms of power are exercised.[6]

The relationship between the police and the public is of utmost importance in the functioning of a democracy and must be predicated on the basis of public service. In other words, the policeman must invoke and exercise his authority in the spirit of public service, not in response to the pressures of his own or his group's social, political, racial or religious feelings. Only the former use of authority enlists the support of the public and maintains its attitude toward the police as one of a force for the good, peace, comfort and safety of society and not as an abusive or intrusive force designed to maintain the inequities and hardships of society.

Reiss and his associates have studied the relationship of police and public closely and have found distinct patterns. First, most police activity is citizen initiated; that is, the police act primarily when they are requested to perform a certain function by a citizen or a group of citizens.

> Citizens exercise considerable control over the policing of everyday life through their discretionary decisions to call or not to call the police.[7]

Studies of police activities in high-crime-rate areas found that 87% of all such activities were citizen initiated; only 13% were police initiated. Therefore, in almost nine instances out of ten a police officer is acting in response to a civilian request for action. The citizens play another significant role in police work, that of guiding the activities of the police. Not only do they initiate police action, but for the police to be effective, they must remain in the area and indicate to the police what the problem is or what function they wish the police to perform. When the policeman enters a situation in which no civilian guidance is present, the study indicated, he will do very little and may do nothing at all.[8]

This citizen initiation invests the police with the proper authority they need to perform their functions and assures, in most cases, civil citizen-police relations.

Second, when police initiate an action themselves, and not upon request by citizens, the police must first establish their authority. Citizens do not automatically accept the police assumption of authority. In almost every case, they judge, even if silently, this assumption of authority. Depending upon the nature of the police action and the manner in which they establish their authority, citizen-police relations may or may not be cordial.

In police-citizen encounters, social interactions play a significant role. When citizens are calm, the police are calm; when citizens are agitated, the police are generally agitated.[9] In Reiss's study, almost 75% of police-citizen encounters found the police behaving in a businesslike, routine and civil manner. In 15% of the cases, they went beyond this standard to become more personable in manner and to exhibit a more personal interest. In only 11% of the cases reviewed were they hostile, authoritarian or derisive.[10] The majority of citizens in encounters with police were found to be calm or detached. Three in ten could be characterized as agitated, but only one in ten was antagonistic or hostile.

Civil relations between police and public require the observance of several rules.

1. Citizens must be civil in their relations with one another.
2. Citizens must grant legitimacy to police authority and respect their legal intervention.
3. Police must be accountable to civil authority and the citizen must be protected from police tyranny.[11]

It goes without question, of course, that these rules are to be observed in all police-public relationships. There may be no alteration, modification or diminution of these rules on the basis of any change in the composition of the public. Especially in large cities, where there are likely to be distinct areas and neighborhoods characterized by differing racial, religious or ethnic composition, the police must maintain an even-handed and judicious approach to their role.

Unfortunately, in general, no such even-handed treatment is practiced. In their sensitivity to the feelings conveyed to them and their estimation of the impression they make, the police have divided their public into five distinct groups.

1. Children
2. Better class of people
3. Slum people
4. Negroes
5. Criminals[12]

The police conduct themselves differently when they come into contact with different groups. They are usually kinder, more polite and deferential to the "better class of people," whom they define as those with education, affluence and residence in the better parts of town. They are harsher with people in the slums. They view them "as lacking in morality, ready to commit a crime, ignorant of the law," and believe that these people "respond only to fear."[13]

COMMUNITY RELATIONS

In discussions of police dealings with the public, three terms are often used interchangeably and incorrectly. These terms are *community relations, public relations* and *minority relations.* While there is some connection between the terms, they have special connotations which should be observed.

Community relations refers to the interaction of the police with the community, largely in the form of public involvement in police programs and activities. Public relations refers to the efforts of the police to present themselves to the public in a manner that enhances their image. It requires a combination of programmed activities and the presentation of information. In many ways community relations and public relations are intertwined, especially in the area of police-sponsored community programs, such as Police Athletic League, Block Watchers, and so forth. Minority relations is a branch of community relations, involving the police in the special requirements of any distinct minority within the police jurisdiction. In the larger cities, this is concerned primarily with establishing and maintaining good relations between the police and the black, Hispanic, Chicano or even American Indian minorities. Basically, a community program differs from a minority program by being more encompassing. It is designed to bring all members of a community into active involvement with the police.

Police public relations programs are maintained usually by assigning a number of officers to appear before various public

Community relations refers to the interaction of police with the community, largely in the form of public involvement in police programs and activities. *Photo courtesy of the Nassau County Police Department.*

groups, at churches, Kiwanis, Rotary and Lion clubs, Chambers of Commerce, schools, Boy Scout and Girl Scout troops. Unfortunately, this is largely window dressing. The fallacy of this approach is that the appeal for understanding, cooperation and support is being made to those segments of society which are predisposed to supporting the police without any such special appeal.

Such a program is invariably interwoven with the "hard sell" approach of a public relations agency. However, the goal of the police department should be to make every segment of the community aware of its responsibility to the police agency, to convince every member of the community that the excellence of the department is dependent upon his or her cooperation, and that the excellence of the department translates itself into the citizen's health, safety and welfare.

The President's Task Force Report advises the adoption of a set of basic formulas that should eventually be accepted by all communities.

1. The community should be given a formal role in upper-level policy formulation.
2. Minority members of any community should be represented on policy-making boards.
3. Police patrols should be integrated.
4. Where required, and with the understanding of and acceptance by the community, there should be saturation patrols.[14]

The implementation of such a program requires the unequivocal support of police management, including all upper-level officers and civilian commissioners. Part of the program should be the establishing of a well-defined educational program for the recruit and the in-service officer. These programs should include instruction by civilian sociologists, psychologists, historians and other academics. In many areas, these programs can take the form of police officer attendance at colleges and universities either for specific courses or in search of degrees.

Two programs designed to establish closer police-community relations have been given a good deal of attention in recent years. Neither is acceptable in any degree either to the individual officer or the police agency and is generally anathema to both.

The first is the Civilian Complaint Review Board. This is a unit which consists of a majority of civilian members with representative members of the police department. Their function is to review, make recommendations and institute charges (if necessary) against a police officer whenever any complaint is lodged concerning his actions. The efficiency of such a board still has not been determined.

Philadelphia was the first city to establish one; proponents point with pride to its successful operation. A review board was established in New York City on a preliminary basis. Dr. Algernon Black, universally respected as a leader in civil rights, who was mutually acceptable to both the minority groups and the police department, served as chairman. The review board functioned ably and no fault could be found with any of Dr. Black's recommendations. Nevertheless, it was subsequently defeated in a public referendum.

Police agencies are well aware of the sensitivity of communities to Civilian Review Boards. In order to prevent such institutions, they have compromised. The department usually has its own unit that handles civilian complaints and makes every effort to determine the plausibility of each complaint and the degree of involvement of the accused officer. These units are usually directly answerable and responsible to the police chief and sincerely attempt to determine objectively the police officer's guilt or innocence. Nevertheless, in the foreseeable future, because of citizen suspicion of such attempts, we can anticipate that civilian review boards will supplant police agency units. The present and future training of police officers emphasizing college study, perhaps eventually requiring a college degree, with a concentration in the areas of sociology and psychology, will undoubtedly have an important impact in limiting such an eventuality.

The other proposal is the institution of complete community control of the police agency. This is the goal of all dissident organizations. In actuality this means that a board consisting of elected community residents would be the controlling factor in a police department. It would determine police selection and training, and the chief of the department would be a subordinate officer whose sole duty would be the implementation of the policies of the board. Recent elections in Berkeley, California, gave a substantial number of votes to dissident members of the community. One of their avowed policies was the institution of such a board. At the present writing, there is no indication as to whether or not it has been instituted, or whether it will be accepted when and if it is.

MINORITY RELATIONS

In present day America minority relations refers to the relations between the police and such minorities as blacks, Puerto Ricans, Chicanos and American Indians. While there remain many distinct ethnic minorities in many cities and towns—Polish, Italian, Irish, and so forth—we are not referring to them when we speak of minority relations. For the most part, the members of these groups are considered part of the mainstream of middle-class American cultural and social life. While at one time in the early days of their immigration to the United States these groups and others suffered all the outrages of a hostile environment, they are now generally integrated and have significant numbers of their members among the police forces. Part of the answer to the problems of police-minority relations lies in the enrollment of members of the minority in the ranks of the police.

A minority relations program, therefore, takes on other aspects than those of a community relations program. The need for a definitive and specific program in this area is acute. Polarization exists not only between a police agency and a minority group, but within the police department itself. The reasons for this lack of understanding and communication between the police and minority groups and the intransigence of both groups lie largely in the differences in origin between the police and the minority society. Alleviation of this perilous situation will depend in part upon educating the police to an appreciation of the hopes and aspirations of this society.

What the policeman must understand above all is that most of the people in any minority area want to live in the same peace and safety that the majority of the population enjoys, and they welcome any legitimate police effort that furthers this desire. What they see too often and resent most deeply is that police interactions "with lower socioeconomic groups involves, for the most part, preserving the integrity of private order."[15] The members of every minority group, as the primary victims of the crime and corruption in their areas, welcome police protection, but they do not, as James Baldwin says in *The Fire Next Time,* welcome the policeman as a member of an occupying army keeping them in their place.

Relations between the police and the black community are probably most important and critical in the area of minority relations, since blacks comprise the most numerous minority, have been in the forefront of the civil rights movement, have enrolled more of their members in the ranks of the police, and have seen more of their number attain the professional, social and financial achievements of the majority white culture. Unfortunately, a great number of police harbor the feeling that "the Negro epitomizes the slum dweller, and he is considered inherently criminal both culturally and biologically."[16]

Westley's *Violence and the Police* studied the attitudes of the police in a large Northeastern city, and these may very likely be assumed to be the norm among the police nationally. A majority of the police characterized themselves as anti-Negro. Almost half of them thought of blacks as biologically inferior. Their characterizations of Negroes are stereotypical. Statistically, the study reveals the following police attitudes towards the Negro: 39% thought they were corrupted by their living conditions; 25% thought they were naturally lazy and irresponsible; 19% thought they were still savages; 8% thought they were born criminals.[17] It is no wonder, if these attitudes are typical, that relations between the police and the black citizen are in so much need of improvement.

One aspect of police-citizen encounters in black neighborhoods is significant. Since in so many big cities blacks live in crowded ghetto areas, and since this crowding forces a good proportion of teeming city life to take place on the streets, the policeman, when he is called into action in a black neighborhood, is likely to encounter more people than he will in a white neighborhood. The greater number of people involved becomes, in and of itself, a cause for special care and alertness on the part of the police officer.

The lifestyles of the black and Hispanic communities cannot possibly be understood by a white police officer. One particular example, presented merely to underline this lack of understanding, is the numbers racket. Numbers gambling is extensive in

New York City's ghettos; it may almost be said that it is the very stuff of life in the ghettos. To the law enforcement establishment, numbers is gambling and thus contrary to law. The officially stated reason for constant police action against numbers is that this form of gambling drains the members of the ghetto of their salaries and savings, and they must be protected from such deprivation. However, the popularity of numbers is not based solely upon the fact that a participant can hope to recoup a tremendous amount of money. He does not delude himself as to the odds against him and as to the amount he may win. The "play" is merely a conversation piece—something that can be discussed endlessly, reflecting the hope and ambition that by winning any amount, however small, a black can be a winner. As a matter of fact, when he does win, he is more than likely to buy drinks for all and sundry assembled at the bar, eventually spending more than he has won. This is immaterial, for it proves to him that at least once he is not a loser. The Puerto Rican community of New York refers to the numbers as "bolita," and it has the same strong feelings about numbers as does the black community.

Since the police officer is enjoined to suppress illegal gambling of all types, he must, when he can, arrest the numbers runner. Yet the consternation of the citizens of the black and Puerto Rican communities is understandable too. As long as drug pushers and other "real" criminals roam the streets with impunity, they feel, the numbers runner, who gives them their slight connection to happiness and fortune, should also be allowed to go free and unfettered.

A similar situation exists in New York's Chinatown. The Chinese are inveterate gamblers, but gambling is merely a means of escape for them. The Chinese work long hours, usually at heavy manual labor, and an inordinate number of them are bachelors, or at least recent immigrants who have left wives and families behind. Because of the problems of vastly different languages and cultures, their means of entertainment and relaxation are severely circumscribed. Card games such as fantan are their escape, their enjoyment, their entertainment. Naturally, they find it incomprehensible that they should be arrested for engaging in an activity that does not threaten or interfere with anyone outside their own group.

Minorities, therefore, view much police activity with suspicion.

Many of their interactions with the police are interpreted as indicative that the usual police preoccupation with their social activities is an abuse of police power. Therefore, the police presence in the ghettos is often viewed with suspicion and mistrust. In spite of the fact that the police presence, often in saturation force, ensures residents that they are receiving protection against violent crime, the residents often feel that this presence represents "selective enforcement." In police parlance, this method of enforcement in the ghetto is "discretionary." The distinction is lost on the ghetto resident and antipathy toward the police officer becomes patently visible, resulting in a two-edged sword of prejudice and distrust. Prejudices, biases, fears and hatreds have prevented communications and have sharpened the polarization between the police and various minority groups.

However, the issues are not insurmountable and can be overcome. They require the police officer to add another talent to his qualifications—compassion, the principle of "sympathetic effort." The officer should develop this sensitivity. Once he has developed it, if at all, he will not necessarily be embraced by minority groups. We merely suggest that when an officer develops this "compassionate feeling," he can view confrontations more objectively. It should reduce the traumatic, challenging effect of confrontation and reduce the possibility of overt action that could be regretted.

A PLAN FOR MINORITIES

Obviously, one solution would be the establishment of communications between the police agency and minority groups. Contact must be made and prove to be mutually acceptable. However, the initial move must be made by the police agency itself and it must invite the participation of the residents of the ghetto. These residents should include various leaders, regardless of their political and social philosophies, and especially if these clash with those of the majority of the police officers themselves. These leaders may represent political, religious and social forces or may be charismatic or militant reformers.

These leaders should be informed of the goals of the program. The need for their cooperation in the success of the program should be stressed. Before invitations are issued, the support and cooperation of the city's political leaders must be enlisted, and a preparatory unit should be formed to establish the following elements:

1. The ranking officer of the special minority relations unit should be responsible only to the chief of police or commissioner and should be acceptable to the ghetto leaders.
2. The subordinate members of the unit should have certain qualifications:
   a) Education—college degree preferable, but some college education acceptable, with an emphasis on studies in sociology, psychology, or the behavioral sciences.
   b) Temperament—emotional objectivity, innate courtesy and empathy for the community.
   c) Abilities—Spanish-speaking.
3. The unit must attain a certain degree of prestige within the minority group.

It should be noted from the start that the creation of such a unit and its acceptance by the community will not overcome deep-seated minority prejudices and hatred. Members of the unit should be prepared for the community's critical, cynical and even hostile reception, but should not be put off by it. They should be especially wary of giving up too soon, of writing off their efforts as useless. The community's reaction to the unit should be anticipated and the unit should be prepared to offer specific suggestions leading to the improvement of communications and dialogue. Members of the unit should be prepared to guide criticism into constructive channels. The primary factor that should always be in the forefront of concern is the establishment of dialogue. The means by which the police and the minority group can be brought to a state of mutual understanding and respect are difficult, but not impossible. Since the committee consists of important figures from the community, their support should be forthcoming, as the committee will provide an important rostrum for the airing of their views.

The next step is the scheduling of social functions in which members of the committee (and their spouses) and members of the minority relations unit (and their spouses) meet informally. Subsequent meetings should involve the children of members of the committee and the special unit. If these preliminary overtures meet some degree of success, they can be expanded to include other members of the minority group.

The concept of the understanding officer visiting playgrounds and distributing lollipops as contributing towards a rapport between minorities and police agencies is valueless. However, the use of the Community Service Officer, as suggested by the Crime Commission Report, would be of inestimable value. He would be meeting with the community and becoming to an extent a member of it.

It should be borne in mind that these proposals are particularly pertinent to minority groups and may or may not have applicability to a general community relations program as a whole.

THE HIERARCHY OF BASIC NEEDS

A distinguished social psychologist, Abraham H. Maslow, formulated a theory of the importance of an individual's basic needs. Although the theory is applicable to anyone, it has particular significance for the patrolman.

In essence, everyone's basic needs are as follows:

1. Physiological (food, shelter, sex, matters of life and death).
2. Safety (security, stability).
3. Love, or identification with society; social conscience, a place in the group, a sense of belonging.
4. Esteem (desire to further oneself; need or desire for a stable, friendly base, usually being an evaluation of oneself; self-respect or self-esteem, and for the esteem and respect of others.)
   a) Desire for strength, achievement, adequacy, mastery or competence, confidence, independence.
   b) Reputation, prestige, status, dominance, recognition, importance, attention, appreciation.
5. Self-actualization (desire for actualization of fulfillment of potential).

This hierarchy of needs, as indicated, is applicable to every person, but is singularly significant to the police officer, since ". . . frustration of these needs [may be] psychopathogenic," and "destructiveness or aggression may occur as one of the concomitant reactions to basic threat."[18] Thus, any threat or thwarting of the basic needs, any threat to the defensive or coping system, any threat to the general way of life is likely to be reacted to by anxiety, by "hostility, which means that hostile, aggressive, or destructive behavior may very frequently be expected in such reactions."[19]

We will now examine the specific applicability of this hierarchy of basic needs to the police officer. We begin with item 3, since it is safe to assume that the officer's physiological and safety needs have been satisfied by his becoming a member of the department.

The next most important need is for identification (a love need), and a sense of belonging, which is denied to the officer by society in general but is granted to him in full measure by the department. He now feels himself an accepted member and brother of either ethnic, racial or religious societies within the department, and this furnishes him with a variety of social functions that further fulfill this particular need.

These societies are also a source of problems to the commander of any department large enough to accommodate a number of such organizations. In addition to satisfying a psychological need, these groups serve also as an instrument in attempting to force the commander to favor certain members of their group for special assignments, which at times places him in an embarrassing and difficult position.

Thus, the first three needs are satisfied rather quickly and effectively. The officer's fourth need now becomes a matter of greater importance, since it gives his daydreams and ambitions a direction and an "almost-fulfillment." There are a number of aspects of this fourth need as noted in the subdivisions. All of them are partially fulfilled by departmental recognition, such as conferring of medals, letters of commendation, praise at roll calls and so forth. The administrator should take this into consideration when thinking of ways to improve the morale of his department.

Another psychological factor that may be considered in this category would be the carrying of a weapon. The policeman's pistol is the obvious symbol of his adequacy, importance and dominance. He attributes his need for a weapon to the violence that surrounds him. In actuality, close to 95 percent of patrolmen killed in the line of duty are shot either from ambush or when they had no opportunity to use their weapon. An assumption may be made that this implies a suggestion that patrolmen be relieved of their weapons. Quite the contrary, they are absolute necessities, but not for the reasons the patrolmen give. They are part of his psychological armor, as are the uniform and the shield. However, each police officer must be aware that his weapon is as much a part of him as his uniform and that it is not meant to be used to cover his inadequacies.

The last of the basic needs, that of "self-actualization," goes beyond merely the advantages of being a superior officer and the financial advantages accruing therefrom. Superior rank is the culmination of all of the patrolman's desires and dreams. The drive for further study is obvious. The moment that the patrolman enters the profession he begins his studies for the next promotional opportunity. He never stops studying; it is a continuing process. Again, the driving force is not only for visible and ordinary tokens of success, but for proof of his own superiority and worth.

ANOMIC CYNICISM

The term *anomie* was introduced by the French sociologist Emile Durkheim. It has been given various interpretations, including a confusion of values in the group and a consequent insecurity. According to Weston and Wells it is "the normlessness of striving to win outside the rules of the game, to win at any cost."[20] Psychologically, we refer to anomie as a breakdown of values and a feeling of isolation. Although this feeling was attributed to cultures and individuals within it, there seems, nevertheless, to be a peculiar affinity in these descriptions to the police officer's feelings.

A generalized behavioral view outlined by Alfred Adler approximates this term with the police officer's dilemma: ". . . A man is endowed with social needs and these needs will not find satisfying fulfillment in any existing society. Born with a need to relate and establish his own identity, he enters a world which shapes his nature to fit society's mold. . . . [21] Durkheim restates this more understandably when he relates anomie to a situation whereby "social norms are at variance with the individual."[22]

This is elucidated still further by another sociologist, Albert Solomon, who states: "If society loses its regulating vitality, anomie arises. This state is further heightened by the passions that are unleashed when men are denied discipline and social authority."[23]

Anomie is usually associated with withdrawal from society. However, there is still another aspect of the patrolman's behavioral psychology, and that is his cynical attitude. He has become exceedingly distrustful of everyone's motives, disbelieving them as a matter of course. We cannot separate the terms anomie and cynicism insofar as the policeman is concerned. Both are part and parcel of his existence. Niederhoffer made this distinction clear; however, the author prefers using the term *anomic cynicism*.

The inference may be drawn from this that the police officer is psychotic. Quite the contrary, the officer has learned to live with his pressures and has adjusted to them. The average citizen who becomes anomic would probably need some type of therapy, having no working area in which to unload his frustrations. In fact, this quality gives the officer a greater conception of his obligations; a deeper understanding of the frailties of mankind; a degree of compassion he would not otherwise have.

SUMMARY

Unlike almost all other members of society, the policeman is involved with his role on a 24-hour-a-day basis, and this requires of him an unending concern for the society in which he functions.

One of the distinguishing aspects of the policeman's role is his exercise of authority. Though this is granted to him by virtue of his role, he must assert it constantly. Asserting it successfully is attributable partially to his role, his uniform, his professional demeanor and activity. It is also attributable to the validity with which he asserts authority.

Police-citizen relations depend in large measure on the citizen; the policeman's actions and attitudes largely reflect those of the citizens. Most relations are civil and even cordial, but when they are not, the policeman finds it necessary to invoke whatever measure of force he deems necessary to accomplish his task.

The nature of police relationships varies with the people encountered, tending to be friendlier and more deferential to those the police see as the "better class of people" and harsher toward minority group members. Although they don't necessarily act upon them, most police harbor deep-seated prejudices towards blacks.

Police must improve their relations with the public and enlist their support in the fight against crime. They are most successful in community relations, especially when ethnically, socially and culturally the police are representative of the community. They are also successful in public relations, the effort to convince the public of the value and validity of the work the police are doing. They are least successful in, and must bend most of their future effort to improving, minority relations. Part of their effort will be in enrolling in their numbers members of the various ethnic minorities. Much of their effort should be in the direction of becoming more sympathetic to the problems, needs and desires of the minority groups.

In performing his functions, the police officer is fulfilling his hierarchy of basic needs, as outlined by Abraham Maslow. These range from physiological needs through safety, love and esteem to the need for self-actualization.

Most police officers are marked by and need to cope effectively with two distinct traits, anomie and cynicism. These are so much a part of the armor he girds himself with that he may be thought to be experiencing anomic cynicism.

Understanding himself and his needs in relationship to the general public only enhances the effectiveness of the police officer. Learning to live with pressures and psychological conditions which would be debilitating to the average citizen is a part of the training and experience for which a police officer can not only feel proud, but he can also feel confident of his ability to do the job society has imposed on him.

NOTES

1. Albert J. Reiss, Jr. *The Police and the Public*. New Haven: Yale University Press, 1971, p. 2.
2. *Ibid.*, p. 46.
3. *Ibid.*, p. 55.
4. *Ibid.*, p. 150.
5. *Ibid.*, p. 142.
6. William A. Westley, *Violence and the Police*. Cambridge, Mass.: The

MIT Press, 1970, p. 118.
7. Reiss, *op. cit.*, pp. 69–70.
8. *Ibid.*, p. 14.
9. *Ibid.*, p. 53.
10. *Ibid.*, p. 51.
11. *Ibid.*, p. 175.
12. Westley, *op. cit.*, p. 104 ff.
13. *Ibid.*, p. 99.
14. *Task Force Report: The Police.* The President's Commission on Law Enforcement and the Administration of Justice. Washington, D.C., Government Printing Office, 1967, p. 150 ff.
15. Reiss, *op. cit.*, p. 17.
16. Westley, *op. cit.*, p. 99.
17. *Ibid.*, p. 101.
18. Abraham H. Maslow, *Motivation and Personality,* New York: Harper & Row, 1954, p. 187.
19. *Ibid.*
20. Paul B. Weston and Kenneth M. Wells, *Law Enforcement and Criminal Justice.* Pacific Palisades, Calif.: Goodyear Publishing Company, 1972, p. 102.
21. Alan J. Butler, "The Sociological Aspects of Police Training," unpublished Master's thesis. Long Island University, 1970, p. 4.
22. *Ibid.*, p. 41.
23. *Ibid.*

STUDY QUESTIONS

1. What are the differences between *social interrelationships, social interaction* and *social control?*
2. Under what conditions are police officers most likely to have their authority accepted? Or challenged?
3. What are the differences between *community relations, minority relations* and *public relations?* Which is most important for effective police work?
4. Will enrollment of minority group members in the ranks of the police contribute to a successful minority relations program?
5. What is "the hierarchy of basic needs"?
6. What are some of the definitions of "anomie"?
7. What are the major elements in civil police-citizen relations?
8. How does the citizen control the working and performance of the police officer?
9. How do police respond to various groups? Is the response affected by age, sex, occupation, social status, color?
10. What are the pros and cons of civilian complaint review boards?

9

Police Administration and Command

The organization of police departments varies across the country with the size of the jurisdiction. In the smallest towns and villages the police may be represented by only one man, or one man in command of a few others. As the cities grow larger, the police structure becomes more complex. There are precincts, districts, commands, and there is a hierarchy of rank rising from the patrolman to sergeant, lieutenant, captain, and various ranks of inspector. At the top is the chief of police, the highest ranking uniformed officer, who may be subordinate to a civilian commissioner. The larger and more complex the organization, the greater the problems of administration and command.

In this chapter we examine police administration and command. The first part is devoted to a study of purposes and principles and the need to set a list of priorities. Then we look at the division of a police organization according to line, staff and supportive functions, giving details on those operations that are categories of each function. We also outline police management theory, concentrating on span of control, chain of command and unity of command as major principles.

After some discussion of authority and responsibility and principles of management, we look at the rank of sergeant as the key element in all police administration.

The final section of the chapter is given over to methods of evaluating performance, with special emphasis on a newly devised system of scoring that is attuned to crime prevention and is based on the evaluation of hazard factors.

PURPOSES AND PRINCIPLES

A police department is usually thought of as a military organization, and outwardly the analogy is correct. Both are marked by distinct structures, ranks and uniforms. Yet a police department incorporates more of the features of a business organization than it does of a military unit. The chief of police more nearly resembles the head of a corporation who is answerable to a board of directors, though he is the ultimate authority as far as the employee of the corporation is concerned, than he does a general. A police chief may be appointed or he may have secured his position through a civil service examination. He is answerable to a higher authority, which may be the mayor, city manager, safety director, police commissioner or municipal commission. He is (and must be) sensitive to the desires of his civilian superiors and to the demands of the community, including all ethnic, racial, religious, political, business, homeowner and tenant groups. All demand attention, sometimes all at the same time, and sometimes with mutually contradictory goals. So the chief must often walk a delicate tightrope.

The chief's problems from outside the department are often compounded within the department: by police officers' lack of understanding of the chief's responsibilities to the community, by their militancy, sometimes by their lack of morale. The difficulties facing the chief may often appear insurmountable, yet he must make an effort to overcome them, and his main weapon in this effort is the formulation of distinct plans and procedures handed down to his department and designed to deal with every aspect of the police mission in society.

Getting the job done requires, first of all, the setting of goals. From among the multitude of demands made upon him, the chief must set a list of priorities, so that he can assign his commanders and their line officers a specific roster of duties. First and foremost, both for the department and for the general public, is the goal of dealing with crime in the two primary areas of prevention and repression. Beyond this are the more workaday requirements of traffic management, control of liquor violations, suppression of gambling and vice, tracing lost and stolen property, supervision of private clubs, checking the security of residential and business areas, monitoring juvenile gang activities, preventing traffic in drugs and quelling public disturbances. These are among the more public and obvious functions of a police department, but there are a host of others, which the general public is usually only mildly aware of. Among these are:

1. *Training.* Administering the police academy and the continuing education and instruction of police officers.
2. *Recruitment.* Attracting qualified men and women, and members of minority groups, to police service through adjustment of physical and educational requirements consistent with the fulfillment of police services.
3. *Equipment.* Acquisition and maintenance of motor vehicles from patrol cars through personnel carriers to rescue vans.
4. *Communications.* Acquisition and maintenance of call boxes, walkie-talkies, radios, computers and new developments in technically sophisticated systems.
5. *Detention.* Securing detainees and arrestees until they are booked and released or sent to prison.
6. *Community relations.* Maintaining a regular program of contact with the community and all segments within it to keep the public aware of the police role, their need for cooperation and their efforts to serve the community.
7. *Lost and found.* Taking possession of and securing all sorts of lost articles and restoring them to their owners.
8. *Special units.* Organizing and running such special units as harbor and helicopters, horse-mounted police, and scuba divers.

ORGANIZATION

Achieving the goals mentioned above depends on successful organization. A police organization can usually be divided according to *line, staff* and *supportive* functions.

The line units include the usual patrol functions. The line units are the backbone, the workhorse, the most important units of any police department. The chief must be aware of the importance of his uniformed officers, much as the general of an army division is

A police organization can usually be divided according to *line*, *staff*, and *supportive* functions. The structure shown in this chart is typical of that found in many police agencies.

aware of his riflemen, the soldiers that count in battle. The line functions may be divided along these general lines:

1. *Patrol.* Preliminary investigations, surveillance of potential hazards, public service, crowd control.
2. *Investigation.* Recovery of stolen property, arresting suspects, questioning witnesses, securing evidence, writing reports.
3. *Regulation of vice.* Prostitution, gambling, illicit liquor and tobacco sales, narcotics violations.
4. *Traffic.* Maintainence of safe vehicular and pedestrian traffic; investigation and aid in accidents.
5. *Juvenile.* Protection of dependent children.

Secondary line activities include ambulance and rescue, civil defense, animal and pet licensing, guard services, auxiliary volunteer reserve.

Staff functions relate mainly to planning, inspection, training and budget. They too may be divided into primary and secondary functions. Among the primary functions are:

1. *Personnel and training.* Attracting, testing and educating candidates for the force, with emphasis on getting the best men (and women) possible for the force.
2. *Planning and research.* Keeping abreast of political, social, scientific and technical developments so as to keep the department always responsive to and capable of coping with whatever problems may arise.
3. *Financial.* Determining how much money is needed to allow the department to fulfill all its functions and how this money is to be divided among men, machines and equipment.
4. *Public relations.* Presenting to the public the best possible image of the policeman and his contribution to the welfare of society.
5. *Community relations.* Involving the members of each community in the work of the police and the police in the needs and aspirations of the community.
6. *Civilian personnel.* Enlisting and training citizens to perform a variety of technical and/or clerical functions so as to free more police officers for line duty.

Secondary staff functions include maintenance and operation

of a crime lab, detention centers, records and identification apparatus, communications, property and equipment maintenance, and transportation facilities.

Supportive units are involved in internal police activities: inspection and investigation of personnel, civilian complaints, allegations of department vice or corruption.

The subdivisions may vary in their responsibilities assigned, depending on the chief and his needs. The one unalterable fact is that the uniform patrol division is the most important unit in any police agency and that its line functions are the most essential of all police activities.

Once the chief has established his goals, he determines the distribution of manpower. He must, however, be aware of certain pitfalls. We are accustomed to the phrase "empire-building." This is usually associated with private enterprise and institutions of higher learning. It is just as prevalent, however, in the police profession. Empire-building is often referred to as "Parkinson's theory," which postulates, especially in the civil service, that any

Communications is a crucial secondary staff function.
Photo courtesy of the Nassau County Police Department.

unit will discover innumerable reasons (supported, of course, by facts and figures) for an increase in personnel. As time goes on the need for ever more personnel becomes inevitable and indisputable. Although it might appear that any administrator would be aware of such a tendency, he will find difficulties in attempting to challenge this tendency. The chief, when submitting his budget, will attempt to justify his request for more personnel based on the need for auxiliary and supportive units. He is prompted by his knowledge of the necessities of his force and he attempts to relay this to his superiors. City officials usually appear to be more impressed by the importance of these auxiliary and supportive units than they are with the need to expand line units. This is understandable, since the media tend to glamorize the detective and all sorts of special agents.

The police chief is continually badgered by special divisions, such as detective, juvenile, traffic and so on, as to the necessity for more personnel.

COMMAND IN THE DEPARTMENT

Management

In police management theory, there are three areas of major concern: *span of control, chain of command,* and *unity of command.* These are time-honored phrases, as valid today as they were when coined years ago by the police profession. Administrators and supervisors are well aware of them, and the patrolman should become aware of them too, for several reasons:

1. To increase his ability to answer the questions usually given in examinations for promotion.
2. To gain a better understanding of his responsibilities in the department.
3. To comprehend the department's policies as they relate to him personally.
4. To better understand the chief's and the department's problems.
5. To avoid being unknowledgeable.

Span of Control

This term denotes the number of subordinates that any supervisor can effectively control: the number of patrolmen a sergeant can supervise, the number of sergeants a lieutenant can give direction to, and so on. The number of men supervised by the superior officer depends on a number of factors which the commanding officer must be aware of:

1. *Empire-building.* Various line organizations strive to increase promotional opportunities for their favored members, and will favor the establishing of as many supervisory positions as possible.
2. *Actual necessity.* This is a variable that is hard to determine, for where human beings are involved so many contending factors come into play. Even a computer could probably not determine this, for its input would be controlled by these same contentious humans.
3. *Budget allotments.* The perennial problem in any department is convincing those who set the budget within any jurisdiction to allot sufficient funds for all the men, materiel and equipment needed.

Span of control refers not only to physical control of those in the presence of or within sight or hearing of the supervisor, but of communications control as well. With the technically sophisticated communications equipment in use today, it is quite possible to think in terms of subordinates under the control of superior officers at command posts or headquarters miles away. Of course, a breakdown in communications is accompanied by a loss of control, which is less of a problem when control is exercised by persons on the scene of any accident. When communications are broken, control is absent, and each patrolman establishes his own self-control. He must then rely on his own education, training and judgment to make sometimes crucial decisions, sometimes without knowing all the factors available to a central command. In such cases, it is understandable that the patrolman may be confused and hesitant, and his actions will often reflect this. Justifiably or not, the patrolman's actions will affect the chief more than they will him, for the chief bears the responsibility for the actions of all his men, come what may.

Chain of Command

This denotes the responsibility of each individual officer to a higher-ranking officer. The chain of command is a two-way street, in that policy, directives and orders are sent down the chain, with each successive subordinate required to assume responsibility for the person below him in the chain and required to answer for the failure of any subordinate. The chain of command provides continuous communication up and down the line. It gives the police chief control and is used to pinpoint variations or changes in orders.

A complication may arise when the immediate supervisor is absent. This is usually anticipated, however, and allowed for in departmental orders. Substitutions and reassignments are made, as necessary, but the chain of command should never be broken.

Unity of Command

The patrolman assigned to a specific duty or incident expects to report to and be responsible to a superior who has been designated as the person responsible for detail. He has received his orders and is aware of his responsibility. Should a superior officer not associated with the patrolman's unit appear on the scene and countermand the orders given, the patrolman would only be confused. The problem for the patrolman is deciding whether he should obey the instructions given to him by his superior in the chain of command or obey the new instructions given him by an officer of superior rank who is not a link in his chain of command. Does he refuse to obey these new orders, inform the superior who gave him his original instructions or telephone headquarters?

This dilemma can be extended to those assignments involving officers of equal rank. In the event of an incident that involves members of the uniformed patrol units and of the detective divisions, the question of who is in charge is a delicate one. Assuming that the commander of the uniformed patrol needs more men and that the only ones available are in the detective division, he is faced with these questions:

1. Can he assign them to specific duties?
2. Does he have the authority to make these assignments?
3. What does he do in case his orders are refused?

The commander of a detective division faces the same problem when the extra men assigned to him are from uniformed patrol.

Let us assume that both commanders are on the scene, that one of them needs more men, and that he is refused these men by the other commander. This refusal will not be lost on the patrolmen or detectives; if the matter is brought to a superior officer for adjudication, compromise will be difficult and delicate.

AUTHORITY AND RESPONSIBILITY

The principles of authority and responsibility are incorporated in the division of authority, which is closely related to and part of the principles listed above.

A good rule is that authority can be delegated but that ultimate responsibility cannot be. The chief and the supervisor should always keep this in mind. A possible exception is that some responsibility can be delegated, but only as much as is commensurate with the authority delegated. Assume that a supervisor in command of a detail is given orders and the authority to implement these orders. His responsibility extends no further than the authority implied in his orders. In all situations outside those covered by his orders, authority reverts to the commander with the ultimate responsibility.

A police chief may accept the philosophy that there can be delegation of authority with qualified responsbility, but he should —*must*—be aware that, under all circumstances, he is the one who will eventually assume the burden and the final responsibility.

Although we have discussed police administrators and other higher officers, we are also concerned with the patrolman, who has both authority and responsibility. As far as the ordinary citizen is concerned, the patrolman *is* authority. His actions should be governed with the following points in mind:

1. The citizens he comes in contact with view him as the ultimate authority for his action.
2. His action affects the citizens' opinion of him, his department and the law enforcement establishment in general.
3. His actions are regarded as final decisions which are meant to stand and which cannot safely or sucessfully be challenged.

The patrolman, therefore, appears to the citizen as an entire department rolled into one person, and he must conduct himself with the full implications of this judgment in mind.

PRINCIPLES OF MANAGEMENT

The basic principles of police management were formulated years ago and are still considered valid guidelines for police officers. They have to be studied and memorized by those seeking promotions as much as by those already in positions of command. They are presented here not only to inform the patrolman about problems that may await him, but to give him a greater understanding of the problems in the higher echelons. These problems do not appear to be relevant to the patrolman's primary duties, but his ordinary functions are part of a superior officer's responsibilities. The officer cannot function unless he is aware of his subordinate's performance, and his duties then become manifest. He must continually analyze and appraise the activities of the patrol force and make decisions accordingly.

The patrolman must be aware that his performance will directly affect his superiors. He cannot assume—whatever his patrol duties—that they are of no concern to the higher echelon.

The patrolman may also find himself in the position of a superior officer. This situation usually develops at the scene of an unusual occurrence where no ranking officer is present. The patrolman may be assigned to a situation because of his experience, seniority and/or common sense. The officer is thus obligated to know police management processes in order to understand the assignment he has been given, his relationship to other members and officers in the department, his assumed authority and responsibility and his obligations. This understanding should help him to contribute to his department, since he will be aware that his conduct affects his partners, the department and the profession.

The following managerial topics are usually dealt with in depth in various courses. The authoritative *Municipal Police Administration* lists these subjects, which cover the entire field of police management:

1. Planning.
2. Organization.
3. Staffing.
4. Training.
5. Budgeting.

6. Equipment.
7. Coordination.
8. Public information.
9. Reporting.
10. Directing.

These represent the administrative problems the police commander must be concerned with. His problems are compounded by the fact that he must distribute his limited patrol force according to time, place and function. He must keep abreast of the situation by using charts—administrative, personnel and functional. In addition, he should use a pin chart, with each pin denoting an incident. There has been some argument over whether to use charts and maps instead of computerization using special cards. No matter how inclusive the information on the computer card is, the system cannot compete with the immediacy of pin maps.

In addition, with the information now available to him, by using either computers or pin maps, the officer must now apportion his men according to the time element involved. Traditionally, there are three shifts, or platoons, with the manpower equally divided, regardless of the circumstances. This tradition is so powerful that few supervisors dare to tamper with it. There have been experiments in which platoons or shifts were changed. One of these involves the short swing, in which a patrolman has only eight hours between the time he goes off duty and reports on again. The short swing has largely disappeared, though it remains in a few police departments. Another experiment is that of the 10-hour shift. Neither the short swing nor the 10-hour shift has proved effective, however.

A new method is being tried by the New York City Transit Police, in which a fourth platoon works from 8:00 P.M. to 4:00 A.M. (a high-crime period). Although it has worked well, there is no doubt that this shift is unpopular, so to implement the plan the department has offered two alternatives: first, those with the least seniority are assigned to this shift and eventually, because of normal attrition, they are then assigned to normal rotating shifts; second, the men on the shift are given additional time off, plus an extra weekend day during the month. So that there would be no misunderstanding, the chief requested that the men sign a statement acknowledging their acceptance of these tours.

The system has worked well to reduce dramatically the amount of crime during this late night to early morning shift. It has been mentioned favorably in the Crime Commission Report, and a number of other departments have instituted the fourth-platoon system with good results. The three-platoon system is so deeply ingrained, however, that police commanders are hesitant to disturb it, both for the additional problems of command that it presents and for the agreements that would need to be worked out with the various police unions.

THE SERGEANT

The most important supervisor in the police administrative structure is the sergeant. He is as important to the organization as the uniformed patrol division is to the administrative structure as a whole. The sergeant is the bridge between the patrolman and the higher echelons. He is the buffer which absorbs blows from both sides. He is the main contact for the patrolman, and his ability to compromise, advise and/or make suggestions can considerably lessen the problems the commander has to deal with.

The most important supervisor in the police administrative structure is the Sergeant.
Magnum Photos

Policies, orders and directions usually follow a pattern. How they are accepted by the "line" depends on how the sergeant implements them. This implementation, in turn, depends on his common sense, loyalty and understanding of his duties.

The sergeant is the rank to which every patrolman aspires, an aspiration that can influence the patrolman's current attitudes. The patrolman studies continually, sacrifices personal time, neglects his family—all because of this ambition. The sergeant represents the entire police department as far as the patrolman is concerned.

The patrolman's attitude toward his sergeant differs markedly from the attitude of the sergeant's superior officers. For example, his superior officers address him by his first name, rather than by his rank and surname. Sometimes he is patronized by them and reminded of his inferior rank. Supposedly, this behavior is meant to demonstrate a certain bond of fellowship, but, unfortunately, it violates the self-esteem of the police officer. "All the people in our society . . . have a need or desire for . . . self-respect, or self-esteem, and for the esteem of others."[1] This principle is thus violated by a lack of understanding of what motivates not only the patrolman but the sergeant as well. A superior officer, without being aware of this—and perhaps innocently, out of a personal relationship that exists between him and the sergeant—might call him by his first name. However, he should always address him by his title, especially in the presence of patrolmen. This formality should be observed at all times. Such observance will underscore the respect to be accorded to the sergeant. It will also convey to him a sense of his own importance.

The sergeant must be respected by both lower and higher echelons. If he is not, and the patrolman feels that his immediate superior is considered of little consequence, the sergeant's orders may not be heeded. The commanding officer must recognize his responsibilities to this rank.

EVALUATING PERFORMANCE

An important factor that has always plagued the administrator is the objective evaluation of a patrolman's performance. The usual ratings are based on stereotyped forms containing boxes to be checked off by the administrator and reviewed by a superior who usually agrees with the administrator's evaluation. There are so few exceptions to this procedure that we may accept it as a generalization. These forms, nevertheless, reflect opinion rather than objective evaluation. The usual guides for the officer who fills them out are:

1. Number of summonses or citations issued.
2. Number of arrests.
3. Number of convictions.
4. Letters of Commendation.
5. Civilian complaints against.

It should be noted particularly that the areas of police action of concern here are those directed toward apprehending criminals and to the prevention of crime. The evaluation record is more important to those who want to be promoted than to the commander himself. He is interested, but only so far as the evaluation affects his department.

Promotional evaluations are based first on a written examination, second on seniority and third on the individual's record in the department. This evaluation is of great importance to the patrolman and his supervisor.

A scientific formula relative to performance has been devised by Inspector Sidney Tatz of the New York City Transit Police.[2] It has been said that the primary duties of the law enforcement officer are apprehension and prevention. The basis of this premise is that an arrest is, in effect, a failure to prevent a crime. In other words, the standard evaluation is based on the arrests a patrolman makes and neglects altogether his other major duty: crime prevention. This problem places the administrator and the rating officers in a dilemma. It is easy to measure an officer's performance in terms of the arrests he has made and the number of citations he has handed out. But the evaluation of immediate concern to the patrolman is how to evaluate the prevention of criminal activity by aggressive patrol. This can be determined somewhat by studying the factors below, which are a part of objective evaluation.

The use of hazard factors, with which police administrators are familiar, such things as size of area, type of area, population, and the record of criminal activity within the area determines the size, intensity and type of patrol posts. It is possible to rate each post so as to reflect these factors. The patrol posts are compared and rated numerically against a chosen norm.

Complaints about crimes are given numerical values which reflect their severity. According to theory, given these equalizing "handicaps" or scoring devices, officers who consistently prevent crimes rather than make arrests after a crime has been committed will rate low numerically. This is the true crime-prevention officer, compared to the high scorer, the lock-'em-up cop.

As an example of this system: Patrolman A is assigned to a high-crime post and Patrolman B to a low-crime post. Patrolman A and his post are given a minus 2 rating, reflecting the hazards of the post. Patrolman B and his quiet post are given a zero rating. When there is a crime on B's quiet post and no arrest is made, B earns a plus 3 rating for the crime he failed to prevent. If Patrolman A succeeds in preventing crime during his tour on hazardous duty, he earns another minus 2. In the event that Patrolman B develops information that leads to an arrest, he is given a minus 2 and winds up with a plus 1 for his tour. But Patrolman A, who received a minus 4 for his tour, still has a better crime-prevention score than Patrolman B.

This concept is most effective where crime statistics are computerized. Roll calls are also performed by a computer. In small departments, the member assigned to make up the roll call can also keep a current account of each officer's crime-prevention rating.

This is not solely an evaluative tool; it is also a strong instrument to encourage and motivate a police department to concentrate on its main objective—crime prevention. It helps counter the belief that police work can be measured only by records of arrests. It also helps bring about a crime-prevention program and a completely objective evaluation of the operation of the department as a whole and of each of its individual police officers.

SUMMARY

Police departments across the country vary in size and complexity, but in their organization and functions they more nearly resemble business enterprises than, as is commonly thought, military units. Like business enterprises they are goal-oriented and arrange their functions according to a set of priorities.

Achieving standard police goals is usually accomplished by dividing the organization according to line, staff and supportive functions. Major line functions include patrol, investigation, regulation of vice, traffic control, juvenile aid and services. Basic staff functions include personnel and training, planning and research, finances, public relations, community relations, and utilization of civilian personnel. Supportive functions are concentrated on major internal police activities.

Command in the department is based on management theory that is built around three major concepts: *span of control, chain of command* and *unity of command.* Span of control refers to the number of subordinates that any superior officer can effectively control. Chain of command refers to the responsibility up and down the line of each officer to the next officer either above or below him in rank. Unity of command refers to the need to maintain control of operations by having superior officers give their orders and instructions only to those assigned to their command and, conversely, by having line officers required to accept assignments and command only from those higher ranking officers in whose units they serve.

Two other concepts that are of major concern are authority and responsibility, the former conferred and the latter accepted. Both of these are important to the uniformed patrol officer, because in almost every situation it is he who represents the organization whose uniform he wears.

Police management requires the commander to be expert in the following areas: planning, organization, staffing, training, budgeting, equipment, coordination, public information, reporting and directing.

The key man in any police organization is the sergeant. He is the central figure between the ranking officers above and the line officers below. Effective police work depends on his ability to convey to the line officers the requirements of the ranking officers and must be based on respect for the sergeant both from above and below.

One of the most difficult areas of police administration is the evaluation of performance. Most rating systems are based on input of crime repression information. A more accurate and effective system, devised by a ranking officer of the New York City Transit Police, is based on success in crime prevention and functions around the concept of hazard factors. According to this system, a lack of activity—arrests, summonses, citations—is an indication of success in preventing crime and produces a higher rating.

NOTES

1. Abraham H. Maslow, *Motivation and Personality*. New York: Harper and Row, 1970, p. 45.
2. Sidney Tatz, "A Positive Approach to Crime Prevention: An Innovative Plan," *Police*, March–April 1970, pp. 69–72.

STUDY QUESTIONS

1. What are the major functions of the police organization?
2. What are the differences between *line, staff* and *supportive* functions?
3. What is span of control?
4. What is chain of command?
5. What is unity of command?
6. Why are these concepts important?
7. Why does the sergeant play such a central role in a successful police organization?
8. What is "empire-building"?
9. What is the best way of evaluating police performance?
10. Why does the police officer need to know the principles of police management?

10

Police Agencies: Federal, State, and Private

In this final chapter we examine the various federal, state and private organizations that provide police services. The study of the federal agencies indicates that most of them have been established over the years in response to perceived needs and that only a few of them have been prescribed in the Constitution. Most of the police agencies function within the cabinet-level administrative departments, the military services and the regulatory agencies and commissions.

Study of the state agencies indicates that many of these have come into being fairly recently, largely as a result of the introduction of the automobile, which required an agency with statewide jurisdiction. Other state agencies are patterned after federal agencies and perform similar functions.

We end the chapter by looking at the private agencies that provide guard, alarm, protective and investigative services that are required by private individuals, manufacturing, retail and insurance companies.

One of the most striking features of the American police system is its fragmentation or lack of national unity. Unlike many other nations, the United States has no national police force. Despite a growing trend toward the sharing and dissemination of information on all sorts of police matters and coordination by such national organizations as the Federal Bureau of Investigation and the Law Enforcement Assistance Administration, there is not likely ever to be a national force.

This is in large measure the result of several factors in the American heritage. Foremost, of course, is the several centuries of English history that were characterized by the constant struggle against an encroaching central authority in the institution of the crown. Local administration of the law in Anglo-Saxon times was replaced by national administration with the Norman conquest, and the increasingly repressive nature of this administration was halted only with the signing of Magna Carta. But the tendency for the crown to assert its rule quickly reappeared and grew stronger with time. Parliament struggled against it constantly, but did not win its final battle until the acceptance of the English Bill of Rights by James II in 1689. This experience is the primary factor in the establishment of this nation as the United States of America, which means exactly that, in structure as well as in concept: this is a nation of separate states that have joined together in a federation and have surrendered to that federation only as much of their sovereignty as is necessary for that federation to function as a nation alongside other nations. This federation of states is set forth in the Constitution, which, among its many notable features, outlines only limited police functions for the federal government, and specifies none for the states which, together with cities, towns and counties have established their police organizations under the terms of the "reserved powers" clause in Article X.

Out of this background has grown the fragmented arrangement of town, county, state and federal police organizations, each with its specific jurisdiction, and each guarding its jurisdiction jealously. Only within the last generation, with the increasing national attention on the crime problem, has there been any attempt to coordinate police functions and administration.

FEDERAL AGENCIES

As indicated in an earlier chapter, the Constitution prescribes only a very few police functions for the federal government, in the areas of currency, postage and customs. Federal police agencies have grown primarily in response to perceived needs; as a problem requiring police attention was discovered, the duty of coping with that problem was assigned to an already existing unit or to a new unit established specifically in response to the problem. At the present time the federal police structure numbers several thousand persons working in dozens of major and minor law enforcement or investigative agencies in the major cabinet level federal departments and the major regulatory agencies.

Department of State

The intelligence gathered by the CIA and other agencies, together with its own studies and research, is coordinated for the Department of State and other federal agencies by the Bureau of Intelligence and Research. A deputy undersecretary for administration is responsible, among other things, for divisions that administer the granting of passports and visas, a Division of Protective Services and a Division of Security.

Department of the Treasury

Some of the oldest federal police units are located within the Department of the Treasury.

The Internal Revenue Service was created in 1862, although the internal revenue system has functioned under the jurisdiction of the Department since 1789. The Intelligence Unit superintends the assessment and collection of all taxes imposed by any law providing internal revenue. The Alcohol and Tobacco Tax Division administers and enforces the laws and regulations relating to alcohol, alcoholic beverages, tobacco and firearms. This division enforces the National Firearms Act, which regulates the possession of automatic weapons and determines which firearms it is illegal to possess.

The United States Secret Service was created in 1865 to combat an increasing wave of counterfeiting. Within five years it had succeeded in reestablishing the integrity of the "greenback." It is now concerned with the following functions: protecting the President of the United States, members of his immediate family, the President-elect, and the Vice President; suppressing the counterfeiting of coins, currency, stamps, and other United States obligations and securities; investigating criminal violations of the Gold Reserve Act of 1934, Federal Deposit Insurance Act, Federal Land Bank Act, Federal Farm Loan Act; investigating thefts of government property under control of the Treasury Department.

The Bureau of Customs was created in 1927, but it had predecessors, the United States Customs Service established in 1789 and a Division of Customs established in a reorganized Treasury Department in 1875. Its principal roles are in assessing and collecting duties and taxes on imported merchandise, controlling carriers and merchandise imported into or exported from the United States and preventing smuggling and frauds on the revenue process. Customs agents guard baggage enclosures, ships, trucks and railroad cars, and patrol docks, terminals and airfields.

Department of Defense

Each of the major divisions of the Department of Defense operates and maintains its own law enforcement and intelligence units.

The Army's Deputy Chief of Staff supervises the Provost Marshal General, who is responsible for plans, policy and procedure for military police, crime prevention programs, apprehension programs, care of prisoners of war, security at defense installations including supervision of civilian guards, and administration of the restoration, clemency and parole of military prisoners.

The Chief of the National Guard Bureau participates in the formulation and administration of a program designed to develop and maintain the National Guard and the Air National Guard.

The Judge Advocate General supervises the system of military justice throughout the army and serves as legal advisor to the Secretary of the Army, the Chief of Staff and all staff agencies.

The Navy's Bureau of Naval Personnel is concerned with questions of naval discipline, return and punishment of deserters, places of confinement and prisoners. The office of the Judge Advocate General reports on legal features of courts-martial, courts of inquiry and boards of investigation and inquest.

The Marine Corps' Inspector General conducts inspections and investigations.

In addition, each of the services operates its own uniformed patrol: the Military Police for the Army, the Shore Patrol for the Navy, and the Security Police for the Air Force. Police investigations and intelligence, akin to the plainclothes and detective units of civilian police units, are the function of the Military Police Criminal Investigation Division for the Army, the Office of Naval

Intelligence for the Navy, and the Office of Special Investigation for the Air Force.

Department of Justice

The primary federal agency concerned with law enforcement is the Department of Justice, headed by the Attorney General; it has several major sub-units.

The Federal Bureau of Investigation is the investigative arm of the Department and is not a police agency as such. It is responsible for the investigation of all violations of federal law, except those that have been placed by statute under the jurisdiction of another federal agency. It has jurisdiction over incidents of espionage, sabotage, treason, and other matters concerned with the internal security of the United States. It is also concerned with the following matters of criminal law: kidnapping, extortion, bank robbery, burglary, and larceny; crimes on Government or Indian reservations; thefts of Government property; interstate transportation of stolen motor vehicles, aircraft and cattle; interstate transmission or transportation of wagering information or devices; fraud against the Government; election law violations; matters of civil rights; and assaults on or murder of a federal official or officer. The FBI, in cooperation with the International Association of Chiefs of Police, compiles annually the *Uniform Crime Reports,* issues a monthly *Law Enforcement Bulletin,* maintains a central fingerprint file and assists local police agencies through its crime laboratory.

The Immigration and Naturalization Service was created as a separate agency in 1891. It was transferred to the Department of Justice in 1940. It administers the immigration and naturalization laws pertaining to the admission, exclusion and deportation of aliens, and the naturalization of aliens lawfully present in the United States. It investigates alleged violation of these laws and advises whenever prosecution is to be recommended. Through the Border Patrol, its enforcement agency, it controls and prevents the illegal entry of aliens into the United States.

The Bureau of Narcotics and Dangerous Drugs was created in 1968 by the consolidation of the Department of the Treasury's Bureau of Narcotics and the Department of Health, Education and Welfare's Bureau of Drug Abuse Control. The bureau's primary role is the investigation, detection and prevention of violations of various federal narcotic and marijuana laws, the Opium Poppy Control Act of 1942 and the Drug Abuse Control Amendments of 1965. The agents of this agency work closely with state and local police agencies and often work underground.

Post Office Department

The Bureau of the Chief Postal Inspector directs the execution of policies, regulations and procedures governing investigations, inspections and audits. The Chief Postal Inspector directs the selection, training and supervision of inspection service personnel, and maintains liaison with other investigative and law enforcement agencies of the government.

The Postal Inspection Service is one of the oldest federal agencies, having been established in 1775. Postal inspectors are concerned mainly with two types of investigation: the use of the postal service in illegal or fraudulent activities and attempts to withhold postal revenues.

Department of the Interior

The nation's natural resources within the continental United States and its territories, almost 900,000,000 acres of land, are under the management of the Department of the Interior. The department is charged with the task of conserving and developing water mineral resources; promoting mine safety; conserving, developing and utilizing fish and wildlife; administering the nation's nearly 200 parks, monuments and historic sites; administering programs for the welfare of almost 350,000 Indians; reclaiming arid lands; and managing hydroelectric power systems.

The Division of Inspection has the responsibility for all the investigative and inspection services of the department; the Division of Security is responsible for establishing and maintaining security within the division. Major divisions of the Department include the National Park Service, which maintains a staff of Rangers who police the National Parks, and the United States Fish and Wildlife Service, which enforces the laws concerning migratory game birds, fish and wildlife restoration acts. The Bureau of Mines enforces federal regulations involving mine accidents, fires and explosions. The Bureau of Indian Affairs polices the nation's Indian reservations and controls illegal liquor and drug traffic.

Department of Agriculture

The Department of Agriculture administers more than fifty laws designed to protect the farmer and the consuming public. It regulates programs of animal disease prevention and eradication, animal quarantine, meat inspection, and enforces regulations to prevent harmful insects from entering and spreading through the United States. The Forest Service administers more than 150 national forests in 40 states and Puerto Rico and protects them from fire, insects and disease. It also manages and controls livestock grazing and watersheds.

The Commodity Exchange Authority conducts investigations to prevent price manipulation affecting agricultural commodities, false and misleading crop and market information, and to protect users of the commodity futures markets against cheating, fraud and manipulative practices.

Department of Commerce

The primary responsibility of this department is fostering the business interests of the United States, promoting and developing foreign and domestic commerce, the mining, manufacturing and shipping industries, and the nation's transportation facilities. The department's Office of Security Control is responsible for developing policies and procedures for physical security and personnel safety.

Department of Labor

The safety, welfare and working conditions of wage earners in the United States is under the jurisdiction of the Department of Labor. The Office of the Solicitor coordinates all investigative activities and handles violations of the Fair Labor Standards Act, which are criminal cases, the Public Contracts Act, which are civil cases and the Davis-Bacon Act, which establishes labor standards for federally financed construction. It also enforces laws relating to manpower, minimum wages and maximum hours, child labor, employment security, veteran's readjustment assistance program, workmen's compensation, veterans' reemployment rights and apprenticeship training.

Department of Health, Education and Welfare

This mammoth department is concerned with the promotion of

the general welfare. Among its major agencies are the Social Security Administration, Public Health Service and Food and Drug Administration. The Food and Drug Administration was created in 1930 and it is charged primarily with promoting and maintaining the purity, potency and truthful identification and labeling of essential ingredients found in food and drugs.

Department of Transportation

The major agency of this department is the United States Coast Guard, begun in 1790, and thus one of the oldest of the federal agencies. The Coast Guard is a military service and operates as a part of the Navy in time of war or by presidential decree. It comprises a unified service made up out of the old Revenue Cutter Service, the Lifesaving Service, the Lighthouse Service and the Bureau of Marine Inspection and Navigation. It maintains a port security system and enforces or assists in enforcing federal laws on the high seas or waters subject to United States jurisdiction.

Until 1967, when it was transferred to the Department of Transportation, the Coast Guard functioned as a division of the Treasury Department and was responsible for port security, maritime safety, and the enforcement of maritime law.

The Federal Aviation Administration promulgates and enforces safety regulations by inspecting, certifying and rating the activities of airmen; by enforcing the regulations relating to the manufacture, registration, safety and operation of aircraft; and by inspecting the air navigation facilities of the United States.

The Federal Highway Administration is charged with the promotion of highway safety. The National Highway Safety Bureau administers a national highway safety program to reduce deaths, injuries and property damage resulting from highway traffic crashes.

Other Federal Agencies

Numerous independent agencies and regulatory commissions of the federal government contain their own law enforcement units. Among the larger units are those within the General Services Administration, the Atomic Energy Commission, the Civil Aeronautics Board, the United States Information Agency and the

Veterans Administration. The Civil Service Commission administers the federal Civil Service laws, conducts investigations preliminary to employment and performs similar investigative functions for NASA and other federal agencies. The Federal Communications Commission enforces the Communications Act, which regulates the licensing and operation of radio and television broadcasting stations. The Federal Trade Commission oversees the equitable functioning of businesses engaged in interstate commerce and investigates allegations of unfair competition, price-fixing and deceptive, collusive or monopolistic practices. The Interstate Commerce Commission regulates common carriers in interstate transport and investigates railroad accidents. The Securities and Exchange Commission investigates and prosecutes illegal activities in the securities and financial markets.

STATE AGENCIES

Each of the states has its own law enforcement apparatus, and though the structure and functions of these various state agencies may vary, they generally fulfill some of the regulatory and investigative roles of the federal agencies and some of the uniformed patrol roles of the local agencies. In general, state police and highway patrols have developed later than both federal and local agencies. They have developed in part, as the name "highway patrol" indicates, only in this century, as the phenomenal increase in the use of the automobile indicated the need for a police unit with statewide jurisdiction to maintain highway safety. In some states, the statewide police agency still fulfills no wider function than this. They have also developed in response to the recognition that a decentralized local police operation is handicapped in dealing with crime and traffic problems that span hundreds of miles across dozens of local jurisdictions.

State Police

Generally, these are organized along two lines. Some, like the Michigan State Police, have general police powers and enforce all state laws. Others, like the California Highway Patrol, direct most of their attention to the enforcement of laws which govern the operation of vehicles upon public highways. California's State Police retain jurisdiction on state college and university campuses, in state buildings and on state grounds. Each state police unit has developed in its own way, and there is no common assignment of duty. In Pennsylvania, New York, New Jersey and West Virginia the state police are fire, fish and game wardens; in other states they are required to execute civil processes in actions to which the state is a party; in still other states they are required to act as court attendants; and in other states they conduct examinations for motor vehicle operator licenses.

Highway Patrol

State highway patrols have as their main function the enforcement of all laws governing state traffic and the operation of motor vehicles. Their duties include:

1. Enforce laws governing the operation of motor vehicles.
2. Patrol the highways to enforce speed limits and encourage safe driving habits.
3. Direct the flow of traffic and relieve congestion when it occurs.
4. Investigate all traffic accidents.

Motor Vehicle Bureau

State motor vehicle bureaus have three major duties:

1. Register all motor vehicles and maintain registration records.
2. Test and license drivers and maintain license records.
3. Administer the laws regulating financial responsibility.

The bureau also has a staff of investigators who look into auto thefts, illegal transfer of ownership, forged or counterfeit registration certificates or drivers' licenses.

Identification Units

State police sometimes operate as clearinghouses of identification. In varying degrees, these units compile and analyze criminal statistics, maintain fingerprint and record files, and cooperate with local law enforcement units in the dissemination of information useful to investigation and enforcement activity.

Crime Labs

The laboratory examines, identifies and compares all types of physical evidence.
Magnum Photos

Crime Labs

With increasing frequency, states are maintaining crime laboratories to aid local law enforcement units. The laboratory examines, identifies and compares all types of physical evidence; provides expert testimony for prosecution; and scientifically examines crime scenes in major cases. Some state units are mobile and available upon request.

Liquor Control Boards

Every state has some form of board or commission whose duty it is to license and regulate the alcoholic beverage industry and assess and collect taxes upon the sale of alcoholic beverages. Among the duties of these boards and commissions are investigating persons who apply for licenses and enforcing the liquor control acts of the state which prohibit or regulate the sale, use, possession, adulteration, dilution, misbranding or mislabeling of alcoholic beverages. In most states investigators for those boards have full peace officer status and are empowered to make arrests. They often investigate sales to minors, sales after hours and sales to obviously intoxicated persons.

Conservation Agencies

Every state has some law enforcement unit charged with protecting and conserving the natural resources of the state. State parks maintain their own law enforcement units to protect the parks, beaches, trails, recreational areas and historical landmarks. State Foresters protect the timber and watershed areas, prevent and suppress fires, and protect forests from insects and diseases. State Fish and Game Wardens conserve and protect birds, animals and fish, license anglers and hunters, and enforce the fish and game codes of the state. Wardens investigate complaints of wildlife damage to crops, advise landowners on how to control wildlife, arrange for feeding game birds and animals during severe weather conditions, assist in planning controlled hunts and issue kill permits. They also promote safety programs for hunters and fishermen.

Public Health Units

These have the responsibility of investigating and enforcing all state statutes relating to communicable diseases, licensing of hospitals and nursing homes, adulteration of food and drugs, pollution of public water and public sanitation.

Health and Safety Units

Various states have enacted into law health and safety codes. These often provide for a state fire marshal, who is responsible for the elimination of fire hazards, the investigation of fires, the enforcement of fire and panic safety regulations, the development of fire prevention programs, the establishment of safety requirements, the issuance of fire clearances and licenses.

State Militia or National Guard

The second Amendment to the Constitution provides that "A well regulated militia, being necessary to the security of a free state, the right of the people to keep and bear arms, shall not be infringed." In keeping with this all the states have organized and maintain a military force, the National Guard and the Air National Guard. These units have dual federal and state status and are available both to the federal and state government in case of need. The National Guard and Air National Guard are organized according to the laws of the state and the regulations of the Army and Air Force, with the governor as commander in chief and the adjutant general as chief of staff and commander of all military forces. This military force is not a standing army, but a group of citizens, under training, who can be summoned in cases of violence that cannot be contained by ordinary governmental law enforcement units. Such violence can take the form of war, insurrection, rebellion, riot, breach of the peace, major catastrophe, or resistance to the laws of the state or the United States. When such violence requires the summoning of the militia or the national guard by the executive branch of the government, martial law may be invoked, the declaration of which can involve whatever means the executive deems necessary to insure or restore public order and safety, including the suspension of such bulwarks of the civil law as habeas corpus and the due process provisions of the Constitution.

PRIVATE AGENCIES

Thousands of persons earn their livelihood in some form of private law enforcement service. Some of the service is limited and is not often thought of as being part of law enforcement. Doorkeepers and watchmen working at large housing, industrial and commercial facilities fall into this category. Others operate in fairly specialized areas, such as arson investigation for insurance companies. With increasing frequency, persons in these private areas work in close cooperation with regular governmental law enforcement units. Where their roles require the performance of duties similar to those of a uniformed service, including the carrying of weapons, they are licensed by the state.

Armored Car Services

Large amounts of cash, securities and valuables including gold, jewelry and art objects, are often transferred under the armed escort of an armored car service, such as Brinks and Wells Fargo.

Protective Alarm Agencies

Many homes, factories, stores and offices have installed a wide variety of protective alarm devices. Specialized agencies offer burglar alarms, safe alarms, entrance alarms, boiler alarms, fire alarms and other sophisticated systems involving photoelectric, microwave and ultrasonic activation. The alarms are often connected directly to the police agency communication center, making fast response possible. The alarm is often set so that a loud bell or siren is sounded upon any intrusion, but in many cases the alarm is silent.

Security Services

For a variety of reasons private citizens require protection and attention of a nature greater than the regular governmental agency can provide. Private guard and patrol services are available to provide personnel for special events; protection at housing developments, construction sites, supermarkets and department stores, and college campuses; and crowd management at nightclubs, theatres, ball parks, or other special entertainment or sports events. They also provide special protective patrol of houses and grounds with armed or unarmed guards, often accompanied by trained guard dogs.

Retail Security

Many large merchandising establishments have found it necessary to set up their own security units to lessen unnecessary loss of inventory, to prevent and investigate cases of shoplifting, to evaluate liability claims, to screen prospective employees and to maintain order and safety within the premises.

Plant Protection

Industrial concerns also have need for a service that will provide security. Sometimes they hire these services from a private agency; if they are large enough they usually set up their own units. In many cases the service is provided by a watchman on daytime or nighttime duty, who does little more than watch for fires and for illegal intrusion. In other cases the services are complex, including accident prevention and investigation, traffic control, screening and escorting of vendors and visitors, protection against pilfering and vandalism.

Industrial Security

Companies engaged in defense contract work are required by the government to meet very exacting regulations relating to the security of the facility, its manufacturing processes, personnel and all classified material. Physical security at these facilities is extensive, including fences, lighting and alarm systems, isolation of restricted areas. Personnel security includes the processing and clearance of employees, pass and badge systems, lock and key systems, special procedures for handling vehicles, visitors, vendors, incoming and outgoing packages. The security of classified information includes attention to the mechanics of record security, the transportation, utilization and destruction of classified material, and investigation of violations.

Private Detective Agencies

Several thousand individuals and small firms provide private investigative services to private citizens, attorneys, and industrial and commercial enterprises. Their specialties include investigating theft, fraud and extortion; industrial, home and motor vehicle accidents; domestic and matrimonial disputes; missing persons; child custody and juvenile cases. Depending upon the time and money available, private citizens can investigate the backgrounds of members or potential members of their family, job applicants and prospective business partners. Attorneys often use them to provide information about clients, witnesses, suspects and jurors. Industrial and commercial entrepreneurs often need information concerning competition, employees, executives and credit applications.

Insurance Investigation Units

Large companies handling liability insurance have an enormous need for establishing the legitimacy of all claims made by their clients. They have, therefore, hired large and well-trained staffs to investigate the facts in liability cases, to interview claimants and to determine whether any fraud may be involved in a claim.

SUMMARY

The uniformed town, city or county police officer is our most obvious symbol of law enforcement but he is not the only police functionary. His counterparts, both in and out of uniform, in the federal and state governments and in private services swell the number of persons performing police functions in the United States to well over a million.

The Constitution does not provide for either federal or state police units. For the federal government it prescribes enforcement functions in the areas of currency, customs and postage. For the state governments it prescribes no specific functions and so most state agencies, like local agencies, are established under the "reserved powers" clause of Article X.

The federal agencies that maintain police or investigative units and personnel are predominantly the cabinet level federal departments and the major regulatory agencies and commissions. Among these are the departments of State; Treasury; Defense; Justice; Post Office; Interior; Commerce; Health, Education and Welfare; Agriculture; Labor and Transportation. Among the independent agencies and regulatory commissions are the General Services Administration, the Atomic Energy Commission, the Civil Aeronautics Board, the Federal Communications Commission, the Interstate Commerce Commission, the Federal Trade Commission and the Securities and Exchange Commission.

The primary state agencies are usually either uniformed state police or highway patrols; their organization, functions and jurisdictions vary from state to state. In addition to these uniformed services, the states maintain some agencies to regulate specific activities. Among them are motor vehicle bureaus, liquor control boards, identification units, crime labs, conservation agencies, public health units, job health and safety units, militia or guard units.

Private agencies fulfill all the needs that individuals or private manufacturing, industrial and commercial enterprises cannot obtain from governmental agencies. These include armored car services, protective alarm agencies, security services for retail establishments, plants and industrial sites, private investigative services and insurance investigation units.

STUDY QUESTIONS

1. What are the historical factors that have influenced the organization of American law enforcement agencies as they are presently constituted?
2. Should the United States have a national police force?
3. What are the duties of the Alcohol and Tobacco Tax Division?
4. What are the duties of the Secret Service?
5. What are the duties of the Federal Bureau of Investigation?
6. What are the duties of State Liquor Control Boards?
7. What police role is played by the state militia or national guard?
8. What two types of investigation is the Postal Service concerned with?
9. How does the Department of Agriculture serve the needs of the consumer and citizen?
10. What are the two main types of police organization typically employed by the states?

The Constitution of the United States

We the People of the United States, in Order to form a more perfect Union, establish Justice, insure domestic Tranquility, provide for the common defence, promote the general Welfare, and secure the Blessings of Liberty to ourselves and our Posterity do ordain and establish this CONSTITUTION for the United States of America.

ARTICLE I

Section 1. All legislative Powers herein granted shall be vested in a Congress of the United States, which shall consist of a Senate and House of Representatives.

Section 2. (1) The House of Representatives shall be composed of members chosen every second Year by the People of the several States, and the Electors in each State shall have the Qualifications requisite for Electors of the most numerous Branch of the State Legislature.

(2) No Person shall be a Representative who shall not have attained to the Age of twenty-five Years, and been seven Years a Citizen of the United States, and who shall not, when elected, be an Inhabitant of that State in which he shall be chosen.

(3) [Representatives and direct Taxes[1] shall be apportioned among the several States which may be included within this Union, according to their respective Numbers, which shall be determined by adding to the whole Number of free Persons, including those bound to Service for a Term of Years, and excluding Indians not taxed, three fifths of all other Persons.][2] The actual Enumeration shall be made within three Years after the first Meeting of the Congress of the United States, and within every subsequent Term of ten years, in such Manner as they shall by Law direct. The

---

[1]The Sixteenth Amendment replaced this with respect to income taxes.
[2]Repealed by the Fourteenth Amendment.

Number of Representatives shall not exceed one for every thirty Thousand, but each State shall have at Least one Representative; and until such enumeration shall be made, the State of New Hampshire shall be entitled to choose three, Massachusetts eight, Rhode-Island and Providence Plantations one, Connecticut five, New-York six, New Jersey four, Pennsylvania eight, Delaware one, Maryland six, Virginia ten, North Carolina five, South Carolina five, and Georgia three.

(4) When vacancies happen in the Representation from any State, the Executive Authority thereof shall issue Writs of Election to fill such Vacancies.

(5) The House of Representatives shall choose their Speaker and other Officers; and shall have the sole Power of Impeachment.

Section 3. (1) The Senate of the United States shall be composed of two Senators from each State, [chosen by the Legislature][3] thereof, for six Years; and each Senator shall have one Vote.

(2) Immediately after they shall be assembled in Consequence of the first Election, they shall be divided as equally as may be into three Classes. The Seats of the Senators of the first Class shall be vacated at the Expiration of the second Year, of the second Class at the Expiration of the fourth Year, and of the third Class at the Expiration of the sixth Year, so that one-third may be chosen every second Year; [and if Vacancies happen by Resignation, or otherwise, during the Recess of the Legislature of any State, the Executive thereof may make temporary Appointments until the next Meeting of the Legislature, which shall then fill such Vacancies].[4]

(3) No person shall be a Senator who shall not have attained to the Age of thirty Years, and been nine Years a Citizen of the United States, and who shall not, when elected, be an Inhabitant of that State for which he shall be chosen.

(4) The Vice President of the United States shall be President of the Senate, but shall have no Vote, unless they be equally divided.

(5) The Senate shall choose their other Officers, and also a President pro tempore, in the absence of the Vice President, or when he shall exercise the Office of President of the United States.

(6) The Senate shall have the sole Power to try all Impeachments. When sitting for that Purpose, they shall be on Oath or Affirmation. When the President of the United States is tried, the Chief Justice shall preside: And no Person shall be convicted without the Concurrence of two thirds of the Members present.

(7) Judgment in Cases of Impeachment shall not extend further than to removal from Office, and disqualification to hold and enjoy any Office of

---

[3]Repealed by the Seventeenth Amendment, Section 1.

[4]Changed by the Seventeenth Amendment.

honor, Trust or Profit under the United States: but the Party convicted shall nevertheless be liable and subject to Indictment, Trial, Judgment and Punishment according to Law.

Section 4. (1) The Times, Places and Manner of holding Elections for Senators and Representatives, shall be prescribed in each State by the Legislature thereof; but the Congress may at any time by Law make or alter such Regulations, except as to the Places of Choosing Senators.

(2) The Congress shall assemble at least once in every Year, and such Meeting shall [be on the first Monday in December,][5] unless they shall by Law appoint a different Day.

Section 5. (1) Each House shall be the Judge of the Elections, Returns and Qualifications of its own Members, and a Majority of each shall constitute a Quorum to do Business; but a smaller number may adjourn from day to day, and may be authorized to compel the Attendance of absent Members, in such Manner, and under such Penalties as each House may provide.

(2) Each House may determine the Rules of its Proceedings, punish its Members for disorderly Behavior, and, with the Concurrence of two thirds, expel a Member.

(3) Each House shall keep a Journal of its Proceedings, and from time to time publish the same, excepting such Parts as may in their Judgment require Secrecy; and the Yeas and Nays of the Members of either House on any question shall, at the Desire of one fifth of those Present, be entered on the Journal.

(4) Neither House, during the Session of Congress, shall, without the Consent of the other, adjourn for more than three days, nor to any other Place than that in which the two Houses shall be sitting.

Section 6. (1) The Senators and Representatives shall receive a Compensation for their Services, to be ascertained by Law, and paid out of the Treasury of the United States. They shall in all Cases, except Treason, Felony and Breach of the Peace, be privileged from Arrest during their Attendance at the Session of their respective Houses, and in going to and returning from the same; and for any Speech or Debate in either House, they shall not be questioned in any other Place.

(2) No Senator or Representative shall, during the Time for which he was elected, be appointed to any civil Office under the Authority of the United States, which shall have been created, or the Emoluments whereof have been increased during such time; and no Person holding any Office under the United States, shall be a Member of either House during his Continuance in Office.

---

[5]Changed by the Twentieth Amendment, Section 2.

Section 7. (1) All Bills for raising Revenue shall originate in the House of Representatives; but the Senate may propose or concur with Amendments as on other Bills.

(2) Every Bill which shall have passed the House of Representatives and the Senate, shall, before it become a Law, be presented to the President of the United States; If he approve he shall sign it, but if not he shall return it, with his Objections to that House in which it shall have originated, who shall enter the Objections at large on their Journal, and proceed to reconsider it. If after such Reconsideration two thirds of that House shall agree to pass the Bill, it shall be sent, together with the Objections, to the other House, by which it shall likewise be reconsidered, and if approved by two thirds of that House, it shall become a Law. But in all such Cases the Votes of both Houses shall be determined by Yeas and Nays, and the Names of the Persons voting for and against the Bill shall be entered on the Journal of each House respectively. If any Bill shall not be returned by the President within ten Days (Sundays excepted) after it shall have been presented to him, the Same shall be a Law, in like Manner as if he had signed it, unless the Congress by their Adjournment prevent its Return, in which Case it shall not be a Law.

(3) Every Order, Resolution, or Vote to which the Concurrence of the Senate and House of Representatives may be necessary (except on a question of Adjournment) shall be presented to the President of the United States; and before the Same shall take Effect, shall be approved by him, or being disapproved by him, shall be repassed by two thirds of the Senate and House of Representatives, according to the Rules and Limitations prescribed in the Case of a Bill.

Section 8. (1) The Congress shall have Power To lay and collect Taxes, Duties, Imposts and Excises, to pay the Debts and provide for the common Defense and general Welfare of the United States; but all Duties, Imposts and Excises shall be uniform throughout the United States;

(2) To borrow money on the credit of the United States;

(3) To regulate Commerce with foreign Nations, and among the several States, and with the Indian Tribes;

(4) To establish an uniform Rule of Naturalization, and uniform Laws on the subject of Bankruptcies throughout the United States;

(5) To coin Money, regulate the Value thereof, and of foreign Coin, and fix the Standard of Weights and Measures;

(6) To provide for the Punishment of counterfeiting the Securities and current Coin of the United States;

(7) To establish Post Offices and post Roads;

(8) To promote the Progress of Science and useful Arts, by securing for

limited Times to Authors and Inventors the exclusive Right to their respective Writings and Discoveries;

(9) To constitute Tribunals inferior to the supreme Court;

(10) To define and punish Piracies and Felonies committed on the high Seas, and Offenses against the Law of Nations;

(11) To declare War, grant Letters of Marque and Reprisal, and make Rules concerning Captures on Land and Water;

(12) To raise and support Armies, but no Appropriation of Money to that Use shall be for a longer Term than two Years;

(13) To provide and maintain a Navy;

(14) To make Rules for the Government and Regulation of the land and naval Forces;

(15) To provide for calling forth the Militia to execute the Laws of the Union, suppress Insurrections and repel Invasions;

(16) To provide for organizing, arming, and disciplining the Militia, and for governing such Part of them as may be employed in the Service of the United States, reserving to the States respectively, the Appointment of the Officers, and the Authority of training the Militia according to the discipline prescribed by Congress;

(17) To exercise exclusive Legislation in all Cases whatsoever, over such District (not exceeding ten Miles square) as may, by Cession of particular States, and the acceptance of Congress, become the Seat of the Government of the United States, and to exercise like Authority over all Places purchased by the Consent of the Legislature of the State in which the Same shall be, for the Erection of Forts, Magazines, Arsenals, dock-Yards, and other needful Buildings;—And

(18) To make all Laws which shall be necessary and proper for carrying into Execution the foregoing Powers, and all other Powers vested by this Constitution in the Government of the United States, or in any Department or Officer thereof.

Section 9. (1) The Migration or Importation of such Persons as any of the States now existing shall think proper to admit, shall not be prohibited by the Congress prior to the Year one thousand eight hundred and eight, but a tax or duty may be imposed on such Importation, not exceeding ten dollars for each Person.

(2) The privilege of the Writ of Habeas Corpus shall not be suspended, unless when in Cases of Rebellion or Invasion the public Safety may require it.

(3) No Bill of Attainder or ex post facto Law shall be passed.

(4) No capitation, or other direct, Tax shall be laid, unless in Proportion to the Census or Enumeration herein before directed to be taken.[6]

[6]Changed by the Sixteenth Amendment.

(5) No Tax or Duty shall be laid on Articles exported from any State.

(6) No Preference shall be given by any Regulation of Commerce or Revenue to the Ports of one State over those of another: nor shall Vessels bound to, or from, one State, be obliged to enter, clear, or pay Duties in another.

(7) No Money shall be drawn from the Treasury, but in Consequence of Appropriations made by Law; and a regular Statement and Account of the Receipts and Expenditures of all public Money shall be published from time to time.

(8) No Title of Nobility shall be granted by the United States: And no Person holding any Office of Profit or Trust under them, shall, without the Consent of the Congress, accept of any present, Emolument, Office, or Title, of any kind whatever, from any King, Prince, or foreign State.

Section 10. (1) No State shall enter into any Treaty, Alliance, or Confederation; grant Letters of Marque and Reprisal; coin Money; emit Bills of Credit; make any Thing but gold and silver Coin a Tender in Payment of Debts; pass any Bill of Attainder, ex post facto Law, or Law impairing the Obligation of Contracts, or grant any Title of Nobility.

(2) No State shall, without the Consent of the Congress, lay any Imposts or Duties on Imports or Exports, except what may be absolutely necessary for executing its inspection Laws: and the net Produce of all Duties and Imposts, laid by any State on Imports or Exports, shall be for the Use of the Treasury of the United States; and all such Laws shall be subject to the Revision and Control of the Congress.

(3) No State shall, without the Consent of Congress, lay any duty of Tonnage, keep Troops, or Ships of War in time of Peace, enter into any Agreement or Compact with another State, or with a foreign Power, or engage in War, unless actually invaded, or in such imminent Danger as will not admit of delay.

ARTICLE II

Section 1. (1) The executive Power shall be vested in a President of the United States of America. He shall hold his Office during the Term of four Years, and, together with the Vice-President, chosen for the same Term, be elected, as follows

(2) Each State shall appoint, in such Manner as the Legislature thereof may direct, a Number of Electors, equal to the whole Number of Senators and Representatives to which the State may be entitled in the Congress; but no Senator or Representative, or Person holding an Office of Trust or Profit under the United States, shall be appointed an Elector.

[The Electors shall meet in their respective States, and vote by Ballot for two persons, of whom one at least shall not be an Inhabitant of the same State with themselves. And they shall make a List of all the Persons voted for, and of the Number of Votes for each; which List they shall sign and certify, and transmit sealed to the Seat of the Government of the United States, directed to the President of the Senate. The President of the Senate shall, in the Presence of the Senate and House of Representatives, open all the Certificates, and the Votes shall then be counted. The Person having the greatest Number of Votes shall be the President, if such Number be a Majority of the whole Number of Electors appointed; and if there be more than one who have such Majority, and have an equal Number of Votes, then the House of Representatives shall immediately choose by Ballot one of them for President; and if no Person have a Majority, then from the five highest on the List the said House shall in like Manner choose the President. But in choosing the President, the Votes shall be taken by States, the Representation from each State having one Vote; A quorum for this Purpose shall consist of a Member or Members from two-thirds of the States, and a Majority of all the States shall be necessary to a Choice. In every Case, after the Choice of the President, the Person having the greatest Number of Votes of the Electors shall be the Vice-President. But if there should remain two or more who have equal Votes, the Senate shall choose from them by Ballot the Vice-President.][7]

(3) The Congress may determine the Time of choosing the Electors, and the Day on which they shall give their Votes; which Day shall be the same throughout the United States.

(4) No person except a natural born Citizen, or a Citizen of the United States, at the time of the Adoption of this Constitution, shall be eligible to the Office of President; neither shall any Person be eligible to that Office who shall not have attained to the Age of thirty-five Years, and been fourteen Years a Resident within the United States.

(5) In case of the Removal of the President from Office, or of his Death, Resignation, or Inability to discharge the Powers and Duties of the said Office, the same shall devolve on the Vice-President, and the Congress may by Law provide for the Case of Removal, Death, Resignation or Inability, both of the President and Vice-President, declaring what Officer shall then act as President, and such Officer shall act accordingly, until the Disability be removed, or a President shall be elected.[8]

(6) The President shall, at stated Times, receive for his Services, a Compensation, which shall neither be increased nor diminished during the Period for which he shall have been elected, and he shall not receive within that Period any other Emolument from the United States, or any of them.

(7) Before he enter on the Execution of his Office, he shall take the following Oath or Affirmation:—"I do solemnly swear (or affirm) that I will faith-

[7]This paragraph was superseded in 1804 by the Twelfth Amendment.
[8]Changed by the Twenty-fifth Amendment.

fully execute the Office of President of the United States, and will to the best of my Ability, preserve, protect and defend the Constitution of the United States."

Section 2. (1) The President shall be Commander in Chief of the Army and Navy of the United States, and of the Militia of the several States, when called into the actual Service of the United States; he may require the Opinion in writing, of the principal Officer in each of the executive Departments, upon any subject relating to the Duties of their respective Offices, and he shall have Power to Grant Reprieves and Pardons for Offenses against the United States, except in Cases of Impeachment.

(2) He shall have Power, by and with the Advice and Consent of the Senate, to make Treaties, provided two-thirds of the Senators present concur; and he shall nominate, and by and with the Advice and Consent of the Senate, shall appoint Ambassadors, other public Ministers and Consuls, Judges of the supreme Court, and all other Officers of the United States, whose Appointments are not herein otherwise provided for, and which shall be established by Law: but the Congress may by Law vest the Appointment of such inferior Officers, as they think proper, in the President alone, in the Court of Law, or in the Heads of Departments.

(3) The President shall have Power to fill up all Vacancies that may happen during the Recess of the Senate, by granting Commissions which shall expire at the End of their next Session.

Section 3. He shall from time to time give to the Congress Information of the State of the Union, and recommend to their Consideration such Measures as he shall judge necessary and expedient; he may, on extraordinary Occasions, convene both Houses, or either of them, and in Case of Disagreement between them, with Respect to the Time of Adjournment, he may adjourn them to such Time as he shall think proper; he shall receive Ambassadors and other public Ministers; he shall take Care that the Laws be faithfully executed, and shall Commission all the Officers of the United States.

Section 4. The President, Vice President and all civil Officers of the United States, shall be removed from Office on Impeachment for, and Conviction of, Treason, Bribery, or other high Crimes and Misdemeanors.

ARTICLE III

Section 1. The judicial Power of the United States, shall be vested in one supreme Court, and in such inferior Courts as the Congress may from time to time ordain and establish. The Judges, both of the supreme and inferior Courts, shall hold their Offices during good Behavior, and shall, at stated Times, receive for their Services a Compensation which shall not be diminished during their Continuance in Office.

Section 2. (1) The judicial Power shall extend to all Cases, in Law and Equity, arising under this Constitution, the Laws of the United States, and Treaties made, or which shall be made, under their Authority;—to all Cases affecting Ambassadors, other public Ministers and Consuls;—to all Cases of admiralty and maritime Jurisdiction;—to Controversies to which the United States shall be a Party;—to Controversies between two or more States;—[between a State and Citizens of another State];[9] —between Citizens of different States;—between Citizens of the same State claiming Lands under Grants of different States, and [between a State, or the Citizens thereof, and foreign States, Citizens or Subjects].[10]

(2) In all Cases affecting Ambassadors, other public Ministers and Consuls, and those in which a State shall be Party, the supreme Court shall have original Jurisdiction. In all the other Cases before mentioned, the supreme Court shall have appellate Jurisdiction, both as to Law and Fact, with such Exceptions, and under such Regulations as the Congress shall make.

(3) The trial of all Crimes, except in Cases of Impeachment, shall be by Jury; and such Trial shall be held in the State where the said Crimes shall have been committed: but when not committed within any State, the Trial shall be at such Place or Places as the Congress may by Law have directed.

Section 3. (1) Treason against the United States, shall consist only in levying War against them, or in adhering to their Enemies, giving them Aid and Comfort. No Person shall be convicted of Treason unless on the Testimony of two Witnesses to the same overt Act, or on Confession in open Court.

(2) The Congress shall have power to declare the Punishment of Treason, but no Attainder of Treason shall work Corruption of Blood, or Forfeiture except during the Life of the Person attained.

ARTICLE IV

Section 1. Full Faith and Credit shall be given in each State to the public Acts, Records, and judicial Proceedings of every other State. And the Congress may by general Laws prescribe the Manner in which such Acts, Records and Proceedings shall be proved, and the Effect thereof.

Section 2. (1) The Citizens of each State shall be entitled to all Privileges and Immunities of Citizens in the several States.

(2) A Person charged in any State with Treason, Felony, or other Crime, who shall flee from Justice, and be found in another State, shall on demand of the executive Authority of the State from which he fled, be delivered up, to be removed to the State having Jurisdiction of the Crime.

---

[9] Restricted by the Eleventh Amendment.

[10] Restricted by the Eleventh Amendment

(3) [No Person held to Service or Labor in one State, under the Laws thereof, escaping into another, shall, in Consequence of any Law or Regulation therein, be discharged from such Service or Labor, but shall be delivered up on Claim of the Party to whom such Service or Labor may be due.][11]

Section 3. (1) New States may be admitted by the Congress into this Union; but no new State shall be formed or erected within the Jurisdiction of any other State; nor any State be formed by the Junction of two or more States, or parts of States, without the Consent of the Legislatures of the States concerned as well as of the Congress.

(2) The Congress shall have Power to dispose of and make all needful Rules and Regulations respecting the Territory or other Property belonging to the United States; and nothing in this Constitution shall be so construed as to Prejudice any Claims of the United States, or of any particular State.

Section 4. The United States shall guarantee to every State in this Union a Republican Form of Government, and shall protect each of them against Invasion; and on Application of the Legislature, or of the Executive (when the Legislature cannot be convened) against domestic Violence.

ARTICLE V

The Congress, whenever two-thirds of both Houses shall deem it necessary, shall propose Amendments to this Constitution, or, on the Application of the Legislatures of two-thirds of the several States, shall call a Convention for proposing Amendments, which, in either Case, shall be valid to all Intents and Purposes, as part of this Constitution, when ratified by the Legislature of three-fourths of the several States, or by Conventions in three-fourths thereof, as the one or the other Mode of Ratification may be proposed by the Congress; Provided that no Amendment which may be made prior to the Year One thousand eight hundred and eight shall in any Manner affect the first and fourth Clauses in the Ninth Section of the first Article; and that no State, without its Consent, shall be deprived of its equal Suffrage in the Senate.

ARTICLE VI

(1) All Debts contracted and Engagements entered into, before the Adoption of this Constitution, shall be as valid against the United States under this Constitution, as under the Confederation.

(2) This Constitution, and the Laws of the United States which shall be made in Pursuance thereof; and all Treaties made, or which shall be made, under the Authority of the United States, shall be the supreme Law of

---

[11]This paragraph has been superseded by the Thirteenth Amendment.

the Land; and the Judges in every State shall be bound thereby, any Thing in the Constitution or Laws of any State to the Contrary notwithstanding.

(3) The Senators and Representatives before mentioned, and the Members of the several State Legislatures, and all executive and judicial Officers, both of the United States and of the several States, shall be bound by Oath or Affirmation, to support this Constitution; but no religious Test shall ever be required as a Qualification to any Office or public Trust under the United States.

ARTICLE VII

The Ratification of the Conventions of nine States, shall be sufficient for the Establishment of this Constitution between the States so ratifying the Same.

DONE in Convention by the Unanimous Consent of the States present the Seventeenth Day of September in the Year of our Lord one thousand seven hundred and Eighty seven and the Independence of the United States of America the Twelfth. In Witness whereof We have hereunto subscribed our Names.

Go WASHINGTON

President and deputy from Virginia

ARTICLES IN ADDITION TO, AND AMENDMENT OF, THE CONSTITUTION OF THE UNITED SATES OF AMERICA, PROPOSED BY CONGRESS, AND RATIFIED BY THE LEGISLATURES OF THE SEVERAL STATES, PURSUANT TO THE FIFTH ARTICLE OF THE ORIGINAL CONSTITUTION.

ARTICLE I[12]

Congress shall make no law respecting an establishment of religion, or prohibiting the free exercise thereof; or abridging the freedom of speech, or of the press; or the right of the people peaceably to assemble, and to petition the Government for a redress of grievances.

ARTICLE II

A well regulated Militia, being necessary to the security of a free State, the right of the people to keep and bear Arms, shall not be infringed.

ARTICLE III

No Soldier shall, in time of peace be quartered in any house, without the consent of the Owner, nor in time of war, but in a manner to be prescribed by law.

---

[12]The first ten amendments were adopted in 1791.

ARTICLE IV

The right of the people to be secure in their persons, houses, papers, and effects, against unreasonable searches and seizures, shall not be violated, and no Warrants shall issue, but upon probable cause, supported by Oath or affirmation, and particularly describing the place to be searched, and the persons or things to be seized.

ARTICLE V

No person shall be held to answer for a capital, or otherwise infamous crime, unless on a presentment or indictment of a Grand Jury, except in cases arising in the land or naval forces, or in the Militia, when in actual service in time of War or public danger; nor shall any person be subject for the same offence to be twice put in jeopardy of life or limb; nor shall be compelled in any criminal case to be witness against himself, nor be deprived of life, liberty, or property, without due process of law; nor shall private property be taken for public use, without just compensation.

ARTICLE VI

In all criminal prosecutions, the accused shall enjoy the right to a speedy and public trial, by an impartial jury of the State and district wherein the crime shall have been committed, which district shall have been previously ascertained by law, and to be informed of the nature and cause of the accusation; to be confronted with the witnesses against him; to have compulsory process for obtaining witnesses in his favor, and to have the Assistance of Counsel for his defence.

ARTICLE VII

In suits at common law, where the value in controversy shall exceed twenty dollars, the right of trial by jury shall be preserved, and no fact tried by a jury, shall be otherwise reexamined in any Court of the United States, than according to the rules of the common law.

ARTICLE VIII

Excessive bail shall not be required, nor excessive fines imposed, nor cruel and unusual punishments inflicted.

ARTICLE IX

The enumeration in the Constitution, of certain rights, shall not be construed to deny or disparage others retained by the people.

ARTICLE X

The powers not delegated to the United States by the Constitution, nor prohibited by it to the States, are reserved to the States respectively, or to the people.

ARTICLE XI[13]

The Judicial power of the United States shall not be construed to extend to any suit in law or equity, commenced or prosecuted against one of the United States by Citizens of another State, or by Citizens or Subjects of any Foreign State.

ARTICLE XII[14]

The Electors shall meet in their respective states and vote by ballot for President and Vice-President, one of whom, at least, shall not be an inhabitant of the same state with themselves; they shall name in their ballots the person voted for as President, and in distinct ballots the person voted for as Vice-President, and they shall make distinct lists of all persons voted for as President, and of all persons voted for as Vice-President, and of the number of votes for each, which lists they shall sign and certify, and transmit sealed to the seat of the government of the United States, directed to the President of the Senate; —The President of the Senate shall, in presence of the Senate and House of Representatives, open all the certificates and the votes shall then be counted; —The person having the greatest number of votes for President, shall be the President, if such number be a majority of the whole number of Electors appointed; and if no person have such majority, then from the persons having the highest numbers not exceeding three on the list of those voted for as President, the House of Representatives shall choose immediately, by ballot, the President. But in choosing the President, the votes shall be taken by states, the representation from each state having one vote; a quorum for this purpose shall consist of a member or members from two-thirds of the states, and a majority of all the states shall be necessary to a choice. [And if the House of Representatives shall not choose a President whenever the right of choice shall devolve upon them, before the fourth day of March next following, then the Vice-President shall act as President, as in the case of the death or other constitutional disability of the President.][15] —The person having the greatest number of votes as Vice-President, shall be the Vice-President, if such number be a majority of the whole number of Electors appointed, and if no person have a majority, then from the two highest numbers on the list, the Senate shall

---

[13]Adopted in 1798.

[14]Adopted in 1804.

[15]Superseded by the Twentieth Amendment, Section 3.

choose the Vice-President; a quorum for the purpose shall consist of two-thirds of the whole number of Senators, and a majority of the whole number shall be necessary to a choice. But no person constitutionally ineligible to the office of President shall be eligible to that of Vice-President of the United States.

ARTICLE XIII[16]

Section 1. Neither slavery nor involuntary servitude, except as a punishment for crime whereof the party shall have been duly convicted, shall exist within the United States, or any place subject to their jurisdiction.

Section 2. Congress shall have power to enforce this article by appropriate legislation.

ARTICLE XIV[17]

Section 1. All persons born or naturalized in the United States, and subject to the jurisdiction thereof, are citizens of the United States and of the State wherein they reside. No state shall make or enforce any law which shall abridge the privileges or immunities of citizens of the United States; nor shall any State deprive any person of life, liberty, or property, without due process of law; nor deny to any person within its jurisdiction the equal protection of the laws.

Section 2. Representatives shall be apportioned among the several States according to their respective numbers, counting the whole number of persons in each State, excluding Indians not taxed. But when the right to vote at any election for the choice of electors for President and Vice-President of the United States, Representatives in Congress, the Executive and Judicial officers of a State, or the members of the Legislature thereof, is denied to any of the male inhabitants of such State, being twenty-one years of age, and citizens of the United States, or in any way abridged, except for participation in rebellion, or other crime, the basis of representation therein shall be reduced in the proportion which the number of such male citizens shall bear to the whole number of male citizens twenty-one years of age in such State.

Section 3. No person shall be a Senator or Representative in Congress, or elector of President and Vice-President, or hold any office, civil or military, under the United States, or under any State, who, having previously taken an oath, as a member of Congress, or as an officer of the United States, or as a member of any State legislature, or as an executive or judicial officer of any State, to support the Constitution of the United States, shall have engaged in insurrection or rebellion against the same, or given aid or comfort to the

---

[16]Adopted in 1865.
[17]Adopted in 1868.

enemies thereof. But Congress may by a vote of two-thirds of each House, remove such disability.

Section 4. The validity of the public debt of the United States, authorized by law, including debts incurred for payment of pensions and bounties for services in suppressing insurrection or rebellion, shall not be questioned. But neither the United States nor any State shall assume or pay any debt or obligation incurred in aid of insurrection or rebellion against the United States, or any claim for the loss or emancipation of any slave; but all such debts, obligations and claims shall be held illegal and void.

Section 5. The Congress shall have power to enforce, by appropriate legislation, the provisions of this article.

ARTICLE XV[18]

Section 1. The right of citizens of the United States to vote shall not be denied or abridged by the United States or by any State on account of race, color, or previous condition of servitude—

Section 2. The Congress shall have power to enforce this article by appropriate legislation.

ARTICLE XVI[19]

The Congress shall have power to lay and collect taxes on incomes, from whatever source derived, without apportionment among the several States, and without regard to any census or enumeration.

ARTICLE XVII[20]

The Senate of the United States shall be composed of two Senators from each State, elected by the people thereof, for six years; and each Senator shall have one vote. The electors in each State shall have the qualifications requisite for electors of the most numerous branch of the State legislatures.

When vacancies happen in the representation of any State in the Senate, the executive authority of such State shall issue writs of election to fill such vacancies: *Provided,* That the legislature of any State may empower the executive thereof to make temporary appointments until the people fill the vacancies by election as the legislature may direct.

This amendment shall not be so construed as to affect the election or term of any Senator chosen before it becomes valid as part of the Constitution.

---

[18]Adopted in 1870.
[19]Adopted in 1913.
[20]Adopted in 1913.

ARTICLE XVIII[21]

Section 1. After one year from the ratification of this article the manufacture, sale, or transportation of intoxicating liquors within, the importation thereof into, or the exportation thereof from the United States and all territory subject to the jurisdiction thereof for beverage purposes is hereby prohibited.

Section 2. The Congress and the several States shall have concurrent power to enforce this article by appropriate legislation.

Section 3. This article shall be inoperative unless it shall have been ratified as an amendment to the Constitution by the legislatures of the several States, as provided in the Constitution, within seven years from the date of the submission hereof to the State by the Congress.

ARTICLE XIX[22]

The right of citizens of the United States to vote shall not be denied or abridged by the United States or by any State on account of sex.

Congress shall have power to enforce this article by appropriate legislation.

ARTICLE XX[23]

Section 1. The terms of the President and Vice-President shall end at noon on the 20th day of January, and the terms of Senators and Representatives at noon on the 3d day of January, of the years in which such terms would have ended if this article had not been ratified; and the terms of their successors shall then begin.

Section 2. The Congress shall assemble at least once in every year, and such meeting shall begin at noon on the 3d day of January, unless they shall by law appoint a different day.

Section 3. If, at the time fixed for the beginning of the term of the President, the president elect shall have died, the Vice-President elect shall become President. If a President shall not have been chosen before the time fixed for the beginning of his term, or if the President elect shall have failed to qualify, then the Vice-President elect shall act as President until a President shall have qualified; and the Congress may by law provide for the case wherein neither a President elect nor a Vice-President elect shall have qualified, declaring who shall then act as President, or the manner in which one who is to act shall be selected, and such person shall act accordingly until a President or Vice-President shall have qualified.

---

[21]Adopted in 1919. Repealed by Section 1 of the Twenty-first Amendment.
[22]Adopted in 1920.
[23]Adopted in 1933.

Section 4. The Congress may by law provide for the case of the death of any of the persons from whom the House of Representatives may choose a President whenever the right of choice shall have devolved upon them, and for the case of the death of any of the persons from whom the Senate may choose a Vice-President whenever the right of choice shall have devolved upon them.

Section 5. Sections 1 and 2 shall take effect on the 15th day of October following the ratification of this article.

Section 6. This article shall be inoperative unless it shall have been ratified as an amendment to the Constitution by the legislatures of three-fourths of the several States within seven years from the date of its submission.

ARTICLE XXI[24]

Section 1. The eighteenth article of amendment to the Constitution of the United States is hereby repealed.

Section 2. The transportation or importation into any State, Territory, or possession of the United States for delivery or use therein of intoxicating liquors, in violation of the laws thereof, is hereby prohibited.

Section 3. This article shall be inoperative unless it shall have been ratified as an amendment to the Constitution by conventions in the several States, as provided in the Constitution, within seven years from the date of the submission hereof to the States by the Congress.

ARTICLE XXII[25]

Section 1. No person shall be elected to the office of the President more than twice, and no person who has held the office of President, or acted as President, for more than two years of a term to which some other person was elected President shall be elected to the office of the President more than once. But this Article shall not apply to any person holding the office of President when this Article was proposed by the Congress, and shall not prevent any person who may be holding the office of President, or acting as President, during the term within which this Article becomes operative from holding the office of President or acting as President during the remainder of such term.

Section 2. This article shall be inoperative unless it shall have been ratified as an amendment to the Constitution by the legislatures of three-fourths of the several States within seven years from the date of its submission to the States by the Congress.

---

[24]Adopted in 1933.
[25]Adopted in 1951.

ARTICLE XXIII[26]

Section 1. The District constituting the seat of Government of the United States shall appoint in such manner as the Congress may direct:

A number of electors of President and Vice-President equal to the whole number of Senators and Representatives in Congress to which the District would be entitled if it were a State, but in no event more than the least populous State; they shall be in addition to those appointed by the States, but they shall be considered, for the purposes of the election of President and Vice-President, to be electors appointed by a State; and they shall meet in the District and perform such duties as provided by the twelfth article of amendment.

Section 2. The Congress shall have power to enforce this article by appropriate legislation.

ARTICLE XXIV[27]

Section 1. The right of citizens of the United States to vote in any primary or other election for President or Vice-President, for electors for President or Vice-President, or for Senator or Representative in Congress, shall not be denied or abridged by the United States or any state by reasons of failure to pay any poll tax or other tax.

Section 2. The Congress shall have power to enforce this article by appropriate legislation.

ARTICLE XXV[28]

Section 1. In case of the removal of the President from office or of his death or resignation, the Vice-President shall become President.

Section 2. Whenever there is a vacancy in the office of the Vice-President, the President shall nominate a Vice-President who shall take office upon confirmation by a majority vote of both Houses of Congress.

Section 3. Whenever the President transmits to the President pro tempore of the Senate and the Speaker of the House of Representatives his written declaration that he is unable to discharge the powers and duties of his office, and until he transmits to them a written declaration to the contrary, such powers and duties shall be discharged by the Vice-President as Acting President.

Section 4. Whenever the Vice-President and a majority of either the principal officers of the Executive departments or of such other body as Congress may by law provide transmit to the President pro tempore of the Senate and the

---

[26]Adopted in 1961.
[27]Adopted in 1964.
[28]Adopted in 1967.

Speaker of the House of Representatives their written declaration that the President is unable to discharge the powers and duties of his office, the Vice-President shall immediately assume the powers and duties of the office as Acting President.

Thereafter, when the President transmits to the President pro tempore of the Senate and the Speaker of the House of Representatives his written declaration that no inability exists, he shall resume the powers and duties of his office unless the Vice-President and a majority of either the principal officers of the Executive departments or of such other body as Congress may by law provide transmit within four days to the President pro tempore of the Senate and the Speaker of the House of Representatives their written declaration that the President is unable to discharge the powers and duties of his office. Thereupon Congress shall decide the issue, assembling within forty-eight hours for that purpose if not in session. If the Congress, within twenty-one days after receipt of the latter written declaration, or, if Congress is not in session, within twenty-one days after Congress is required to assemble, determines by two-thirds vote of both houses that the President is unable to discharge the powers and duties of his office, the Vice-President shall continue to discharge the same as Acting President; otherwise, the President shall resume the powers and duties of his office.

ARTICLE XXVI[29]

Section 1. The right of citizens of the United States, who are 18 years of age or older, to vote shall not be denied or abridged by the United States or any state on account of age.

Section 2. The Congress shall have power to enforce this article by appropriate legislation.

ARTICLE XXVII[30]

Section 1. Equality of rights under the law shall not be denied or abridged by the United States or by any State on account of race.

Section 2. The Congress shall have the power to enforce, by appropriate legislation, the provisions of this article.

Section 3. This amendment shall take effect two years after the date of ratification.

---

[29]Adopted in 1971.

[30]Approved by Congress in 1972 and sent to the states for ratification. As of November, 1974, 33 had ratified this "equal rights amendment," 5 short of the necessary 38 ratifications.

Professional Associations

American Correctional Association (ACA)
Woodridge Station
P.O. Box 10176
Washington, D.C. 20018

American Federation of Police (AFP)
1100 N.E. 125th Street
North Miami, Fla.

Americans for Effective Law Enforcement (AELE)
33 North Dearborn Street
Chicago, Ill. 60602

International Association of Chiefs of Police (IACP)
1319 18th Street, N.W.
Washington, D.C. 20036

International Conference of Police Associations (ICOPA)
1241 Pennsylvania Avenue, S.E.
Washington, D.C. 20003

International Footprint Association (IFA)
1095 Market Street
San Francisco, Calif. 94103

International Narcotic Enforcement Officers' Association (INEOA)
178 Washington Avenue
Albany, N.Y. 12210

National Council on Crime and Delinquency (NCCD)
44 East 23rd Street
New York, N.Y. 10010

National Police Officers' Association of America (NPOAA)
1890 S. Tamiami Trail
Venice, Fla. 33595

National Sheriffs' Association (NSA)
Suite 209, 1250 Connecticut Avenue
Washington, D.C. 20036

Society of Professional Investigators
Box 1107, Church Street Station
New York, N.Y. 10008

Journals in Law Enforcement

American Journal of Correction. Issued bimonthly jointly by the American Correctional Association and the Bruce Publishing Company, 1821 University Avenue, Saint Paul, Minn. 55104.

American Sociological Review. Published bimonthly by the American Sociological Association, 1001 Connecticut Avenue, N.W., Washington, D.C. 20036.

Bulletin on Narcotics. Issued quarterly by the United Nations, Sales Section, New York, N.Y. 10017.

Correctional Research. Issued by the Massachusetts Correctional Association, 33 Mount Vernon Street, Boston, Mass. 02108.

Crime and Delinquency. Issued by the National Council on Crime and Delinquency, 44 East 23rd Street, New York, N.Y. 10010.

Crime and Delinquency Abstracts. Issued bimonthly by the Superintendent of Documents, U.S. Government Printing Office, Washington, D.C. 20402.

Crime and Delinquency Literature. Published six times annually by the National Council on Crime and Delinquency.

Criminologica. Published quarterly by the American Society of Criminology, Dept. of Sociology, Catholic University of America, Washington, D.C. 20017.

Criminologist. Issued quarterly by the Forensic Publishing Company, Ltd., 9 Old Bailey, London, E.C.4, England.

Criminology. Issued by the Department of Criminology and Corrections, Florida State University, Tallahassee, Fla. 32306.

FBI Law Enforcement Bulletin. Issued monthly by the FBI, U.S. Department of Justice, Washington, D.C. 20535.

FBI Uniform Crime Reports. Issued quarterly and annually by the FBI.

Federal Probation. Issued by *Federal Probation Quarterly*, Supreme Court Building, Washington, D.C. 20544.

Georgia Juvenile Association Newsletter. Issued by the Corrections Division, Institute of Government, University of Georgia, Athens, Ga. 30601.

INSCAPE. Issued by Southern Illinois University, Center for the Study of Crime, Delinquency and Corrections, Carbondale, Ill. 62901.

INTERPOL. Issued monthly by the General Secretariat, *Interpol*, 26 Rue Armengaud, 92 Saint Cloud, France.

Journal of Criminal Law, Criminology and Police Science. Issued quarterly by Williams and Wilkins Company, 428 E. Preston Street, Baltimore, Md. 21202.

Journal of Forensic Psychology. Issued annually by the International Academy of Forensic Psychology, Paul Quinn College, Waco, Tex.

Law and Order. Issued monthly by *Law and Order Magazine*, 72 West 45th Street, New York, N.Y. 10036.

National Sheriff. Issued bimonthly by the National Sheriffs' Association, Suite 209, 1250 Connecticut Avenue, Washington, D.C. 20036.

Police. Issued bimonthly by Charles C Thomas, Publisher, 302-327 East Lawrence Avenue, Springfield, Ill. 62703.

Police Chief. Issued monthly by the International Association of Police Chiefs, 1319 18th Street, N. W., Washington, D. C. 20036.

Police Journal. Issued monthly by Butterworth and Company, Ltd., 14 Curity Avenue, Toronto, Canada.

Prison Journal. Issued semiannually by the Pennsylvania Prison Society, Room 302, Social Service Building, 311 South Juniper Street, Philadelphia, Pa. 19107.

Probation. Published quarterly by the National Association of Probation Officers, 6 Endsleigh Street, London, W.C.1, England.

Social Problems. Issued quarterly; can be ordered from *Social Problems*, Business Office, P.O. 190, Kalamazoo, Mich. 49005.

Traffic and Digest Review. Issued monthly by the Traffic Institute, Northwestern University, 1804 Hinman Avenue, Evanston, Ill. 60204.

BIBLIOGRAPHY

Adorno et al. *The Authoritarian Personality*. New York: Harper & Row, 1950.

Ahern, James F. *Police in Trouble*. New York: Hawthorn Books, Inc., 1971.

Allport, Gordon. *The Nature of Prejudice*. Garden City, N.Y.: Doubleday, 1958.

American Trial Lawyers Association. "The Police and the Law." In *Trial Magazine*. Boston, 1969.

Amsterdam News. September 13, 1969.

Anderson, Walter H., and Anderson Gus Carr. *Anderson on Sheriffs*. Buffalo, N.Y.: Dennis and Co., 1941.

Aristotle. *Politics and Nichomachean Ethics*.

Asch, Sidney H. *Police Authority and the Rights of the Individual*. 3rd ed. New York: Arco Publishing Company, Inc., 1971.

Berger, Peter L. *An Invitation to Sociology: A Humanistic Perspective*. Garden City, N.Y.: Doubleday, 1963.

Black, Henry Campbell. *Black's Law Dictionary*. West Publishing Co., 1933.

Botein, Bernard. *Our Cities Burn*. New York: Simon and Schuster, 1972.

Campbell, James S., Joseph R. Savid, and David R. Stang, eds. *Law and Order Reconsidered*. New York: Bantam, 1970.

Cavan, Ruth Shonle, ed. *Readings in Juvenile Delinquency*. 2nd ed. Philadelphia: Lippincott, 1969.

Chapman, Samuel G. ed. *Police Patrol Readings*. Springfield, Ill.: Charles E. Thomas, 1970.

Chevigny, Paul. *Police Power*. New York: Pantheon Books, 1969.

Cipes, Robert M. *The Crime War*. New York: The New American Library, 1968.

Cray, Ed. *The Big Blue Line*. New York: Coward-McCann, Inc., 1967.

Durkheim, Emile. *The Rules of Sociological Method*. Trans. Sarah A. Solovay and John W. Mueller. New York: Free Press, 1938.

———. *Suicide*. Trans. John A. Spaulding and George Simpson, ed. George Simpson. New York: Free Press, 1951.

———. *Essays in Sociology and Philosophy*. Trans. Kurt Wolff. New York: Harper & Row, 1960.

Encyclopedia Brittanica. 11th ed. New York: The Encyclopedia Company, 1910.

Farrand, Max. *The Framing of the Constitution of the United States*. New Haven: Yale University Press, 1964.

Fox, Vernon. "Sociological and Political Aspects of Police Administration." In *Sociology and Social Research*, vol. 51, no. 1 (October 1966).

———. *Introduction to Corrections*. Englewood Cliffs, N.J.: Prentice-Hall, 1972.

Frankel, Marvin E. *Criminal Sentences*. New York: Hill and Wang, 1973.

Glueck, Sheldon, and Eleanor Glueck. *Unravelling Juvenile Delinquency*. Cambridge, Mass.: Harvard University Press, 1950.

Graves, Frank Pierreport. *A History of Education: Before the Middle Ages*. New York: Macmillan, 1918.

Hahn, Paul H. *The Juvenile Offender and the Law*. Cincinnati: W. H. Anderson Co., 1971.

Handbook of Social Psychology, 2nd ed. Reading, Mass.: Addison-Wesley, 1968.

Harris, T.O. "Alternatives in Solving the Juvenile Problem." *Police Chief Intellect,* vol. 101, no. 2344 (November 1972).

Heaps, Willard A. *Juvenile Justice*. New York: The Seabury Press, 1974.

International Association of Chiefs of Police, Inc. *IACP Law Enforcement Legal Review,* no. 12 (June 1973).

International City Managers' Association. *Municipal Police Administration*. 5th ed. Chicago, 1961.

Irwin, John. *The Felon*. Englewood Cliffs, N.J.: Prentice-Hall, 1970.

Jenkins, Herbert. *Keeping The Peace*. New York: Harper and Row, 1970.

Jet Magazine. October 1969.

Kelly, Alfred H. and Winfred A. Harbison *The American Constitution*. 4th ed. New York: W.W. Norton, 1970.

Klotter, John C. and Jacqueline R. Kanovitz. *Constitutional Law for Police*. Cincinnati: W.H. Anderson Co., 1971.

Liddell, Henry G. *A History of Rome*. New York: Harper and Brothers, 1886.

Martindale, Don. *The Nature and Types of Sociological Theory*. Boston: Houghton Mifflin, 1960.

Maslow, Abraham H. *Motivation and Personality*. New York: Harper & Row, 1954.

McNamara, John H. "Uncertainties in Police Work: The Relevance of Police Recruits, Backgrounds, Training." In *The Police — Six Sociological Essays,* ed. David J. Bordua. New York: Wiley, 1967.

Menninger, Karl. *The Crime of Punishment*. New York: The Viking Press, 1968.

Morris, Norval and Gordon Hawkins. *The Honest Politician's Guide to Crime Control*. Chicago: The University of Chicago Press, 1970.

National District Attorneys' Association Bulletin. *Confessions and Interrogations after* Miranda. Chicago, 1970.

Newsweek. August 4, 1969.

New York Post. October 10, 1973; September 17, 1973.

New York Times. September 28, 1969.

Niederhoffer, Arthur. *Behind the Shield: The Police in Urban Society*. New York: Doubleday, 1967.

Niederhoffer, Arthur and Abraham S. Blumberg. *The Ambivalent Force*. Waltham, Mass.: Ginn, 1970.

Oxford Companion to American History. New York: Oxford University Press, 1966.

Peter, Laurence J. *The Peter Prescription*. New York: Bantam, 1972.

Plato. *The Dialogues of Plato*. Trans. B. Jowett. vol. 5. London: Oxford University Press, 1892.

Poole, A.L. *From Domesday Book to Magna Carta, 1087–1216*. 2nd ed. Oxford, Eng.: Oxford University Press, 1955.

President's Commission on Law Enforcement and Administration of Justice. *The Challenge of Crime in a Free Society*. Washington, D.C.: U.S. Government Printing Office, 1967.

———. *Task Force Report: Juvenile Delinquency and Youth Crime*. Washington, D.C.: U.S. Government Printing Office, 1967.

———. *Task Force Report: The Police*. Washington, D.C.: U.S. Government Printing Office, 1967.

Quinney, Richard. *The Social Reality of Crime*. Boston: Little, Brown, 1970.

Reiss, Albert J., Jr. *The Police and the Public*. New Haven: Yale University Press, 1971.

The Report of the National Commission on the Causes and Prevention of Violence. *Violent Crime*. New York: George Braziller, 1969.

Rose, Arnold M. *Sociology, the Study of Human Relations*. New York: Knopf, 1967.

Rothman, David J. *The Discovery of the Asylum*. Boston: Little, Brown, 1971.

Seymour, Whitney North, Jr. *Why Justice Fails*. New York: William Morrow & Company, Inc., 1973.

Sumner, W.G. *Folkways*. Boston: Ginn, 1906.

Smith, Goldwin. *A Constitutional and Legal History of England*. New York: Scribner's, 1955.

Timasheff, Nicholas S. *Sociological Theory: Its Nature and Growth*. New York: Random House, 1955.

Tatz, Sydney. "A Positive Approach to Crime Prevention: An Innovative Plan." *Police*, March-April 1970.

Westley, William A. "The Police: A Sociological Study of Law, Custom, and Morality." Unpublished doctoral diss., University of Chicago, 1957.

———. *Violence and the Police*. Cambridge: The MIT Press, 1970.

Wormser, Rene A. *The Story of the Law*. New York: Simon and Schuster, 1962.

Index